D1242825

ANGLO~ AMERICAN FEMINIST CHALLENGES TO THE RHETORICAL TRADITIONS

VIRGINIA WOOLF MARY DALY ADRIENNE RICH

BY KRISTA RATCLIFFE

SOUTHERN ILLINOIS UNIVERSITY PRESS
Carbondale & Edwardsville

Printed in the United States of America

Edited by John K. Wilson
Designed by Bob Nance
Production supervised by Natalia Nadraga

99 98 97 96   4 3 2 1

Library of Congress Cataloging-in-Publication Data

Ratcliffe, Krista, 1958–
Anglo-American feminist challenges to the rhetorical traditions:
Virginia Woolf, Mary Daly, and Adrienne Rich / Krista Ratcliffe.
p. cm.
Includes bibliographical references and index.
1. American literature—Women authors—History and criticism.
2. Feminism and literature—Great Britain—History—20th century.
3. Feminism and literature—United States—History—20th century.
4. English literature—Women authors—History and criticism.
5. Woolf, Virginia, 1882–1941—Political and social views.   6. Rich,
Adrienne Cecile—Political and social views.   7. Persuasion
(Rhetoric)   8. Daly, Mary.   9. Feminism.   I. Title.
PS152.R33   1996
810.9'9287'0904—dc20   94-40053
ISBN 0-8093-1934-9   CIP

The paper used in this publication meets the minimum
requirements of American National Standard for Information
Sciences—Permanence of Paper for Printed Library Materials,
ANSI Z39.48-1984. ⊗

To Mary, Elaine, Win, . . . and Kevin

I thought as I wiped my eyes on the corner of my apron:
Penelope did this too.
And more than once: you can't keep weaving all day
And undoing it through the night;
Your arms get tired, and the back of your neck gets tight;
And long towards morning, when you think it will never
  be light,
And your husband has been gone, and you don't know
  where for years,
Suddenly you burst into tears;
There is simply nothing else to do.

And I thought, as I wiped my eyes on the corner of my
  apron:
This is an ancient gesture, authentic, unique,
In the very best tradition, classic, Greek;
Ulysses did this too.
But only as a gesture—a gesture which implied
To the assembled throng that he was too moved to speak.
He learned it from Penelope . . .
Penelope who really cried.

—Edna St. Vincent Millay
"An Ancient Gesture"

Contents

Preface

Sometimes we drug ourselves with dreams of new ideas.
The head will save us. The brain alone will set us free.
But there are no new ideas waiting in the wings to save
us as women, as human. There are only old and forgotten
ones, new combinations, extrapolations and recognitions
from within ourselves—along with the renewed courage to
try them out.
—Audre Lorde, "Poetry Is Not a Luxury"

I remember my second quarter in graduate school at Ohio State,
almost a decade ago, when I was simultaneously reading Virginia Woolf and Aristotle. I was reading Woolf's *Mrs. Dalloway*
for Marlene Longenecker's "Woman as Hero" seminar and Aristotle's *Rhetoric* for Ed Corbett's history of rhetoric survey. Although it has since crossed my mind that the history of rhetoric
course could easily have been retitled "Man as Hero," I remember
being equally excited about both classes. And as the quarter wore
on, my excitement remained, but it became accompanied by perplexity and then by frustration. Where were women's voices in the
history of rhetoric? I would like to say that my quarter ended with
a nice, neat conclusion. But it did not. Instead, I wrote two seminar
papers, one about Margaret Atwood and one about Isocrates, as
if the two had nothing to say to one another. It has taken me a
dissertation, a few articles, several drafts of this book, and innumerable conversations to articulate this frustration. And still I
have no pat answers. What I do have is an idea, a way of extrapolating feminist theories of rhetoric from feminist texts. To demonstrate this idea, I have focused on the three Anglo-American
feminists who have taught me most of what I know about women
(and) writing: Virginia Woolf, Mary Daly, and Adrienne Rich.
Whether or not these feminists would approve of my project, I
cannot say, and while I hope they would, in many ways such a
question does not concern me. What does concern me is how their

gendered claims about writing and their gendered textual practices can inform rhetoric and composition studies.

This project has had a long, meandering path to fruition. Its roots, scarcely recognizable here, are in my dissertation. There I analyze Woolf's and Rich's feminist essays in order to identify their rhetorical strategies. In that endeavor, I owe debts of gratitude to Andrea Lunsford, Edward Corbett, Barbara Rigney, Cindy Cox, Cheryl Glenn, Sue Lape, and Eric Walborn for their generous readings and conversations, all of which helped me think my way toward this book. And while writing this book, I have incurred many other debts of gratitude. I want to thank Curtis Clark, Carol Burns, and John Wilson at Southern Illinois University Press for supporting this project. I want to thank the reviewers (especially Susan Jarratt) for thought-provoking comments that challenged me and ultimately made this project far richer in both process and product. I want to thank the graduate students from my 1991 feminist rhetoric seminar for conversations that still echo in my ears: Marduk Alkaus, Melissa Deutsch, Lisa Higgins, Jim Jackson, Elizabeth Jared, Dana Kinnison, Anna Lovern, Ron Mitchell, Simone Novak, Kevin Parker, Marty Patton, Cathy Quick, Ray Slavens, Bonnie Vegiard, and Chloe Vincent. I want to thank the English Department at the University of Missouri-Columbia for a leave, during which time I reconceptualized this project. I owe special debts of gratitude to Jeanne Colleran, Jill Morstad, Pat Okker, Marty Townsend, and Molly Travis for their support; to Virginia Chappell and Alice Gillam for helping me think through my final revisions; to Chris Farris for endless e-mail conversations; and to Roxanne Mountford for a particularly effective pep talk. And quite simply, without Mary Lago, Elaine Lawless, and Win Horner (and their Friday afternoon "happy hours"), this book would not have been written. Finally, I want to thank Kevin Brown not only for his editing skills but also for his sanity and his laughter.

My parents, too, have always been interested in the writing of this book, so much so that for a period of time I had to ask them to stop asking me when it would be finished. But whenever I felt overwhelmed, I would flash back to a scene with my mother. During one of my visits home, she charged into my bedroom, long after midnight, and announced, "I've been meaning to ask you, what is this *rhetoric* anyway?" It seems Ramona, my mom's next-door neighbor, had been asking about me and my job. I hesitated, wondering how to make my work sensible to my mother so that she, in turn, could make it sensible to Ramona. But I need not have worried. Mother filled the gap for me. "Well," she continued, "I just told Ramona that you read about women and get mad. Then you write about it." Once again, my mother proved herself more sensible than I. For, indeed, it is in "the writing about it" that I have made "sense" of my "madness."

I cannot conclude without offering thanks to the three feminists whose words have inspired this project. Virginia Woolf reminds me that to be an effective writer/teacher I must kill the Angel in my house, the good-girl voice that forever urges me to please. Mary Daly continually re-minds me to Sin Big, that is, to BE. And Adrienne Rich reminds me that the source of my pain may also be the source of my power. These are the hard won lessons that I am continually relearning from these women as I offer their Anglo-American feminist theories of rhetoric to my students and to you.

A portion of chapter 2 was previously published as "Virginia Woolf's Feminist Theory of Rhetoric" in *Virginia Woolf: Themes and Variations* (selected papers from the Second Annual Conference on Virginia Woolf), New York: Pace UP, 1993, 258–67, and small portions of chapters 4 and 5 were previously published as "Reconsidering Essentialism for Feminist Composition Pedagogy: Adrienne Rich's 'Politics of Location' as a Theory of Writerly Agency" in *The Writing Instructor* 13 (Spring 1994): 55–66. My thanks to Theresa Enos, the editor of *Rhetoric Review*, for permission to reprint an excerpt from "A Rhetoric of Textual Feminism: (Re)reading the Emotional in Virginia Woolf's *Three Guineas*," *Rhetoric Review* 11 (Spring 1993): 400–16. And my thanks to Elizabeth Barnett for the epigraph to my book: "An Ancient Gesture" by Edna St. Vincent Millay. From *Collected Poems*, HarperCollins. Copyright © 1954, 1982 by Norma Millay Ellis. Reprinted by permission of Elizabeth Barnett, literary executor.

ANGLO~ AMERICAN FEMINIST CHALLENGES TO THE RHETORICAL TRADITIONS

1

Bathsheba's Dilemma: Defining, Discovering, and Defending Anglo-American Feminist Theories of Rhetoric(s)

> "I have the feelings of a woman," says Bathsheba [Everdene] in *Far from the Madding Crowd*, "but I have only the language of men."
>
> —Virginia Woolf, "Men and Women"

For centuries, Bathsheba's dilemma has troubled women differently in their daily lives, affecting their listening and speaking as well as their reading and writing.[1] But this dilemma need not be read as suggesting that women and men literally speak different languages. Rather, it may be read as exposing, first, that Woman and Man occupy different relationships to language within the symbolic and, second, that each woman occupies a particular subject position within the symbolic, depending on her ever changing intersections of gender, race, class, sexual orientation, history, nationality, culture, and so on.[2] Bathsheba's dilemma is not acknowledged in traditional theories of rhetoric; instead, they perpetuate, among other things, a tradition of gender-blindness. Consider Kenneth Burke's *A Rhetoric of Motives*. To demonstrate that the range of rhetoric includes poetics, Burke invokes Milton's Samson who is "enraged with himself for having 'divulged / The secret gift of God to a deceitful / Woman'" (3). By analyzing Samson's rhetorical situation only in terms of Samson's suffering and violence, Burke leaves readers wondering whether the range of rhetoric includes the unnamed but ever present Delilah. Feminist challenges to the rhetorical traditions are

1

presently emerging to address such genderblindness with the hope of recognizing, validating, and addressing Bathsheba's dilemma.

Although feminist challenges have carved out spaces for themselves within rhetoric and composition circles, they hardly presume theoretical consensus. Indeed, they define Bathsheba's dilemma differently.[3] Some feminist challenges study women's construction of knowledge claims (e.g., Mary Field Belenky, Elizabeth Flynn, Carol Gilligan, Jane Tedesco); others study women's textual strategies (e.g., Pamela Caughie, Mary P. Hiatt, bell hooks); others study how rhetorical theories position women and Woman (e.g., Linda Brodkey, Margaret Fell, Susan Jarratt, Andrea Lunsford and Lisa Ede); others study rhetorical theories that women themselves have constructed (e.g., Cheryl Glenn, Barbara Johnson, C. Jan Swearingen); still others study intersections of rhetorical theory and pedagogy (e.g., Florence Howe, Susan Osborn, Marjorie Curry Woods); or as Virginia Woolf claims about women and literature in *A Room of One's Own*, they may study some combination thereof (3).

Many feminist challenges to the rhetorical traditions draw from studies in other disciplines, interrogating their claims, methodologies, and assumptions in order to determine their implications for the history, theory, and pedagogy of rhetoric and composition studies (Horner 206).[4] An important implication that emerges concerns methodology. Like feminist challenges to literary, historical, and philosophical traditions, feminist challenges to the rhetorical traditions may employ a variety of interwoven moves: (1) recovering, (2) rereading, (3) extrapolating, and (4) conceptualizing.[5]

Recovering involves the archaeological project of discovering lost or marginalized theories of rhetoric. Because Cary Nelson's three axioms for recovering literary texts provide a means not only for expanding canons but also for critiquing the criteria by which canons are constructed, they could easily be adopted for rhetoric and composition projects: (1) retain texts that were popular or influential in particular periods, such as Ida B. Wells' speeches, a move that will reconstruct history; (2) retain texts that people repeatedly claim are worthless—for instance, Eudora Ramsey Richardson's text on women's public speaking—a move that will continually force us to critique our biases; and (3) recover writers and theorists, like Margaret Fell and Audre Lorde, who have dropped out or been left out of rhetorical histories, a move that may force us off the page and into cultural gaps (*Recovery* 51). Once recovered, women's rhetorical theories may be constructed into a separate rhetorical tradition or incorporated into the existing corpus of rhetorical theories. The first option assumes a gynocritical stance that emphasizes differences among women's texts, as exemplified in Andrea Lunsford's *Reclaiming Rhetorica* and Mary Ellen Waithe's two-volume *A History of Women Philosophers*. The second option assumes a desegregated stance that puts women's theories into play "equally" with men's, as attempted in Patricia Bizzell and Bruce Herzberg's *The Rhetorical Tradition*.[6] Although both options serve important functions, they each pose potential pitfalls that must be guarded against: the first could allow women's rhetorical theories to degenerate into a separate but unequal position, and the second could allow women's rhetorical theories to become mere tokens. Moreover, because both methodologies are based on identity, both options focus on recovering specific women and their texts, a strategy that revolves around the question Who is speaking? and relegates unidentified texts into the anonymous category. Barbara Biesecker proposes an alternative means of conceptualizing history, arguing that feminist histories of rhetoric should construct a new narrative. This new narrative would not frame histories around specific subjects as agents—for example, Woolf, Daly, and Rich. Instead, it would foreground the forces that make speaking possible, such as a textual analysis of discursive positions (148). To Biesecker's claim, however, I would add the following question: What forces, including who is (not) speaking, made particular speaking subjects (im)possible?

Rereading entails revising our interpretations of canonical and recovered theories of rhetoric. Rereading canonical theories may not only reaffirm their valuable contributions to rhetorical studies but also explode their patriarchal assumptions and implications for composition studies. Phyllis Lassner provides an example of this latter move in her feminist rereading of Rogerian argument. Rereading canonical theories may give voice to women's/Woman's silenced contributions, shedding light on their visible absences that may be perceived as flitting presences only in prefaces, footnotes, dedications, or margins. Such projects either may focus on real historical women, as in Cheryl Glenn's study of Aspasia's influence on Socrates' concept of rhetoric and Drema Lipscomb's study of Sojourner Truth's influence on public discourse, or they may focus on the analytic category of Woman, as in Page duBois's philosophical project and Susan Jarratt's rhetorical one (*Sophists*). Rereading canonical theories may also result in the construction of feminist theories of rhetoric, as in Dale Bauer's rereading of Bakhtin's discourse theory (*Feminist Dialogics*). Furthermore, rereading women's recovered theories and judging them by contemporary criteria might uncover important contributions to rhetorical studies, as exemplified by Bizzell and Herzberg's inclusion of Sarah Grimke's defense of Anglo-American women's public speaking and by Karlyn Kohrs Campbell's inclusion of Mary Church Terrell's critique of African American women's public speaking (*Man Cannot Speak*). Though not all recovered theories emerge from a feminist ideology, such theories may be reread for feminist purposes, that is, to foreground how gendered claims and strategies affect rhetorical history, theory, and pedagogy.

Extrapolating entails rereading non-rhetoric texts (essays, etiquette manuals, cookbooks, fiction, diaries, etc.) as theories of rhetoric. That is, theories of rhetoric may be extrapolated from women's and/or feminists' critiques of language as well as from the textual strategies of such critiques.[7] For example, Bizzell and Herzberg encourage readers to view Christine de Pisan's *Treasure of the City of Ladies* as both a rhetoric manual and an etiquette book delineating Renaissance women's courtly gestures; Karlyn Kohrs Campbell posits a gender-related theory of feminine style based on the ideas and textual strategies of nineteenth-century feminist orators, such as Maria W. Miller Stewart and Elizabeth Cady Stanton (*Man Cannot Speak*); and Patricia Yaeger conceptualizes a theory of emancipatory style of women's writing based on the ideas and textual strategies in nineteenth- and twentieth-century women's literature. Given that few rhetoric texts by women have been, or are likely to be, recovered and given that much of the modern and contemporary research and personal musings about women and language has occurred outside the field of rhetoric and composition, extrapolation may prove a rich interdisciplinary resource for rhetoric and composition scholars who are interested in constructing women's and feminist theories of rhetoric.

One point about this extrapolating move should be noted, lest an extrapolated theory be mistaken for a positivistic rendering of the nonrhetoric texts: as in ethnographic studies, the person extrapolating the theory influences the resulting theory. Conceptualizing implies writing new theories of rhetoric. The debates that rage about this process parallel debates between liberal and radical feminisms, that is, between working within institutional structures or overturning these structures. Should feminists situate their theories within rhetorical traditions, or should we question any connection with such traditions? Though these two questions appear separate, they are not. Because we are born into language, we cannot escape the dominant discourse of the symbolic.[8] No space exists in which feminists may stand to begin totally anew, for Aristotle writes us as much as we may write (against) him. But because the dominant discourse is not static, it may be revised. Hence, two possibilities arise. The first is that new rhetorical theories and practices may emerge from the old. Roxanne Mountford, however, cautions us about relying too heavily on the old: "appropriating classical rhetorics without deeply transforming them from the point of view of the disadvantaged—those who would seek to enter some kind of public forum, some institutionalized discourse, without the benefit of the elite, white, maleness that classical rhetoric presumes its students to have—is foolhardy" ("Feminist Theory" 2). The second possibility is that the unconceptualized that-which-already-exists may be conceptualized. Karlyn Kohrs Campbell contends that such projects will radically challenge our fundamental assumptions about rhetoric ("Sound of Women's Voices" 214); bell hooks contends that such projects will also force us to ask the questions Who is listening and What is being heard? ("Young Soldier" 14). The potential of these two possible conceptualizing moves puts liberal feminisms and radical feminisms into play. Liberal feminists must recognize that particular changes within structures can change the structures, and radical feminists must recognize that new structures emerge from existing ones, whether that emergence is violent or peaceful, fast or slow, conscious or unconscious. The implications of these conceptualizing moves are enormous. They encourage not a passive acceptance of structural oppression but rather Julia Kristeva's "radical *refusal* of the subjective limitations" of the structure of dominant discourse ("Women's Time" 20). They also reject the desire for a totalizing theory and embrace the possibilities of multiple theories that articulate multiple standpoints and practices.

All four moves—recovering, rereading, extrapolating, conceptualizing, or some combination thereof—offer tremendous potential for challenging our rhetorical traditions. But if the recovery of women's and feminist theories of rhetoric proves as difficult as Bizzell and Herzberg imply (670), then rereading, extrapolating, and conceptualizing may become crucial research functions for rhetoric and composition research about Bathsheba's dilemma.

Focusing on the extrapolating option, I offer the following critical question for this study: How may Virginia Woolf's, Mary Daly's, and Adrienne Rich's Anglo-American feminist theories of rhetoric be extrapolated from their feminist texts about women, language, and culture in ways that productively complicate the genderblindness of traditional rhetoric and composition history, theory, and pedagogy? As one response to this question, I examine the interrelationship between *what* Woolf, Daly, and Rich write and *how* they write; in other words, I extrapolate their feminist theories of rhetoric from their interwoven claims and textual strategies. I offer these extrapolated theories not as positivistic truths lying just under the surface of these feminists' texts, not as the final words on feminism and rhetoric and composition studies, and certainly not as totalizing visions that speak to and for all women. Rather, I offer these extrapolated theories as my readings of three women's texts, readings that inform my rhetoric and composition studies every time I sit down to write or walk into a classroom. I hope this study contributes to the continuing conversations about feminisms and the rhetorical traditions by inviting readers not only to question how Woman, women, and feminists have been located as a part of, and apart from, these traditions but also to explore the implications of such locations for rhetorical history, theory, and pedagogy.

This chapter lays the groundwork for my project by discussing how Anglo-American feminist theories of rhetoric may be defined, discovered, and defended. The defining section establishes the theoretical perspective of this study and defines Anglo-American feminist theories of rhetoric. The discovering section rereads Roland Barthes's essay "The Old Rhetoric: An Aide-Mémoire" to locate gaps in the received tradition that Woolf's, Daly's, and Rich's theories might fill or expand. Finally, the defending section argues that these three theories do indeed provide important Anglo-American feminist challenges to the rhetorical traditions.

Defining Anglo-American
Feminist Theories of Rhetoric(s)

My project, with its focus on Anglo-American feminist theories of rhetoric, offers multiple readings and, as such, demands definitions.[9] My use of the term *feminist* refers to a materialist feminism that can be positioned, in part, in relation to the following terms: *female* is defined as characteristics grounded in biological sex differences, *feminine* as behaviors grounded in socially constructed gender differences,[10] *women* as nonessentialist real-life historical subjects, *Woman* as an analytic category, and *feminist* as an ethical stance that foregrounds sexual and gender concerns as a particularly productive means of demystifying and critiquing the cultural matrix—including the complexities of gender, race, class, sexual orientation, religious preference, geographical location, and so on—within which power relations function.[11]

A materialist-feminist stance cites language as an important arena of political struggle but is skeptical of isolating language and abstractions from other arenas of struggle (Newton and Rosenfelt xxi). Such a stance locates feminism as a site of inquiry from which arise possibilities for (re)visioning multiple concerns within a specific culture. Moreover, this feminist revisioning is not passive. It entails (re)writing the past and the present, not to ignore the roles of men but to draw attention to gendered actions, biases, and assumptions as well as the accompanying inequities of power. Since men's roles have usually been the primary focus in history, since men themselves have usually been the primary interpreters of their roles in history, and since the construction of these "facts" occurs within discourse, an interrogation of language that exposes the constructed "nature" of ideology becomes crucial to the materialist feminist project of revision. Through this feminist revisioning, political stances are translated into action so that personal and collective change is not only imagined but effected. And this imagining and effecting are what introduce the space of rhetoric as well as the need for feminist theories of rhetoric.

The materialist feminism of this study is complicated, however, by the term *Anglo-American*. Even though Woolf is Protestant, Daly is "Nag-Gnostic," and Rich is Jewish, I situate these women within feminist tradition(s) that Toril Moi names Anglo-American. This classification implies a materialist feminism possessed of the ethical stance described above; it also implies a feminism admittedly situated in the white privilege of British and North American traditions. Situated in relation to African American feminist tradition(s), Caribbean American ones, Native American ones, French ones, and so on, the white privilege that is particularly located within the Anglo-American feminist tradition(s) raises certain questions, particularly questions of definition relating to the terms *women* and *Woman*. The problematics of these definitions are well articulated by bell hooks:

> Historically, white patriarchs rarely referred to the racial identity of white women because they believed that the subject of race was political and therefore would contaminate the sanctified domain of "white" woman's reality. By verbally denying white women racial identity, that is by simply referring to them as women when what they meant was white women, their status was further reduced to that of a non-person. . . .
>
> White feminists did not challenge the racist-sexist tendency to use the word "woman" to refer solely to white women; they supported it. For them it served two purposes. First, it allowed them to proclaim white men world oppressors while making it appear linguistically that no alliance existed between white women and white men based on shared racial imperialism. Second, it made possible for white women to act as if alliances did exist between themselves and non-white women in our society, and by doing so they could deflect attention away from their classism and racism. ("Race and Feminism" 140)

Jackie Jones Royster offers one solution to this problem: we must name everybody before we can stop naming anyone.

Considering hooks's critique and Royster's solution, I name my study *Anglo-American* so as to respect the differences among feminists in general and to stipulate my focus on Anglo-American feminist theories of rhetoric in particular. For as Judith Levine has claimed in "White Like Me," Anglo-American feminists have an ethical imperative to deal with race at this particular historical moment, to move beyond discussing race mostly, or only, in terms of "the Other" (23). Such a move exposes what many people with white privilege often forget: that race is marked on Anglo-American women as well as on African American women or Native American women or Chicana women, and that particular differences exist *within* each of these categories. With Levine's claim in mind, I attempt to articulate race and other socially constructed categories in Woolf's, Daly's, and Rich's feminist theories of rhetoric. Because all theories of rhetoric assume particular definitions of subjectivity, these categories are most easily exposed in subsequent chapters where I discuss Woolf's, Daly's, and Rich's uses of the term *woman*. Thus, as Toni Morrison has encouraged literary theorists to do (*Playing* 6), I attempt to articulate how the silences, whispers, images, and arguments about race have contributed to the presence of the Anglo-American identities within Woolf's, Daly's, and Rich's theories.[12]

Even though these feminist theories of rhetoric foreground sex and gender concerns mostly in relation to Anglo-American women, their audience need not be so limited. Rhetoric and composition scholar/teachers who are neither feminist nor Anglo-American may benefit from contemplating the (im)possibilities of these theories, just as I have benefited by contemplating the (im)possibilities of Aristotelian rhetorical theory and their implications not just for studying and teaching but also for daily communication and socialization.

Despite our culture's powerful socializing tendency to define *feminist* as man-hater, my title's emphasis on *challenges* is, first of all, not a separatist move. I do not deny the effectiveness of men's rhetorical theories, whether they be those of Aristotle, Augustine, Burke, Roland Barthes, or Henry Louis Gates. I believe, for instance, that Aristotelian rhetorical theory is so pervasive in our culture that it is inscribed on and in our bodies and that, consequently, we should understand it and use it for our own ends. Yet we must also be honest about its limitations; for example, its genderblindness. My emphasis on *challenges* is, second of all, not a nurturing move, which may seem strange, perhaps not supportive enough, for some feminists and nonfeminists alike. But my goal is to confront conflicts while respecting my readers and students, not to create a "safe space" in theory or in pedagogy. For even though safe spaces seemingly provide temporary harbors from a violent world, they usually exist only in the scholar/teacher's mind. Indeed, such spaces too often deny the very real conflicts inside and outside our minds and, more importantly for our students, inside and outside our classrooms. Susan Jarratt articulates this stance particularly well: "[M]y hopes are pinned on [a theoretical conversation and] a composition course . . . in which students argue about the ethical implications of discourse on a wide range of subjects and, in doing so, come to identify their personal interests with others, understand those interests as implicated in a larger communal setting, and advance them in a public voice" ("Feminism and Composition" 121).

The term *rhetoric* that I employ in this book problematizes Kenneth Burke's concept, which merges "its use of *identification* and its nature as *addressed*" (*Rhetoric of Motives* 45). As Burke himself claims, this rhetorical function pervades all aspects of culture: "We can place in terms of rhetoric all those statements by anthropologists, ethnologists, individual and social psychologists, and the like, that bear upon the *persuasive* aspects of language, the function of language as *addressed*, as direct or roundabout appeal to real or ideal audiences, without or within" (44). This definition posits rhetoric as a conscious and unconscious socializing function of language through which specific subjects, contexts, and texts interact to construct meanings that influence public and private cultural spaces by moving specific subjects to personal and collective action and/or attitude (50). Such a concept of rhetoric and rhetorical analysis exposes the function of ideology in the interwoven textual, personal, and cultural and reminds us that rhetoric has a socializing, hence moralizing, function that influences all texts and all people (39; xiv–xv).

Yet some gaps in Burke's theory (as in many other theories of rhetoric) necessitate the search for feminist theories of rhetoric. First, Burke's theory focuses on points of identification more than points of difference. Burke predicates his concept of identification upon the existence of difference and acknowledges that specific terministic screens will trigger particular worldviews; however, his desire is for rhetoric to erase such differences through consubstantiality and to thereby effect the possibility of communication. He argues that a consubstantial move is possible because different kinds of symbols, including language, promote similarities through socialization (*Language as Symbolic Action* 52). But much is rendered invisible when identification becomes the main rhetorical pursuit. Second, Burke's theory perpetuates a centuries-long tradition of genderblindness. Like many other theories of rhetoric, no mention is made of the differences in men's and women's cultural positions; indeed, little mention is made of women except in the "Courtship" section of *A Rhetoric of Motives* (208). So deeply entrenched in the dominant ideology are such sex and gender biases and erasures that they appear as the natural order of things, not as subjects for investigation. Although women and feminists should not reject Burke's theory or any other phallogocentric theories solely because of such biases or erasures, we do need to expose tacit assumptions about sex and gender and analyze their implications.

To complicate these gaps in Burke's rhetorical function, I call on the theories of Roland Barthes and Julia Kristeva. Because Burke's tension between identification and difference assumes binary structural boundaries that limit the potential play of language and, hence, potential meanings, I invoke Barthes's theory of language function to complicate Burke's theory.[13] Barthes posits language as a sign system that presumes the potentially endless play of the signifier, that is, a signifying process in which signifiers become multiple signifieds that in turn become other signifiers. This language function as transformation becomes a game for Barthes, "the very pleasure of power," the cultural site where various voices intersect to construct "the pensive text" (*S/Z* 59, 217). Despite concerns of certain feminist critics, Barthes's play need not erase the ideological nature of language but may instead foreground it by merging questions of the personal (idiolectal forms) and the political (collective formulas) with the potential for revision (memory) ("Style and Its Image" 98–99).[14] As such, Barthes's doubling of multiplicity and ideology may be read as positing a language function that questions socialization as identification and celebrates socialization as perpetuation of difference. By putting the possibilities of Burke's rhetorical function in play with Roland Barthes's language function, I imagine a rhetorical function that offers possibilities of difference, not just identification, and that assumes multiple interpretive possibilities that, in turn, construct spaces for feminist revisionings.[15] This resulting rhetorical function resembles the particle/wave theory of light in quantum physics: that is, a person's stance, like an electron's *position*, can be noted, or the continual play of the signifier, like an electron's *motion*, can be noted; however, like position and motion, stance and play cannot be observed simultaneously.

To confront the implications of genderblindness in this rhetorical function, I work from Kristeva's third term of feminism, the "*insertion* into history and the radical *refusal* of the subjective limitations imposed by this history's time" ("Women's Time" 20). From this standpoint, many possibilities emerge. First, Kristeva's third term enables feminists to refuse the violent metaphors of killing and scapegoating upon which Burke's rhetorical theory is based (*Rhetoric of Motives* 13; *Language as Symbolic Action* 55). Second, it enables feminists to refuse the binary trap of being forced to identify either with Lakoff's color conscious women or with Cixous's hysterical Medusa (Ryder 531)[16]; indeed, women can use the language of men to express the feelings of women. Third, it enables feminists to (re)theorize rhetorical theories; that is, conventional theories of rhetoric may viewed not as static but as mutable, while new theories may be seen as emerging from the old and making the old unrecognizable. Such possibilities challenge the rhetorical traditions.

Therefore, by complicating Burke's rhetorical function with Barthes's multiplicity and Kristeva's third term of feminism, I construct a rhetorical function that intersects with my materialist feminism. From this position, I construct the following definition: *Anglo-American feminist theories of rhetoric* are those theories that employ Anglo-American materialist feminism(s) as their primary lens of inquiry to expose how language functions through subjects, contexts, and texts to construct meanings that influence public and private cultural spaces by moving specific subjects to personal and collective action and/or attitude. Given that no theory can provide a totalizing vision, Anglo-American feminist theories of rhetoric are admittedly limited; they foreground certain concepts and constituencies while backgrounding others. What becomes visible is how, from an Anglo-American woman's perspective, language affects and is affected by sex and gender.[17] But because sex and gender do not exist in a vacuum, they emerge as a productive means of demystifying and critiquing power relations within the complex cultural matrix. Thus, Anglo-American feminist theories of rhetoric recognize, validate, and address Bathsheba's dilemma by contextualizing gendered discursive practices and by questioning their interwoven claims and strategies as well as their assumptions and implications.

Anglo-American feminist theories of rhetoric assume interwoven relationships of the personal, the textual, and the cultural. Theorizing such interrelationships problematizes the poststructuralist concept of *text*, which is often read as enveloping everything and which is sometimes read as negating the possibility of political positioning. Andrea Nye articulates the necessity of reimagining text as follows: "structuralist and post-structuralist theories of symbolic meaning complete the philosophy of man [by positing] a textual arena where ambivalent relations can be acted out, while at the same time real life continues with its murder and cruelties" (217).[18] To address Nye's complaint, I read the personal, the textual, and the cultural as rhetorical functions that have intersecting, though not identical, properties: the personal constructs and reflects the textual and the cultural, the textual constructs and reflects the personal and the cultural, and the cultural constructs and reflects the personal and the textual. Because all three categories are defined not as static artifacts but as rhetorical functions, specific subjects assume a limited agency, texts assume a potentiality of meanings, and cultures assume a nonstatic structuration. All are read in order to make ideology visible and to locate gaps that disempowered subjects may fill with their heteroglossic words, nonunified voices, and conflictive actions.[19]

Within this framework, rhetorical analyses of personal, textual, and cultural functions are imperative. For texts may emerge differently given different cultural agent(s), space(s), and moment(s). As such, texts are not fetishized but are instead rendered subject to contextualized (re)constructions of meanings at various cultural sites of production and consumption. Texts may disturb personally and culturally accepted ideas as well as effect personal and cultural transformations. At the same time, personal and cultural events may create the space for specific subjects or cultural forces to imagine, write, publish, or read such texts. These intersections of the personal, the textual, and the cultural are important, for they construct spaces wherein the dominant ideology may be continually reinforced, rejected, or reimagined; such intersections force us to recognize that when we question textuality, we also question our cultures and ourselves.

Discovering Sex and Gender Gaps in the Rhetorical Traditions

Until recently, *the* rhetorical tradition commonly evoked such names as Aristotle, Cicero, Quintilian, Augustine, Cassiodorous, Peter Ramus, Hugh Blair, George Campbell, Richard Whately, I. A. Richards, and Kenneth Burke, all of whom have theorized and/or practiced the art of rhetoric. The construction of such a tradition, impressive as it is, has reinforced two trends: a dominance of phallogocentric theories and the marginalization of certain people. Recently, many rhetoric and composition scholars have challenged one another to interrogate the closure implied by this construction and to entertain the possibilities of multiple, diverse rhetorical traditions that not only revise the canon but also question the concept of canon and the assumptions of canon formation (e.g., Patricia Bizzell and Bruce Herzberg, William Covino, Susan Jarratt, Andrea Lunsford, Jaspar Neel). In this study I respond to such challenges by focusing on feminist theories of rhetoric. To lay the groundwork for my response, in this section I identify sex and gender gaps in the received Aristotelian rhetorical tradition(s) that may serve as spaces, or starting points, for conceptualizing feminist theories of rhetoric.

Although a variety of histories would seemingly serve my purpose,[20] I will (re)read Roland Barthes's essay "The Old Rhetoric," compiled in 1964–65 when he became interested in the nineteenth-century "death" of the old rhetoric. Barthes's twentieth-century reception of rhetorical history and theory is heavily Aristotelian, which is appropriate for my purpose here, given that Aristotle's *Rhetoric* remains a dominant thread in twentieth-century "recoveries" of rhetoric. "The Old Rhetoric" not so much reconstructs a linear history as narrates moments of the old rhetoric, questioning traditional rhetorical concepts in terms of class and structuralist language assumptions. For scholars who want to complicate traditional rhetorical concepts in terms of gender, the importance of Barthes's critique is two-fold: it not only models a critical methodology, using class as a criterion, but it also functions as a history text that may be reread for its own gender gaps. In the following paragraphs I complicate Barthes's reading of the old rhetoric in terms of gender gaps; in particular, I examine definitions of *rhetoric* in terms of (1) proofs and appeals, (2) language function, (3) text and the five rhetorical canons, (4) author and audience, (5) rhetorical situation, (6) history, traditions, canons, (7) politics, and (8) pedagogy.

The reason for such a rereading is simple: I want to identify the possibilities and limitations of this Aristotelian rhetorical theory for women and feminists. Like other twentieth-century receptions, Barthes's rendering explores the possibilities of this rhetorical theory, that is, its potential for empowering anyone in any situation to achieve any end. What is not recognized, however, is its limitations for outsiders. Women occupy different cultural spaces than men, and feminists occupy different cultural spaces than nonfeminists. Although infinite possibilities abound for *particular* differences within these various cultural spaces, identifying the limitations of the old rhetoric for these cultural spaces demystifies gendered power plays as well as prevalent stereotypes (e.g., that women are not as logical or as reasonable in their arguments as men). By critiquing both the possibilities and the limitations of Barthes's reception of rhetorical history and theory for women and feminists, I simultaneously discover spaces for, and highlight the need for, feminist theories of rhetoric.

To begin such a project, Barthes's definitions of rhetoric must be examined. He claims that "the world is incredibly full of old Rhetoric" and cites rhetoric's importance as the only theoretical structure that has foregrounded the function of language ("The Old Rhetoric" 11, 15). Though rhetoric has (re)emerged in academic circles during the last half of the twentieth century as an important site of inquiry, the term still suffers from hazy, multi-layered definitions and, consequently, retains some of its power for feminism(s).[21] Barthes acknowledges such a position when he defines rhetoric as a metalangauge and delineates its six different, though sometimes simultaneous, functions: (1) a technique or art, (2) a teaching, (3) a science, (4) an ethic, (5) a social practice, and (6) a ludic practice (13–14). Barthes's multiple definitions can be read and questioned so as to invite women and feminists into the Burkean parlor.

Barthes's rhetoric as *technique* is defined as an " 'art' in the classical sense of the word; the art of persuasion, a body of rules and recipes whose implementation makes it possible to convince the hearer of the discourse . . . , even if what he is to be convinced of is 'false' " ("The Old Rhetoric" 13). For Barthes, rhetoric as *techne* implies a form/content split, despite other rhetoricians' claims to the contrary (Corbett 381). That is, Barthes's rhetoric as *techne* reveals how rhetoric as an "ideology of form" may be learned and employed by anyone in any discourse situation. While the possibilities for empowerment within such a structure are rightly emphasized, we too often forget to question the limitations of this theoretical stance. Particularly, we mystify the fact that different speakers and writers occupy different cultural positions and, hence, different positions of power. By asserting a false sense of equality (i.e., that everyone can learn and employ and be empowered by rhetorical conventions), we assume that the logic underlying this structure is a universal logic shared by all people in all cultures at all points in history, that specific agency alone can overcome structural oppressions, and that content is separated from form. Feminist theories of rhetoric should not only foreground such assumptions but also question them, problematizing rhetoric as an ideology of form in terms of Barthes's other defining categories of rhetoric.

Barthes's rhetoric as *ethic* is posited as "a system of 'rules,' . . . at once a manual of recipes, inspired by a practical goal, and a Code, a body of ethical prescriptions whose role is to supervise (*i.e.*, to permit and to limit) the 'deviations' of emotive language" ("The Old Rhetoric" 13). This ethic points to the cultural construction of rhetorical/ethical intersections, and the specific intersections constructed provide boundaries within which people assume they can function comfortably, that is, prescriptively and predictably. In this way, Barthes's rhetoric as ethic exposes the interwoven relation of theory and praxis. Yet this ethic also functions from assumptions that limit the rhetorical potential of women and feminists, as evidenced by the following questions that may inform feminist theories of rhetoric: Who establishes this ethic? What truth conditions must be accepted for one to believe this ethic? Who benefits from the power structure of this ethic, and how? Where are the boundaries of this ethic? At what points are these boundaries visible and vulnerable? What are the implications of believing in plain and emotive languages? And how can " 'deviations' of emotive language" be recovered or reread for feminist purposes?

Barthes's rhetoric as *social practice* is defined as "that privileged technique (since one must pay in order to acquire it) which permits the ruling class to gain *ownership of speech*" ('The Old Rhetoric" 13–14). This social function exposes class assumptions that control subjects' relative access to rhetoric. It also exposes the constructed "nature" of power relations between subjects within specified cultural spaces; as such, it implies that constructed subjectivities, as opposed to essential natures, may be deconstructed. At the same time, this social function works from assumptions that limit the rhetorical potential of women and feminists, as evidenced by the following questions that should inform feminist theories of rhetoric: What happens to gender when class is the predominant cut made across the social? What happens when the matrix of the social is problematized by sex and gender as a means of interrogating class, race, sexual orientation, religious preference, geography, and so on? How does rhetoric function outside the "ruling class," outside racial barriers, outside geographical circles, and the like? Where do such questions overlap? And, finally, what are the assumptions and implications of believing in the "*ownership of speech*"?

Barthes's rhetoric as *ludic* practice is posed as "games, parodies, erotic or obscene allusions, classroom jokes, a whole schoolboy practice" ("The Old Rhetoric" 14). Rhetoric as ludic provides an ironically effective space for diversion and subversion. Given feminist contexts, rhetoric as ludic provides feminists entrées into dialogues about rhetoric. As with Cixous's laughing Medusa, the play of the ludic becomes the space and the means for feminists to identify, disrupt, and reject the logic of phallogocentric discourse. These disruptions and rejections subvert the dominant ideology by creating gaps that may be filled and expanded with feminists' voices, actions, and theories of rhetoric. What should not be forgotten is that negative material consequences for laughter exist, namely, madness and sometimes death. Yet the ludic also provides a much-needed emphasis in feminist theory, an emphasis on the *pleasures* that women find with(in) language. Borrowing a metaphor from Mary Oliver, Patricia Yaeger provides one such example: "the archetype of the writer as a honey-mad woman, as someone hungry for the honey of speech" (4).

Barthes grounds his multileveled definitions of the old rhetoric primarily in Aristotelian theory: "[It] is above all a rhetoric of proof, of reasoning, of the approximative syllogism (enthymeme); it is a deliberately diminished logic, one adapted to the level of the 'public,' i.e., of common sense, of ordinary opinion. . . . [I]t would be well suited to the products of our so-called mass culture, in which an Aristotelian 'probability' prevails, i.e., 'what the public believes possible.' How many films, pulp novels, commercial articles might take as their motto the Aristotelian rule: 'better an impossible probability than an improbable possibility' " ("The Old Rhetoric" 22). Like William Grimaldi's interpretation of Aristotelian rhetoric, Barthes's Aristotelian "rhetoric of proof" focuses on deductive and inductive arguments with interwoven logical, emotional, and ethical appeals. As scholars too numerous to name have claimed, Aristotle's brilliantly conceived systematic art of rhetoric has greatly influenced Western culture. Yet, to reiterate the point, Aristotle's rhetoric also poses potential pitfalls for women and feminists and, hence, suggests many possible starting points for revisionist theories.

Barthes's Aristotelian rhetoric of proof presumes a deductive logic based on inductive precedent, namely, that which has comfortably come before. To combat this deeply ingrained impulse, feminists must frequently refute received traditions as well as recover lost ones and construct new ones, all in an attempt to construct a space from which to speak effectively. Only when such a space is constructed may they address their immediate arguments and conclusions. Based on Aristotle's enthymeme as defined in his *Rhetoric* and *Prior Analytics*, Barthes's rhetoric of proof also presumes the importance of a deductive logic that relies on publicly accepted (and imagined) probable premises that lead to probable conclusions.[22]

Feminists frequently face particular problems with the logical appeal of Barthes's Aristotelian enthymeme: specifically, the logic of their probable premises often does not reflect the common sense logic of the general public; therefore, the public cannot imagine or will not supply missing premises. As a result, feminists are often obliged to lay out their premises and argue their validity. This time-consuming process often delays political action. Yet even when their premises are outlined, their arguments and conclusions must still confront the judgment of mass logic. And this mass logic often denies the validity of personal experience, especially the personal experiences of women, feminists, and other outsiders, unless of course this personal experience can be validated, preferably by the testimony of two men.[23]

Feminists also confront particular problems with Barthes's Aristotelian emotional appeal. That is, these appeals are largely negated by the logic of Barthes' probable/possible distinctions. The maxim—" 'better an impossible probability than an improbable possibility' "—does not provide space for many feminists' arguments ("The Old Rhetoric" 22). Grounded in women's private/public experiences and skeptical of major/minor distinctions, feminists' arguments frequently emerge as emotional pleas that are too often received neither as probable impossibilities nor as improbable possibilities but as *improbable impossibilities*—that is, improbable within the consensus of public opinion and impossible within the logic of dominant discourse. That these improbable impossibilities (read "private emotional pleas") might possess logics of their own is an unpopular notion that public opinion is not often willing to acknowledge, let alone explore. Jane Tompkins claims that Western epistemology allows no space for the emotional (170), but the emotional does not simply vanish. What Western epistemology does is mystify the power of the emotional by hiding it in the negative and renaming it *il*logical, *ir*rational, *non*sensical, *un*true, *in*valid—all of which occupy space. As a result, emotional appeals are rendered as improbable impossibilities. Because their logic does not neatly fit the dominant logic of the masses, feminists are often labelled "mad" or "angry," accused of giving way to emotional tirades, and dismissed as having no sense of humor. Such labels and accusations deny the validity and importance of feminists' different emotional appeals.

Barthes's Aristotelian ethical appeal also poses problems for feminists. Aristotle restricted his concept of *ethos* to that sense of the speaker which emerges from the text at the site of the audience's listening. This concept of ethos, however, has traditionally not included a space for women whose sex is visibly marked on their bodies. The sight of women or the sound of feminists behind the bar or in the pulpit has almost always evoked resistance before they could ever utter a word, or The Word. Such resistance calls not only upon public opinion but also upon the Law (of God, of the Phallus). Popularly invoked as transcendent Truth that emerges transparently through language, the Law is frequently perceived as impervious to the influences of history and culture. So women and feminists have traditionally had to argue for their right to speak or write in a public forum about private and public concerns (e.g., Margery Kempe, Laura Cereta, Margaret Fell, Angelina and Sarah Grimke, Sojourner Truth, Elizabeth Cady Stanton, Mary Church Terrell). Although Cicero expanded Aristotle's concept of *ethos* to include the reputation of the speaker (*De Oratore* 2.43), his theory further marginalized women and feminists who were not allowed a respectable public reputation.

Clearly, if feminists' enthymemic premises are not imagined or supplied by the public, if their logical appeals prolong political action, if their emotional appeals are hidden within the negative, and if their ethical appeals are given relatively little cultural space, then revisionist feminist theories of rhetoric need to reconceptualize these classical boundaries of proof and appeal to emancipate women from their "old" and "new" rhetorical double binds.

In addition to critiquing definitions, proofs, and appeals of the old rhetoric, Barthes narrates another important rhetorical consideration, language function:

> [T]he art of speech is originally linked to a claim of ownership, as if language, as object of a transformation, condition of a practice, had been determined not from a subtle ideological mediation (as may have been the case in so many forms of art), but from the baldest sociality,

affirmed in its fundamental brutality, that of earthly possession: we began to reflect upon language in order to defend our own. It is on the level of social conflict that was
born a first theoretical sketch of *feigned speech* (different
from fictive speech, that of the poets: poetry was then
the only literature, prose not acceding to this status until
later). ("The Old Rhetoric" 17)

Part of the "subtle ideological mediation" that must be demystified
in the above description is that "we" meant *men* and "our" meant
men's, while women, slaves, and children were relegated to the
category of "earthly possession" for which men bargained (Aristotle, *Politics* 1260a.7). To redefine women's position, feminist theories of rhetoric must critique this concept of language to determine if, and how, it can be made more inclusive. For how we
assume language functions, more than anything else, determines
how we read and write the cultural as well as the textual. When
posited as a simple tool that communicates thought, language functions at the beck and call of unified subjects whose unlimited
agency can determine when, how, and why to speak, listen, read,
or write. When posited as an all-powerful structure that creates
both subjects and thought, language constructs discursive positions *within* which specific subjects are totally determined. But
when posited as a necessary component of rhetorical socialization
and negotiation, language becomes a means through which specific
subjects as rhetorical agents both construct and reflect their personal and collective texts and cultures. The latter position allows women and feminists the possibility of, and space for, social
change. Just as importantly, it demystifies the dangers of celebrating an acultural, autonomous agency, otherwise known as the
bootstrap theory, which frequently traps women and feminists into
feeling inferior, inadequate, mad, or angry for not being able,
singlehandedly, to overcome systemic sexism and its accompanying racism, classism, homophobia, religious prejudice, and so on.
It also demystifies certain death-of-the-author theories that have
emerged just as women, feminists, and other marginalized voices
were becoming powerful in academia, theories that have sometimes
been used to silence them.

Barthes also narrates the concept of text. The significance of the old rhetoric for the new text of modern and contemporary rhetorical theories is elucidated in his opening paragraph:

> At the source—or on the horizon—of this seminar, as always, there was the modern text, *i.e., the text which does not yet exist.* One way to approach this new text is to find out from what point of departure, and in opposition to what, it seeks to come into being, and in this way to confront the new semiotics of writing with the classical practice of literary language, which for centuries was known as Rhetoric. Whence the notion of a seminar on the old Rhetoric: *old* does not mean that there is a new Rhetoric today; rather *old Rhetoric* is set in opposition to that new which may not yet have come into being: the world is incredibly full of old Rhetoric. ("The Old Rhetoric" 11)

Clearly the old rhetoric cannot be ignored, for the new rhetoric must emerge from, or in opposition to, the old. Thus, feminists may construct theories of the new rhetoric by following Virginia Woolf's injunction "to try the accepted forms, to discard the unfit, to create others which are more fitting" ("Men and Women" 195). Woolf's third position echoes Barthes's idea of a "text which does not yet exist," a concept of text that provides the perfect opening for feminist theories of rhetoric. For feminists are concerned with nothing if not arguing that *improbable impossibilities* are indeed *possible.*

Linking *the possible* to gendered textuality has implications for rethinking the canons of rhetoric, which Barthes describes as "*active, transitive, programmatic, operational,*" as not a structure but a "gradual structuration" ("The Old Rhetoric" 50). Although Barthes reduces the five canons to three—invention, arrangement, and style (51–52)—when dealing with written texts, feminist scholars should reclaim all five. For feminist studies of invention, arrangement, and style may help us articulate different thought processes, logics, and shaping of ideas and feelings. Studies of memory may encourage us to ask what is remembered, what is forgotten, who makes such decisions, where, and why. And studies of delivery may disclose cultural gestures that expose textual heteroglossia at all sites of production (e.g., writing, publishing, retailing, advertising, reading). Hence, all five canons are important means of tying the textual to the personal and the cultural, of uncovering the functions of sex and gender in these processes.

Barthes also narrates the rhetorical concepts of author and audience by blurring their boundaries and interweaving them, thus calling into question the concepts of agency, identity, and unified self. When interrogating the concept of author, he distinguishes the *auctor* of the old rhetoric from our contemporary author: "As for the written text, it was not subject, as it is today, to a judgment of originality; what we call the *author* did not exist; around the ancient text, the only text used and in a sense managed, like reinvested capital, there were various functions: 1. the *scriptor* who purely and simply copies; 2. the *compilator* who adds to what he copies, but nothing that comes from himself; 3. the *commentator* who introduces himself into the copied text, but only to make it intelligible; 4. the *auctor*, finally, who presents his own ideas but always by depending on other authorities" ("The Old Rhetoric" 30). The ancient, agonistic auctor poses problems for feminists. He is assumed to be a male "athlete of speech" whose speech emerges as a competition to see who can flex the most rhetorical muscles. His speech "is the object of a certain glamour and of a regulated power," and through this power-play merger of grammar and glamour, his aggression becomes "coded" and invisible (30). These concepts of auctor and auctor's speech celebrate a victor/victim, winner/loser power dynamic based on violence that many feminists are unwilling to accept. Such concepts reinforce a superior/inferior ethics rather than an ethics of difference, and they denigrate personal experiences, emotions, and reasoning by their insistence on "other authorities."

Influenced by Enlightenment concepts of self that have been strengthened by Romantic notions of private visions, the contemporary author also poses problems for feminists. He is an original presence, a unified self in possession of a transcendent signified.[24] This liberal humanist notion of unified self presumes an autonomous agency that uses language as transparent medium to negotiate societal structures and that succeeds or fails on the basis of individual will. When truth and talent are perceived as foundational and transcendent rather than conventional, scapegoating emerges as a popular rhetorical strategy for transferring sin, blame, and responsiblity. With its focus on specific subjects, this concept of author leaves no space for theorizing insititutional oppressions and thus little room for critiquing itself. That is, this closed concept of author does not provide feminists with spaces for questioning the cultural labels of women's discourse (e.g., too personal, too emotional) and the cultural value (e.g., mundane), which emerge in commonsense logics as powerful first premises that are increasingly hard to challenge.

Barthes addresses the limits of auctor/author concepts by repudiating an authorial agency in which the author's presence functions as the sole determinate of meaning ("Death of the Author"; *S/Z*). Instead, he valorizes the continual play of the signifier, a stance about language that simultaneously undermines the concept of authorial presence as agency and posits a readerly agency in which the reader is invited to read and read again, with each reading rendering different possibilities, different texts, that other readers are then invited to (re)read. By blurring the categories of author and reader, Barthes argues that an act of writing is actually an act of reading the world, or as he claims, the death of the author gives rise to the birth of the reader ("Death of the Author" 55). This readerly agency retains a space in which a specific feminist may validate her own experiences by reading/writing the world, but this agency does not enable her to totally control how others receive her readings/writings.[25] This stance allows feminists the possibilities of critique while acknowledging its limitations.[26] My extrapolation of feminist theories of rhetoric joins this discussion. The ideas and textual strategies that inform Woolf's, Daly's, and Rich's feminist theories of rhetoric are theirs; the rhetorical values assigned to them in my extrapolation is mine; further interpretations will belong to the reader.[27] All of these processes will, of course, be influenced by our language and our culture.

Barthes's concern with spatial and temporal influences on reading narrates another rhetorical concept, rhetorical situation. Barthes questions the function of space and time by addressing geographical dimensions of inventive *topoi*: "What is a place? It is, says Aristotle, that in which a plurality of oratorical reasonings coincide. . . . Yet the metaphoric approach to place is more significant than its abstract definition" ("The Old Rhetoric" 64–65). Barthes complicates the function of space with the movement of time when he posits topoi as place, as a method of finding arguments. Although Barthes never uses the term *rhetorical situation*, he does refer to cultural "moments" of production and consumption that are continually being (re)constructed. Within this context, Barthes's rhetorical situation refers to geographic spaces and moments that are both psychological and cultural. This definition opens possibilities for constructing and validating feminist revisionings; indeed, it offers more possibilities for feminists than does Lloyd Bitzer's definition of rhetorical situation as the sum total of exigences, audience, and constraints. Bitzer's positivistic rendering mystifies the influence of time and memory, the constructive nature of history, and, to a degree, the multiple interpretive possibilities of a text.[28] Demystifying these factors, Barthes's concept of reading implies a rhetorical situation, or cultural moment, that is fluid and continually reconstructed.

Barthes's concept of continually reconstructed cultural moments narrates a closely related rhetorical concern, the compilation of these moments into histories. For Barthes, rhetoric cannot be separated from a consideration of history and historiography: "[R]hetoric . . . call[s] into question history itself . . . ; the classification it has imposed is the only feature really shared by successive and various historical groups, as if there existed, superior to ideologies of content and to direct determinations of history, an ideology of form; as if . . . there existed for each society a *taxonomic identity*, a sociologic in whose name it is possible to define another history, another sociality, without destroying those recognized at other levels" ("The Old Rhetoric" 14–15). For feminists, there are both limits and possibilities for change in studying rhetorical history. Limitations emerge in conceiving rhetoric only as "an ideology of form" or static structure that has been relatively untouched by its cultural moments; such a stance may trap women into static cultural, psychological, and linguistic essentialisms. Conceiving rhetoric only as "an ideology of form" also begs a separation of intellectual bodies from stylistic dress; this separation too often implies that language functions only to communicate thought. Yet possibilities for change do exist. Studying the history of rhetoric allows feminists to question the construction and importance of language theory and language function in textual interpretive processes and in cultural power dynamics. It also enables them to question the functions of histories and historiographies, which in turn promotes the possibilities for imagining multiple histories and multiple historiographies. Such actions are imperative if feminists are to read and write their concerns of race, gender, class, sexual orientation, religious preference, and so on, into history.

For Barthes, rhetorical history moves in both diachronic and systematic directions ("The Old Rhetoric" 15). This doubled movement denies the closure of evolutionary historiography to which Knoblauch and Brannon consign classical rhetoric and its potential applications for contemporary composition pedagogy. This doubled movement also calls into question the concepts of tradition and canon. That is, by what criteria are existing rhetorical traditions and canons defined? Do the criteria assume gynocritcal, androcentric, or desegregated canons? Whose interests do these criteria serve? Where should feminist theories of rhetoric be located in relation to these traditions and to these canons? Should feminists establish a separate tradition or expand the canon? What truth conditions inform different traditions, different canons? And what are the limits and possibilities of feminists' embracing the concepts of tradition and canon for their own projects of rewriting rhetorical histories?[29] The paradox of histories that we should always keep in mind, however, is that they have meaning only in the present as they inform our conscious and unconscious thinking, acting, feeling, and being.

When critiquing the knowledge constructed and dispersed within these traditions and canons, Barthes narrates another facet of the old rhetoric, its relation to politics: "It is obviously tempting to conflate this mass rhetoric with Aristotle's politics; which was, as we know, a politics of the happy medium, favoring a balanced democracy, centered on the middle classes, and responsible for reducing antagonisms between rich and poor, majority and minority; whence a rhetoric of good sense, deliberately subordinate to the 'psychology' of the public" ("The Old Rhetoric" 22–23). Barthes's temptation "to conflate this mass rhetoric with Aristotle's politics" echoes Aristotle's impulse to locate rhetoric between logic and ethics/politics (*Rhetoric* 1.4.10). Yet connecting rhetoric to Aristotle's ethics/politics may pose problems for feminists. For example, Aristotle's Ideal States imply a balance, a center agreed upon by *most* people (read "men in power" and "those men who may attain such power").[30] Even if such a relatively conflict-free state were possible, this definition erases the divisions between rich and poor, free and slave, men and women; as such, it privileges the first term—propertied, free, male—while presenting it as the universal subject of rhetorical theory. From a feminist perspective, this ideal state is exposed as ideal only for those with power: the truths of the margins are exposed as less important than the truths of the center, and the stress on conflict-free existence emerges not simply as a desire for harmony but as a desire for maintaining the status quo. Moreover, positing a "rhetoric of good sense" as the dominant discourse of Aristotelian Ideal States poses important questions of power ("The Old Rhetoric" 23). Who gets to define good sense? Will this good sense be constructed as a monolithic category or as a field of difference? Most importantly, why the emphasis on sense, on logic, on the head?

A consideration of good sense located in the head points to the final concern that Barthes narrates: pedagogy. As mentioned above, *a teaching* is one of Barthes's defining categories of rhetoric: "[T]he art of rhetoric, initially transmitted by personal means (a rhetor and his disciples, his clients), was soon introduced into institutions of learning; in schools, it formed the essential matter of what would today be called higher education; it was transformed into material for examination (exercises, lessons, texts)" ("The Old Rhetoric" 13). The *teaching* names a cultural space in which Barthes's other defining categories can be taught and challenged, yet the institutionalization of rhetoric, particularly its relegation to fake exercises and dry handbooks, mystifies the potential of its personal, textual, and cultural powers.[31] Thus, the teaching raises certain questions. What connections exist between institutional and noninstitutional learning, between theory and praxis? Who is allowed access to institutional learning? Where does a student or teacher stand to challenge the dominant rhetoric? And what are the relations among gendered subjects, schools, and culture? Feminists should analyze the history of rhetorical pedagogy, not just to determine how and why women have been included or excluded but also to learn how and why pedagogical power struggles have, and do, undergird the mystifications of rhetoric's potential for changing the personal, the textual, and the cultural.

Barthes concludes his essay by discussing the interwoven possibilities of rhetorical history, theory, and pedagogy: "Yes, a history of Rhetoric (as research, as book, as teaching) is today necessary, broadened by a new way of thinking (linguistics, semiology, historical science, psychoanalysis, Marxism)" ("The Old Rhetoric" 92). To the parenthetical list, I would add feminisms. For an understanding of feminist theory and praxis would enable rhetoric scholars not only to locate gender gaps but also to imagine new texts of rhetorical history, theory, and pedagogy that recognize, validate, and address Bathsheba's dilemma.

Defending Anglo-American Feminist Theories of Rhetoric(s): Woolf, Daly, and Rich

At the 1992 Virginia Woolf Conference, Jane Marcus claimed in her closing address, "I need to make my Virginia Woolf stand for the issues that interest me." In many ways this claim articulates my own feelings about this project. I propose to make my Virginia Woolf, my Mary Daly, and my Adrienne Rich—or rather, the way that I read these women's lives and texts—speak to the issue that interests me in rhetoric and composition studies. That issue is feminism, specifically the ways in which sex and gender come into play in rhetorical history, theory, and pedagogy. As one attempt to articulate this play, I extrapolate Woolf's, Daly's, and Rich's Anglo-American feminist theories of rhetoric from their writings about women, language, and culture.

My extrapolations of these theories emerge from putting these three feminists' texts into play with the sex and gender gaps discovered in the previous discussion of Barthes's essay "The Old Rhetoric." Such an extrapolation process assumes that these feminists' texts are genuinely concerned with rhetorical concepts but that, because these feminist texts have not been constructed from the site of rhetoric and composition studies, their theories of rhetoric must be extrapolated from their nonrhetoric texts, such as their essays, diaries, letters, and poems about women, language, and culture. The limitation of such an extrapolation process is that the eight concepts in the preceding section may be read as a theoretical grid, which forces Woolf's, Daly's, and Rich's Anglo-American feminist theories of rhetoric to conform to previous rhetorical categories and, thus, erases any original contributions these feminists might make. But the possibility of this extrapolation process allows another interpretation: if these eight concepts are interpreted as interwoven functions that merge personal, textual, and cultural concerns, then they may be interpreted as starting points for extrapolating feminist theories of rhetoric. Obviously, these eight concepts are not the only starting points. Thus, my study invites interested scholars to expand my extrapolations and also construct other feminist theories of rhetoric.

This extrapolation process has important implications. First, it challenges the received rhetorical traditions not in order to erase traditional theories nor simply to add women's voices to them but rather to rethink our discipline; that is, this process forces us to ask what happens if we imagine rhetorical history as a map with Aristotle's theory clearly marked and Woolf's, Rich's, and Daly's theories newly charted. Second, it asks how rhetoric and composition studies may be informed not just by the presence of Woman and women but by feminist ideology. Third, it explores how rhetoric and composition studies, specifically the question of Bathsheba's dilemma, may be informed by literary studies, religious studies, and women's studies. And, fourth, it also raises certain questions. Such questions will most likely emerge from the following three grounds, and although I will attempt to anticipate such queries, my responses will, I hope, evoke even more questions.

The first query is often constructed as follows: would studying Woolf, Daly, and Rich in rhetoric and composition studies be appropriate, given that these feminists do not locate themselves within rhetorical traditions and given that traditional histories of rhetoric do not commonly claim the texts of these feminists? My response is simple. Both claims are true. But if someone employs these two claims to prevent interdisciplinary moves, he/she is assuming that authorial intent determines meaning and that canon formation is static. Moreover, these claims ignore Woolf's, Daly's, and Rich's concerns with rhetorical concepts. Their schooling, talents, interests, opportunities, politics, and particular historical moments have led these feminist activists to become a novelist, a philosopher (one who studies "philosophia"), and a poet, respectively. Their concerns about women, language, and writing, however, can be (re)read as Anglo-American feminist theories of rhetoric that challenge the genderblindness of more traditional histories, theories, and pedagogies. To emphasize how these feminists may be read as rhetorical theorists, I have included a section in each subsequent chapter that locates their feminist texts in relation to rhetorical theories, lore, and practice.

The second query usually emerges as follows: would not focusing on French feminist theories be more appropriate, given that they are more sophisticated than Anglo-American theories? Within the logic of this question, Anglo-American feminist theories are denigrated as naive posturings of language use, autonomous wills, and identity politics[32]; they are then compared to French feminist theories, which are hailed as sophisticated critiques of language, subjectivity, closure, writing, and so on. Ironically, this binary reinforces the structure of phallogocentric logic, with French theories occupying the dominant position and Anglo-American theories occupying the subordinate one; this binary also erases the presence of feminists theories that fit into neither category. Within this denigration logic, Anglo-American feminisms are divided into liberal and radical feminisms; in turn, radical feminisms, with which Daly's and Rich's texts are associated and for which Woolf's texts construct a space, are frequently accused of essentialism[33] and separatism.[34] In subsequent chapters, I revise these prevailing readings of Anglo-American feminisms; that is, I reread Woolf, Daly, and Rich to refute claims that an essential female self exists,[35] that gender identity and sexual orientation occur only as conscious choice, and that identification among women is only achieved by a Sartrean bonding as objects (Nye 104).

The third query is perhaps the most serious: would a focus on Anglo-American feminist theory preclude discussions of difference? If we assume that difference occurs only between categories of feminisms, then such a focus would preclude such discussions. But if we assume that difference occurs not only between categories but also *within* them, then my focus on Woolf, Daly, and Rich may be read as exposing differences *within* Anglo-American feminisms. For example, in Woolf's theory the rhetorical canons maintain their structures but posit different definitions; in Daly's

theory the rhetorical canons become Non-canons, feminist reversals of the traditional categories; and in Rich's theory the canons
do not hold but are radically transformed. Foregrounding differences within Anglo-American feminisms is a necessary move if
these theories are to be particularized and recovered from charges
of naïveté. The purpose of such a move is to celebrate Anglo-
American radical feminist theories as *one* of many kinds of feminisms. Yet the ethics of such a move entails our continually asking
ourselves, and addressing, the following questions: what can be
accepted in these theories, what must be discarded, and what needs
to be reconstructed? It also entails asking and addressing: who is
(not) speaking, who is (not) listening, and what is (not) being
heard? Responses to such queries should serve as the impetus for
future research.

By studying Woolf's, Daly's, and Rich's Anglo-American feminist theories of rhetoric, I hope to invite new voices and new
hearings into the history of rhetoric. For by changing contexts
and lines of argument, these three Anglo-American feminists have
reinforced, rejected, or reimagined traditional theories of rhetoric,
whether consciously or unconsciously, to challenge the dominant
ideology and push their own political goals.[36] As challengers of
phallogocentric culture and its dominant discourse(s), these three
writers and their texts have provided a means of recognizing, validating, and addressing women's commonsense experiences, otherwise known as Bathsheba's dilemma. In the process, these writers
and their texts have constructed feminist literacies from which to
enact changes in the interwoven realms of the personal, the textual,
and the cultural. That, I will argue, is the importance of their
Anglo-American feminist theories of rhetoric for rhetoric and
composition studies.

2

Minting the Fourth Guinea:
VIRGINIA WOOLF

[The daughters of educated men] can best help you to prevent war not by repeating your words and following your
methods but by finding new words and creating new methods.

—Virginia Woolf, *Three Guineas*

And she . . . has to devise some entirely new combination
of her resources . . . so as to absorb the new into the old
without disturbing the infinitely intricate and elaborate balance of the whole.

—Virginia Woolf, *A Room of One's Own*

In *Three Guineas* Virginia Woolf constructs a feminist agenda
to subvert the dominant ideology and promote a feminist paci-
fism. She proposes a tripartite economic strategy of donating
three guineas[1] to three worthy causes—the first guinea to women's
colleges, the second to a women's professional society, and the
third to a male antifascist political society. By employing guineas
as the controlling metaphor of her 1938 radical feminist epistolary
essay, Woolf does not pose naive class assumptions (e.g., we can
buy our way out of sexist educational structures, sexist business
practices, and/or war) but rather exposes the insidious implications
of capitalism (e.g., money as power permeates all aspects of
women's and men's lives).[2] Her use of the guinea metaphor implies
that peace and equal rights are "luxury" items that we can no
longer afford not to buy, for they cost us as a culture and as
specific subjects. Yet the material existence of *Three Guineas* implies
an unnamed fourth guinea: a textual strategy of reading and writing against the dominant ideology. Foregrounding this fourth

32

guinea in our reading of Woolf's texts allows us to see how she challenges the dominant ideology from a materialist feminist perspective by weaving an economy of the textual, the cultural, and the psychological. This gendered interweaving, I argue, may be reread as a politicized theory of discourse.

By examining Woolf's critiques of women, language, and culture and by analyzing her own textual strategies, I offer a reading of her texts from the site of rhetoric and composition studies that conceptualizes her contributions to rhetorical history, theory, and practice. My purpose is to extrapolate a feminist theory of rhetoric that challenges the genderblindness of the rhetorical tradition(s). Toward this end, I first locate Virginia Woolf as a rhetorical theorist. Then I posit certain components of Woolf's feminist theory of rhetoric, foregrounding their gender concerns: (1) material conditions, (2) language function, (3) text, (4) author, (5) invention/arrangement/memory, (6) style, and (7) audience. I conclude with examples of theoretical and pedagogical questions made possible by Woolf's Anglo-American feminist theory of rhetoric.

Locating Virginia Woolf as a Rhetorical Theorist

Although Woolf does not locate herself within Western rhetorical traditions,[3] she does name and describe Bathsheba's dilemma: the difficulty women have articulating their feelings in the language of men ("Men and Women" 195). Yet when Woolf explores *how* women read and write within a patriarchal language and society, she does not simply identify problems and rest upon her cleverness.[4] While exploring the writing experiences of herself, other historical women, the fictional Mary Carmichael, and the yet-to-be-born Judith Shakespeare, Woolf argues not only *that* Bathsheba's dilemma must be recognized, validated, and addressed but also *how* this recognizing, validating, and addressing should be done. But before examining her suggested solutions, I want to unpack an assumption embedded in Woolf's discussion of Bathsheba's dilemma: specifically, what is implied by Woolf's use of the term *women*? Obviously, it is complicated by gender; less obviously, by class; and perhaps even less obviously, by race. By exploring such complications in terms of Woolf's claims and images, I hope to expose how her use of the term *women* may resonate in subsequent discussions of her texts and her Anglo-American feminist theory of rhetoric.

Woolf herself exposes how gender assumptions complicate her use of the term *women* in relation to both writing and speaking. In *A Room of One's Own* she makes visible the assumption commonly accepted in 1929 that women have not been, and cannot be, good writers or speakers. She cites Dr. Johnson's comment about the impossibility of women preachers to prove her point: " 'Sir, a woman's [preaching] is like a dog's walking on his hind legs. It is not done well, but you are surprised to find it done at all' " (56). But Woolf refutes this assumption in two ways. First, in *A Room of One's Own* she recovers women writers who are unknown to most of her readers, exemplifying that women have indeed been capable of writing well even if they have not been widely published or canonized. She argues, in fact, that women "ought to let flowers fall upon the tomb of Aphra Behn which is, most scandalously but rather appropriately, in Westminster Abbey, for it was she who earned them the right to speak their minds" (66). Second, Woolf demonstrates via her famous syllogism how interrelated cultural, textual, and psychological assumptions have made writing well an extremely arduous task for women: that is, if material conditions foster intellectual freedom and if intellectual freedom is necessary for poetry, then because women have been poor and lacked intellectual freedom, they "have not had a dog's chance of writing poetry" or sermons or . . . (108). Woolf does note one corollary to these constraints: the novel was still "young enough" when middle-class women started writing in the eighteenth century to be shaped, in part, by their efforts (77). So although women writers and speakers need not be totally determined by commonsense gender assumptions, fighting the effects of such assumptions can be a difficult process, for these assumptions comprise the commonsense premises of daily conversations, arguments, and socialization.

Woolf's term *women* is further complicated by class assumptions. Woolf recognizes the privileges of her own class, which is composed of educated men and the daughters of educated men. But she also claims that the privilege afforded these men and their daughters is vastly different. For example, when discussing her father Leslie Stephen and the literati who flowed in and out of his house at teatime, she talks of how he was elated with such companionship and of how she became imbued with a double consciousness. That is, she learned to criticize literature rigorously in her father's library (because women were not admitted to Oxford); but she learned to flirt, flatter, and concede to young men's opinions at the teatable (Rose 21). For this reason, Woolf asserts in *Three Guineas* that daughters of educated men are less publicly powerful than working class women who, at least, have the power to threaten strikes (12). Although pitting different classes of women against each other and arguing who is more oppressed is probably a counterproductive political move, exposing the cracks in the dream of the middle class is not. For just as middle-class feminists must be careful not to romanticize or colonize working-class women and their concerns, working-class feminists must be equally careful not to assume that middle-class privilege renders sexism less insidious. Perhaps a productive way of reading Woolf's claim is as encouraging feminists of all classes to examine, and respect, how different economic situations affect women differently.

In Woolf's texts, the gender and class assumptions of *women* are even further complicated by race. Sometimes Woolf's texts address the issue directly. In *Three Guineas*, for example, the narrator explicitly mentions race when she stipulates her condition for donating a guinea to a woman's professional society: women who have earned entry into this professional society must, in turn, help other qualified people—"whether man or woman, white or black"—to enter the professions (66). The narrator's stance obviously rejects sexual and racial discrimination; however, it does imply a narrow black/white conception of race. Yet this narrow conception is no doubt complicated by Woolf's knowledge of Hitler's 1938 Germany as well as her marriage to a Jewish man, Leonard Woolf. On the other hand, Woolf's texts address the issue of race indirectly. A character in *The Waves*, for example, demonstrates an unthinking (though not excusable) racism: while eating in a fancy Western restaurant, she refers to colonials as "cannibals." Such passages may be read as Woolf's own bias against colonials, but perhaps more productively, these passages may be read as a move that renders racism visible and, thus, makes rereading that racism possible. In other words, the cannibal comment may be read as exposing that the imperialists are the ones actually doing the cannibalizing (Marcus, "Pathologies").

To explore such ways of reading, the 1993 Virginia Woolf Conference[5] focused on the following questions: what can Woolf studies offer multicultural studies, and what can multicultural studies offer Woolf studies? The keynote speakers pursued these questions. Michelle Cliff examined intersections of empire, race, class, and gender in Woolf's texts. Cliff cited many troublesome passages in Woolf, like the cannibal one above, reflecting on them and calling for further research. Barbara Christian read Woolf through an open letter to Toni Morrison. Christian used Morrison's thesis on Woolf and William Faulkner as a starting point for analyzing connections between Morrison and Woolf. Although Christian cited some stylistic similarities, she argued that the main differences between the two emerge in the concepts they use to envision their texts: Morrison uses *black life* and *black culture*; Woolf uses *women*, which really implies *white women*. Elizabeth Abel read Woolf in conjunction with Alice Walker ("Matrilineage"). After Abel's talk, the discussion circled around the following question: with what authority may white women speak about African American women's experiences? Disagreement ensued, the term of contention being *authority*. Abel concluded the discussion with two claims: one, white women must try to understand and write about the experiences of women in different cultures without presuming the authority of lived experience (after all, minority women have had to do so for years); and two, it is better for white women to make such an attempt and do it badly than not to try at all. The question remaining after the discussion, however, was one of procedure, namely, how?

The above complications make Woolf's use of *women* a loaded term, one that refers primarily to Anglo-American women but one that should be critiqued to explore its multicultural possibilities and limitations. Such critiques should be noted when we read her texts and when we contemplate her solutions to Bathsheba's dilemma. One solution, offered in "Men and Women," is that women writers can challenge textual constraints by attempting "to try the accepted forms, to discard the unfit, to create others which are more fitting" (195). Although the possibilities of these strategies will be explored later, the questions begged here are: do *all* women have access to "the accepted forms," and do *all* women have the power to create "more fitting" forms and to compel others to listen? A second solution, offered in "Women and Fiction," is that women writers can challenge cultural constraints by attaining leisure, money, and a room of their own (52). The questions begged here are these: do all women have the opportunity for leisure, money, and a room of their own, and if not, what other possible cultural conditions may encourage women to write well? A third solution, offered in "Professions for Women," is that women writers can challenge psychological constraints by killing the Angel in the House and by telling the truth about one's body. The questions here include: are all women in all cultures oppressed via the Angel, or does oppression take different forms in different cultures; moreover, what different cultural conceptions of *body* make truthtelling (im)possible? A fourth solution, offered in "Dorothy Richardson," is that women writers can pen themselves into active subjects who assert agency through language via Richardson's model of a "woman's sentence" or a "psychological sentence of the feminine gender" (191). The question begged here is one of procedure: how might such a sentence manifest itself differently in different languages and cultures? A fifth solution, offered in *A Room of One's Own*, is that the Mary Carmichaels of the world can pave the way for the Judith Shakespeares. This solution assumes that agency is neither autonomous nor immaterial; that material barriers can be transformed only by a tradition of writers who are not afraid of, nor obsessed with, their sex; and that women will write well if an androgynous cultural space is carved out for them.[6] Here the question of race is most obvious: if Mary Carmichael and Judith Shakespeare either are or are not assumed to be white, then what can their androgynous tradition offer writers from other cultures? Finally, the purpose for implementing these solutions is offered in *Three Guineas* where Woolf argues that sexism, fascism, and classism arise from the same ideological impulses of *power over* rather than *power to*. Consequently, Bathsheba's dilemma must be resolved if women and men, nations, and the earth are to survive. Although power may manifest itself differently in different cultures, Woolf's proposed means to this survival is an inclusive rhetoric of words, not the failure of rhetoric, which is war. As evidenced by the above claims, Woolf is interested in Bathsheba's dilemma not solely as a textual critique, not solely as a cultural critique, not solely as a psychological critique. Instead, she is interested in an interweaving of the three. Because Woolf explores these interweavings as well as their implications for theory and practice, her texts offer fertile ground from which to extrapolate an Anglo-American feminist theory of rhetoric.

Although no one has previously extrapolated Woolf's feminist theory of rhetoric, debates about Woolf and rhetoric have taken many forms. Jane Marcus erases the rhetorical function of Woolf's texts, arguing that in *Three Guineas* Woolf positions herself as an outsider and, as such, cannot use rhetoric nor take a committed stance ("No More Horses" 269). Pamela Caughie refutes Marcus's claim, asserting that Woolf's rhetorical moves are precisely the reason that her text does not seem to take a committed stance (*Woolf and Postmodernism* 116). Despite their differing definitions of rhetoric, Marcus and Caughie both argue that Woolf sounds uncommitted.[7] I disagree. Instead, I read Woolf as modeling a discursive practice that is at once fluid and committed, a discursive practice that attempts to find and create "new words and new methods" in order to "absorb the new into the old without disturbing the infinitely intricate and elaborate balance of the whole" (*Three Guineas* 143; *Room* 85). From this intersection of fluidity and commitment, of free play and political stance, I will construct Woolf's feminist theory of rhetoric, which is important both for what it does, and does not, provide. What it does not offer is a static list of nonsexist language rules that any person in any situation may employ. What it offers is a heightened awareness of gendered rhetorical concepts as well as strategies that can inform ongoing, gendered critiques of language, culture, and specific subjects.

Woolf's Rhetorical Concepts

MATERIAL CONDITIONS

Woolf's concept of material conditions may be read as a concept of rhetorical situation. For Woolf, language has a material component; so, too, do writers, texts, audiences, and cultures in that they all are influenced by their material conditions. While not functioning as a deterministic grid, material conditions undergird the interwoven textual, cultural, and psychological conditions that inform Woolf's feminist theory of rhetoric. Material conditions of culture (e.g., leisure, money, and a room of one's own) affect the material conditions of specific subjects so that writing is impossible; however, subjects may also assume a limited agency and reconfigure the material conditions so that writing becomes possible for themselves and for others. As argued throughout *A Room of One's Own*, women writing may make women writers possible.

Moreover, Woolf claims that our material conditions are not neutral structures but patriarchal ones: "The cat is out of the bag; and it is a Tom" (*Three Guineas* 52). She argues that evidence for such a claim may be found in biography, autobiography, and daily newspapers (7). Woolf sees private evidence of a patriarchy reflected in her family's Victorian game of manners; as children, her brother George was allowed to perform while she and Vanessa were allowed to watch ("Sketch of the Past" 132). The narrator of *A Room of One's Own* sees public evidence of a patriarchy reflected in the evening paper's headlines: "Somebody had made a big score in South Africa. Lesser ribbons announced that Sir Austen Chamberlain was at Geneva. A meat axe with human hair on it had been found in a cellar. Mr Justice ——— commented in the Divorce Courts on the Shamelessness of Women. . . . A film actress had been lowered from a peak in California and hung suspended in mid-air. The weather was going to be foggy. The most transient visitor to this planet, I thought, could not fail to be aware, even from this scattered testimony, that England is under the rule of a patriarchy" (33). And the narrator of *Three Guineas* cites historical evidence for this claim, noting that patriarchy and the effects of patriarchy repeat themselves, perpetuating voices and images of men's and women's social roles that might seem as familiar to people in 1938 as to those people living in the age of Creon (141).

Woolf's metaphor of patriarchy invokes the sensibility of a white, upper-middle-class, literary British family. Although the limits of such a metaphor have been discussed earlier, the possibilities should not be ignored. Her metaphor exposes that women's cultural spaces and men's cultural spaces are defined differently even though such definitions are difficult to construct ("Women Novelists" 70). Because her metaphor assumes that women and men experience patriarchy differently, the effects of their experiences with the textual, the cultural, and the psychological must also differ. Still, not all men experience patriarchy in the same way. Neither do women: "upsetting though it is, . . . women are apt to differ" (70). Indeed, multiple possibilities exist within each gendered cultural space. Thus, Woolf's metaphor provides a means of talking about women and men in general and in particular.

As the narrator of *Three Guineas* claims, white middle-class women's cultural spaces trap these women in a double bind "between the devil and the deep blue sea": "Behind us lies the patriarchal system; the private house with its nullity, its immorality, its hypocrisy, its servility. Before us lies the public world, the professional system, with its possessiveness, its jealousy, its pugnacity, its greed. The one shuts us up like slaves in a harem; the other forces us to circle, like caterpillars head to tail, round and round the mulberry tree, the sacred tree of property. It is a choice of evils" (74). Although these middle-class women are more privileged than slaves, their cultural spaces are determined within this harem and around this sacred tree of property.

In order for women to revise the complex material conditions of their patriarchal socialization, Woolf recommends the following emancipatory strategies. First, women should embrace four great teachers: poverty, chastity, derision, and freedom from unreal loyalties (*Three Guineas* 79). Specifically, young women should decide to earn enough money to support themselves, to not sell their brains for money, to recognize that censure, ridicule, and obscurity are preferable to praise and fame, and to discard unreal loyalties of national pride, school pride, sex pride, family pride, and so on. (80). Second, in order for young women to contemplate these teachers, they need free time and space to think; that is, they need a room of their own and £500 a year (*Room* 4). Third, being possessed of a room and money is not enough. Women must also consider the questions of how they will decorate the room and with whom they will or will not share it, as well as what criteria they will use to answer such questions ("Professions for Women"

63). If women follow these three strategies, then they have the opportunity to rethink, and perhaps rearrange, the material conditions of patriarchy.

Men's cultural spaces, Woolf argues, usually benefit men more than women's cultural spaces benefit women within patriarchal structures. Men, especially white middle- and upper-class men, often receive better educations, attain more lucrative business positions, achieve more prestigious social status, and get waited upon in their private homes. Yet Woolf recognizes that men, too, are limited by the boundaries of patriarchy:

> Inevitably [the daughters of educated men] look upon societies as conspiracies that sink the private brother, whom many of us have reason to respect, and inflate in his stead a monstrous male, loudof voice, hard of fist, childishly intent upon scoring the floor of the earth with chalk marks, within whose mystic boundaries human beings are penned, rigidly, separately, artificially; where, daubed red and gold, decorated like a savage with feathers he goesthrough mystic rites and enjoys the dubious pleasures of power and dominion while we, "his" women, are locked in the private house without share in the many societies of which his society is composed. (*Three Guineas* 105)

Woolf ponders these limitations, especially the way in which men are socialized to perform expected social roles, and she concludes that these expected roles lead to the nationalism, classism, and sexism that undergird the material manifestations of patriarchy.

After analyzing the material conditions of patriarchy, Woolf concludes that both women and men would benefit from challenging these conditions, for the old consciousness and old traditions have (had) many victims. Women suffer: Woolf cites her alienating experiences at Oxbridge as well as the unpaid institutions of marriage and motherhood (*Room* 24; *Three Guineas* 110–11). But men suffer too: the men at Oxbridge are trapped within their traditions, and the men in the barrister's political society are trapped in their notions of masculinity (*Room* 24; *Three Guineas* 85–144). To counter these situations, Woolf offers different strategies. In *A Room of One's Own*, the narrator encourages women and men to strive for an androgynous vision, a unity of the mind, so that one's mind is rather like a taxi driving off, carrying both a young man and a young woman (104). Such a mind is fertile, active, and noncompartmentalized; so too will be the writing it produces. In *Three Guineas*, the narrator does not so easily believe in an androgynous identification; she represents the communication gap between men and women with ellipses. Nevertheless, she narrates the book in order to articulate these ellipses, an attempt she considers imperative if we are not only to produce art but also to create a peaceful world.

By claiming that men as well as women benefit from revising patriarchy, Woolf constructs a feminism that engages men, even if it does not make them its primary focus. This feminism, in turn, assumes that revising the ideology of patriarchy entails changing its material conditions. Given Woolf's belief that the interwoven cultural, psychological, and textual all have material dimensions, her feminism also assumes that this change may occur through rhetorical functions of language.

LANGUAGE FUNCTION

Woolf's theory of language function may be read in her 1920 essay "Men and Women" in which she ponders the dilemma of Bathsheba Everdene in Thomas Hardy's *Far from the Madding Crowd*: " 'I have the feelings of a woman,' says Bathsheba . . . , 'but I have only the language of men.' From that dilemma arise infinite confusions and complications. Energy has been liberated, but into what forms is it to flow? To try the accepted forms, to discard the unfit, to create others which are more fitting, is a task that must be accomplished before there is freedom or achievement" (195). Woolf's first two strategies—trying accepted forms and discarding unfit ones[8]—position women within the language of men and recognize possibilities for women's agency within this language. Woolf's third strategy—creating other forms that are more fitting—conceptualizes possibilities for that which has not yet been conceptualized.[9] Thus, this third strategy provides the possibility for theorizing our way beyond the formalism as well as the war, scapegoating, and asexual procreation metaphors upon which traditional rhetorical theories are based.

Woolf's tripartite strategy exposes that women cannot escape the language of men, for it constitutes the symbolic as well as women's subject positions (Belsey 48–51; Stimpson, *Meanings* xi–xx). Given that women cannot stand outside this language, they must construct new forms from the old. By implication, conventional forms, theories, and practices are viewed not as static but as mutable, and newly conceptualized forms, theories, and practices make the old ones unrecognizable. Thus, Woolf's strategy provides the possibility for theorizing our way beyond what Mary Ryder defines as the binary trap within feminist language theories: identifying either with Lakoff's overly determined, color conscious women or with Cixous's hysterical Medusa (530–31). Instead, women can use the language of men to find ways of expressing the feelings of a woman, whether pain or pleasure.[10] Once such pain and pleasure are written into language, material conditions change so that revolution becomes a possibility. Like Plato, Woolf has faith in this revolutionary potential of language, which interweaves with the psychological and the cultural; after all, a poem just might change the nature of the republic (Marcus, *Languages of Patriarchy* 16).

Of course, words do not function independently of people. People's interaction with words and their interaction with each other through words constructs subjectivity and meaning. Despite this interactive focus, Woolf would be skeptical of the identification that Kenneth Burke places at the center of his rhetorical theory (*Rhetoric of Motives* 19–29, 55–59). She concedes that a type of identification with words may occur on rare occasions: there is "a feeling of transparency in words when they cease to be words and become so intensified that one seems to experience them; to foretell them as if they developed what one is already feeling" ("Sketch of the Past" 93).[11] She also concedes that a type of identification between people that must be expressed through words may also occur. For example, the visual identification of the female narrator and the male barrister in *Three Guineas* may be put into language: "When we look at those [war] photographs some fusion takes place within us; however different the education, the traditions behind us, our sensations are the same . . . 'horror and disgust' " (11). In such cases, one does not seem to need rhetoric, for the sharing of substance negates the need for rhetoric (89). But such cases, Woolf argues, are rare indeed.

More often, rhetoric is necessary because differences between people, particularly differences between women and men, inhibit their communication and affect their socialization through language. In *Three Guineas* Woolf signifies the distance between men's and women's cultural spaces with ellipses: "But . . . those three dots mark a precipice, a gulf so deeply cut between us that for three years and more I have been sitting on my side of it wondering whether it is any use to try to speak across it" (4). The ellipses indicate that the gulf is unspeakable, incapable of being put into words.[12] Woolf's purpose in *Three Guineas*, however, is to articulate this gulf, which she claims results not from differences in biology but from differences in men's and women's socialization into socially acceptable public and private roles, particularly in the realms of education, professions, and politics. The result of such socialization is that although women and men see the same things, they see them differently (5); thus, the ellipses.

To explain or articulate these ellipses, Woolf conceptualizes gendered terministic screens. But these screens have negative as well as positive ramifications: "The screen making habit is so universal, that probably it preserves our sanity. If we had not this device for shutting people off from our sympathies, we might, perhaps, dissolve utterly. Separateness would be impossible. But the screens are in the excess; not the sympathy" (*Diary* 3: 104). Specific subjects, Woolf argues, protect themselves from words and other people via screens of their own making. For each subject these screens are complicated by particular experiences not only with gender but also with race, class, sexual orientation, education, religion, family, and so on. These particularized screens construct and reflect who each of us are and what each of us knows, feels, thinks, and believes. As these screens indicate, language does not function as a clear, transparent, communicative medium; instead, it helps construct the screen. As such, "the process of language is slow & deluding" in everyday reading and writing as well as in everyday socialization (3: 102).

Because the textual, the cultural, and the psychological are so inextricably intertwined in Woolf's Anglo-American feminist the-

ory of rhetoric, words and the use of words have political implications. Naming assumes special powers.[13] More than just super-
ficial labelling, naming locates spaces of cultural and psychological
power that one functions within or in relation to and that other
people accept, avoid, or renegotiate. For example, Woolf claims
that *miss* "transmits sex; and sex may carry with it an aroma . . . the
swish of petticoats" (*Three Guineas* 50).[14] Interestingly, *feminism*
is a word that Woolf rejects. In 1938 she concludes that it has
had deleterious results and is outdated (101). In conceding this
word, however, Woolf calls for the abolition of other words, such
as *tyrant* and *dictator* (102). Just as the abolition of *feminism* implies that women have made gains over sexism, the abolition of *tyrant* and *dictator* would imply that citizens, both men and women,
have made gains over fascism.

But for Woolf, making gains over sexism or fascism is not the
same as eliminating them. Because words do not simply re-present
things, the strategy of changing words by itself cannot solve all
problems. Cultural and psychological conditions must also be considered in addition to the textual—for example, in addition to the
existing and missing names of concepts: "The old names as we
have seen are futile and false. [Yet] none of these tags and labels
express the real emotions that inspired the daughters' opposition
to the infantile fixation of the fathers, because, as biography shows,
that force had behind it many different emotions, and many that
were contradictory. Tears were behind it, of course—tears, bitter
tears" (*Three Guineas* 137). Woolf's naming process assumes that
the textual constructs and reflects material changes in specific subjects and in the cultural; these changes then allow, and often demand, that new conversations take place in new language and in
a variety of different texts.

TEXT

Woolf's concept of text includes lives of books and lives of
authors, both of which embody gender concerns. She defines a
book as "not made of sentences laid end to end, but of sentences
built . . . into arcades and domes" (*Room* 77). And she explains its
gendered structure via two claims: one, that men have shaped
books such as the epic poem and the drama for and from their

own needs and purposes, and, two, that only the novel is a recent enough invention for women to have influenced it. Woolf's position calls into question the universality of genres and style and argues instead that genre and style differ between women's and men's cultural spaces. Moreover, when Woolf compares the differences between lives of same-sex authors, she celebrates that Mary Carmichael breaks Jane Austen's sentence (91). This celebration argues for the particularity of genres and styles within women's cultural spaces and within men's; it also leaves open possibilities for complications by other cultural structures such as age, race, nationality, and so on. By asserting that women's lives and men's lives influence their writing both consciously and unconsciously, Woolf implies that the resulting texts are gendered; that is, they reflect the shapes of their authors' experiences and their bodies (78).

The intertextuality of these texts—of discourse—is also noted: "books continue each other in spite of our habit of judging them separately" (*Room* 80).[15] This intertextuality constructs a space for uncovering gaps in the claims of apparently seamless texts; that is, it provides a space for demystifying the "normal" of the dominant ideology. This intertextuality also provides a space for discovering arguments to address contradictions about the "normal," as when the narrator of *Three Guineas* lays the letters from the male barrister and the women educators "cheek to jowl" in order to better "understand them" (40). In this way, texts and (inter)textual strategies function not as static, ahistorical artifacts but as processual, material components of history and culture.

Still Woolf insists on a distinction between texts of fiction and texts of fact: "[F]iction is like a spider's web, attached ever so lightly, perhaps, but still attached at all four corners. Often the attachment is scarcely perceptible. . . . But when the web is pulled askew, hooked up at the edge, torn in the middle, one remembers that these webs are not spun in mid-air . . . but . . . are attached to grossly material things, like health and money and the house we live in" (*Room* 41–42). By implication, nonfiction texts might seem even more firmly attached at all four corners. Yet Woolf blurs the separation of fact and fiction, truth and lies, as well as the truth of fiction and the fiction of truth. *A Room of One's Own* is a successful blurring of these categories: "Fiction here is likely to contain more truth than fact. . . . Lies will flow from my lips, but there may perhaps be some truth mixed up with them" (4). *The Pargiters*, however, is a less successful blurring: "the truth of fact and the truth of the imagination simply would not come together in this queer 'marriage of granite and rainbow' " (Leaska xvii). Nevertheless, Woolf's constant obsession with the blurring of categories is important. It questions the dominant logic's obsession with neat definitions and classifications. It also models a method that enables us to appropriate Woolf's ideas about artistic texts and apply them to the politics of students' writing for rhetoric and composition studies.

Yet when appropriating Woolf's spider metaphor, we should remember certain assumptions. The webs of fiction and the webs of fact are both attached, however tenuously, to material things. Both kinds of webs float within an *all*-encompassing ideological membrane. Moreover, within this ideological membrane, texts— whether fictive, factual, or blurred—should be written and read to keep ideological positions visible and in play (Cixous and Clément 145). By keeping such positions visible and in play, writers/readers may scratch holes in the dominant ideology, (con)textually disturbing traditionally accepted ideas and potentially effecting transformations of texts, cultures, and specific subjects. If women and feminists are to speak their feelings and assume power within the symbolic realm, they must discover the gaps or rupture the discourses of the dominant ideology *from within*. They must then fill these gaps and transform these spaces with their own words, their own voices, their own actions.

In this way, Woolf's concept of text is closely interconnected with her concept of author: "The test of a book (to a writer) [is] if it makes a space in which, quite naturally, you can say what you want to say. . . . This proves that the book itself is alive: because it has not crushed the thing I wanted to say, but allowed me to slip it in . . . " (*Diary* 3: 297–98). For Woolf, the life of the text does not presuppose the death of the author.

AUTHOR

If both the author and the text are viable players in the interpretive process, then neither can dictate a closed, unified meaning.

Woolf rejects the author's mind as the sole, or even best, determinate of meaning (*Room* 58). For she claims that an author's writing process is not a wholly conscious activity, that at times it actually benefits from becoming unconscious ("Speech" xxxvii). In addition, she argues that the audience's reading process must be factored in; readers must be allowed then to reach their own conclusions and decide whether the text has any validity (*Room* 4). Woolf makes her point about the negotiation of meaning perfectly clear when contemplating the meaning of *The Waves*: "What it means I myself shan't know till I write another book. And I'm the hare, a long way ahead of the hounds my critics" (*Writer's Diary* 170). Other times, other spaces, other readers, other texts— all continually work not only to (re)construct meaning(s) of texts but also to (re)construct meaning(s) of specific subjects who are potential authors.

Woolf likens a writing subject's attaining new knowledge to a bowl's being constantly (re)filled with water ("Sketch of the Past" 64). This metaphor has constructionist implications for the making of meaning. Every new idea, behavior, and person encountered changes the level and motion of the water. In this way, the present and past merge, and a subject retains an identity (the bowl) while in constant flux (the water) (Schulkind 13–14). This combination of continuity and change is central to Woolf's concept of author. It assumes that specific subjects are not merely essentialist selves (the bowl), not simply discursive positions (the flow of water), but evolving agents who may at times employ language for their own purposes.

Yet a woman's authoring within the language of men is easier said than done. Woolf demonstrates this difficulty when analyzing her own writing process, which she describes as a physical impulse to write that arises whenever there is a jolt or recognition of dissonance in her daily life:

> I feel that I have had a blow; but it is not, as I thought as a child, simply a blow from an enemy hidden behind the cotton wool of daily life; it is or will become a revelation of some order; it is a token of some real thing behind appearances; and I make it real by putting it into words. It is only by putting it into words that I make it

whole; this wholeness means that it has lost its power to hurt me; it gives me, perhaps because by doing so I take away the pain, a great delight to put the severed parts together. Perhaps this is the strongest pleasure known to me. It is the rapture I get when in writing I seem to be discovering what belongs to what. ("Sketch of the Past" 71)

This concept of author is based on the unfortunate but all too real metaphor of anticipating blows, a metaphor grounded in Woolf's childhood and perhaps linked to her sexual abuse.[16] Yet this concept of author also provides a means of turning these blows into positive action, into discovering and writing new ideas. The author's making a thing "real" and "whole" by "putting it into words" does not necessarily have to be read as belief in a Platonic metaphysics or New Critical critique. Instead, it may be read as the basis for a social constructionist theory in which the author continuously constructs a framework that provides her a sense of order and power. But gaining this order and power need not mean conforming to patriarchal assumptions and conclusions; rather, it may mean gaining power through an order that makes sense to the author, sense that emerges from her own experiences, body, logic, and emotions.[17]

Woolf's concept of author may be used to challenge contemporary theoretical cries for the death of the author. In "Craftsmanship" she explores the troubled connections between an historical writer's life and words, a connection that Woolf argues can only really be broken at the author's death: "[There is a] strange . . . diabolical power which words possess . . . to suggest the writer. . . . Why words do this, how they do it, how to prevent them from doing it nobody knows. They do it without the writer's will; often against his will. . . . Even words that are hundreds of years old have this power; when they are new they have it so strongly that they deafen us to the writer's meaning. . . . That is one reason why our judgments of living writers are so wildly erratic. Only after the writer is dead do his words to some extent become disinfected, purified of the accidents of the living body" (202–3). Yet in *Moments of Being* Woolf posits a "philosophy" of meaning that frees the text's meaning from the "diabolical power" of the historical author: "at any rate it is a constant idea of mine; that behind the cotton wool is hidden a pattern; that we—I mean all human beings—are connected with this; that the whole world is a work of art; that we are parts of the work of art. *Hamlet* or a Beethoven quartet is the truth about this vast mass that we call the world. But there is no Shakespeare, there is no Beethoven; certainly and emphatically there is no God; we are the words; we are the music; we are the thing itself" ("Sketch of the Past" 72).

By doubling the importance of an historical author with the importance of an open text, Woolf retains the author as more than a mere discursive position yet allows for multiple meanings for texts. She posits the author as an active agent who haunts her texts within history and culture but who cannot control the reception of her texts. This position is demonstrated by her praise of Aphra Behn and her invocation of Judith Shakespeare in *A Room of One's Own*. But the invoked Judith Shakespeare does not exist, or become an active agent, all on her own. Instead, women must work for her, just as Aphra Behn did, writing and writing and writing again so as to change the material conditions to the extent that Ms. Shakespeare can emerge and, in turn, be challenged. Thus, Woolf provides a means of theorizing a heteroglossic agency within textual, cultural, and psychological structures, an agency that may take different forms in women and men as well as in particular men and particular women.

Women, Woolf claims, face two particular obstacles to their becoming good writers: the first is killing the Angel in the House; the second is telling the truth about their bodies ("Professions for Women" 62). The Angel infects Woolf's own writing process, fluttering about Woolf's body and invading her mind while she composes. Specifically, the Angel informs her decisions about what subjects to examine, what authors to review, what tone to adopt, what style to imitate, and so forth: "I encountered her with the very first words. The shadow of her wings fell on my page. . . . Directly, that is to say, I took my pen in my hand to review that novel by a famous man, she slipped behind me and whispered: 'My dear, you are a young woman. You are writing about a book that has been written by a man. Be sympathetic; be tender; flatter; deceive; use all the arts and wiles of our sex. Never let anybody guess that you have a mind of your own. Above all, be pure' "

(59). The Angel cannot vent anger and frustration through her own voice, if indeed she has one. She certainly cannot describe the experiences of her body, such as sexual relations, menopause, abuse. Ironically, the Angel has to die to possess a body, a feminist reversal of patriarchal transformation in which the body has to die to become an angel.

Woolf claims some success with killing the Angel, but only later in life. Looking back, she sees the Angel's shadow in her *Common Reader* articles and blames her tea-table training for their over-politeness. Too often she found herself passing tea and crumpets to young men, asking them about cream and sugar rather than about their poems and novels ("Sketch of the Past" 129). Telling the truth about her body, however, is something that Woolf feels was harder for her to achieve ("Professions for Women" 62). In fact, she achieved it mostly in private writings: for example, in her diaries she hints at her childhood abuse and adult sexuality; in her posthumously published *Moments of Being* she names herself an incest victim. This truth telling has implications for Woolf's Anglo-American feminist theory of rhetoric, particularly for her conceptualization of three interwoven rhetorical canons.

INVENTION, ARRANGEMENT, AND MEMORY

Woolf is intrigued by the many different ways that women and men construct knowledge claims and truth. She exemplifies these differences in *A Room of One's Own*, specifically in the British Museum scene where the invention processes of the female narrator and the male student seem worlds apart in spite of the fact that they have the same geographical location, the same leisure to study, and the same access to the British Museum, if not to higher education. The narrator relays the scene as follows: "It was impossible to make head or tail of [women's role in history and fiction], I decided, glancing with envy at the [male] reader next door who was making the neatest abstracts, headed often with an A or a B or a C, while my own notebook rioted with the wildest scribble of contradictory jottings. It was distressing, it was bewildering, it was humiliating. Truth had run through my fingers. Every drop had escaped" (30). The "wildest scribble" represents the narrator's mind, which is so overwhelmed by facts and associations and imaginings that it cannot possibly reach a conclusion. This inconclusiveness has unfortunate results. Even though the narrator has discovered her own truth and demonstrated its existence in her own life, she loses her self-confidence and feels alienated from what she perceives to be a male-identified foundational truth (4). Moreover, she berates herself as frivolous for not replicating the systematic research techniques of her male counterpart and for not validating the sacred separation between fact and fiction. Her reactions exemplify how women internalize their socialization, proving the truth of Erica Jong's claim that the best slaves do not need to be beaten, they beat themselves.

Although the narrator is frustrated because she cannot perceive truth directly, her glance aslant does possess a power of its own (*Diary* 3: 264). Her invention process foregrounds associative thought patterns, inductive reasoning, and extended narrative descriptions; it utilizes both conscious and unconscious processes; and it conceptualizes the chaos of facts, the limits of a neat conclusion, the truth of fiction, and the fiction of truth. For example, when conscious analytical logic fails the narrator in the British Museum, unconscious emotional logic sustains her: her doodling reveals to her that the men who have written books about women are angry and that instead of women being overly preoccupied with men, men seem to be overly preoccupied with women (*Room* 31). Thus, her invention process models how to challenge reigning premises of the dominant logic as she calls into question the Socratic imperative to analyze a question systematically.

The narrator's invention process also highlights the differences between the intellectual and class spaces of women and men, of non-university-educated and university-educated. For example, the young male student at the British Museum employs his formal training in his research, defining and classifying with ease. Yet there are limits to this methodical thinking. He obsesses about list and categories, about making things fit, about Truth. Later, at home, the narrator realizes that when a mind is neatly compartmentalized into different chambers so that sound does not travel between them, then the words, ideas, and sentences produced by such an obsessive mind fall flat and unfertile (*Room* 101).

Woolf's concept of invention is inextricably intertwined with her concept of arrangement. For example, the narrator's associative, inductive, and narrative invention process in *A Room of One's Own* formally obscures the classical arrangement strategy. Woolf's five-part strategy resembles the introduction, narration, proof, refutation, and peroration formula that Socrates ridicules in the *Phaedrus*.[18] Yet only in the last chapter does the narrator call attention to this pattern when she claims that convention decrees that she must include a peroration (*Room* 110). By rendering this pattern (in)visible, Woolf's text parodies Plato's parody. By backgrounding a classical arrangement strategy and foregrounding a modernist narrative, Woolf's narrator promotes a particular feminist agenda: blurring boundaries between genres (argumentative essay and narrative fiction), genders ("male rhetoric" and "female rhetoric"), and literary functions (transcendent art and propaganda) as well as calling these very concepts into question.[19]

As a deliberative discourse concerned with a future goal, specifically the emergence of Judith Shakespeare, *A Room of One's Own* demonstrates by its interwoven argumentative and narrative arrangement patterns that just because the narrator is concerned with personal events of daily lives is no indication that she is not also capable of logical argument. But by emphasizing her narration of daily details and downplaying her argumentative arrangement, she challenges the linear, syllogistic structure traditionally celebrated within Western logic. Hence these interwoven arrangement strategies imply that the narrator has adopted a voice of her own with a logic of its own, a voice that has "somehow be[en] adapted to the [experiences of her] body" (78). The narrator's voice does not then become *the* voice of all women; rather the possibility of the narrator's adopting such a voice opens up possibilities for other women to create such a process and adopt their own voices.

Because these interrelated invention and arrangement strategies do not posit *the* feminist alternative to patriarchal strategies that anyone wishing to critique patriarchy may employ, they invite a recognition of difference. The differences implied by these interrelated strategies are directly connected to and productively complicated by Woolf's concept of memory, which is cogently summarized by Jeanne Schulkind: "[M]emory, itself the test of the enduring quality of the moment of being, is invaluable in extending the dimensions of the moment; memory is the means by which the individual builds up patterns of personal significance to which to anchor his or her life and secure it against the 'lash of the random unheeding flail.' Witness the case of Septimus Warren Smith: when he lost his power to recall the past, he lost his will to survive the present" (21). For Woolf, memory encompasses more than reciting a speech. It is what bridges the past and the eternal present, what enables people to know how to keep putting one foot in front of the other, what frees time from its commonsense relegation to strict chronology. This freeing of time has implications for both the personal and the cultural. Particular memories of particular subjects within (un)common cultures cause specific subjects to process ideas and experiences differently. The way that memory is continually influenced by the new and the way that the new is continually influenced by memory is crucial for Woolf's feminist theory of rhetoric. For when memory fails to function, madness and/or death ensue either metaphorically or literally. Once boundaries are gone, specific subjects fragment—as do cultures—unless they can construct new boundaries, ones that integrate cultural and personal influences. Feminists face such a task. Their gendered (re)membering means putting a body of thought back together differently; thus, a culture's tradition and a subject's particularized terministic screen must be revised and make space for themselves.

Although the strategies of invention, arrangement, and memory assume the action of writing, Woolf argues that not writing can also be a productive invention strategy: "seasons of silence, & brooding, & making up much more than one can use, are fertilising" (*Diary* 3: 317); moreover, "strange spaces of silence seem to separate one period of [writing] from another" ("Women and Fiction" 44). Writing something other than a current project can also spur invention. For example, Woolf berates herself for writing in her journal when she should be revising *The Years*, but the journal writing is what enables her to finally go back to her manuscript (*Diary* 5: 17). Although she claims that writing is rewarding, she acknowledges that it is never easy: "One thinks one has learnt to write quickly; and one hasn't. And what is odd, I'm not writing with gusto or pleasure: because of the concentration. I am not reeling it off; but sticking it down" (*Writer's Diary* 143). Regardless whether she is reeling it off or sticking it down, Woolf recognizes not only the interconnections of invention, arrangement, and memory but also their relation to style.

STYLE

For Woolf, women's using the language of men does not mean writing like men. Nevertheless, because women cannot escape the language of men, their writing styles are often "grown about with weeds and bound with briars" of patriarchal language and logic (*Room* 61). When imagining a talented but fictional woman writer named Mary Carmichael, Woolf exults in her style: first Carmichael's style breaks the sentence, then the sequence (81), in order to merge old forms with new form without disrupting the "balance of the whole" (85). By invoking Carmichael's stylistic breaks and balance, Woolf is actually calling for a revolution in style that will enable potentially talented women writers to stop blending into the background and, instead, write themselves into the foreground, highlighting their words, their experiences, their emotions, and their logics (45). But what will spur such a revolution?

Strict imitation of men's texts will not help. Such texts can only teach a woman a few tricks that she must in turn adapt for her own ends (*Room* 76). Moreover, when a woman tries to write like a man, she risks losing sight of her own evolving style (88); for example, Woolf notes that reading Yeats affects her style one way while reading Sterne affects it differently (*Diary* 3: 119). Instead, women's styles should reflect the material conditions of women's bodies, experiences, and cultural spaces. That Jane Austen hid her manuscript from visitors is important to Woolf because these actions shaped Austen's sentences. That Mary Carmichael breaks both the sentence and sequence of Austen's novels is important because such breaks in style and arrangement allow women's styles to differ not only from men's but from one another's (*Room* 91). This point is especially important, for it articulates a rhetoric of the particular, an emphasis often overlooked in many rhetorical theories.

If strict imitation of style isn't desirable, revisionary imitation is.[20] Woolf's own style is an example of this move.[21] As Caughie aptly notes, we cannot analyze Woolf's stylistic strategies empirically and then assign them particular meanings that will apply in all situations (*Woolf and Postmodernism* 107). Instead, we must identify Woolf's strategies and analyze them contextually. That is, we may read Woolf's cumulative sentence at the beginning of *Orlando* as imitating a masculinist literary style; conversely, we may read a similar structure at the end of *Orlando* as parodying this style, or we may read this structure in *A Room of One's Own* as celebrating a feminist invention process. Note, for example, the following passage in *A Room of One's Own* where Mary Seton explores connections between fishing and her own thinking process: "Thought—to call it by a prouder name that it deserved—had let its line down into the stream. It swayed, minute after minute, hither and thither among the reflections and the weeds, letting the water lift it and sink it, until—you know the little tug—the sudden conglomeration of an idea at the end of one's line: and then the cautious hauling of it in, and the careful laying of it out? Alas, laid on the grass how small, how insignificant this thought of mine looked; the sort of fish that a good fisherman puts back into the water so that it may grow fatter and be one day worth cooking and eating" (5). These three sentences demonstrate Woolf's revisionary imitation, how she uses traditional punctuation, grammar, and tropes for her own ends. The dashes separate the narrator's asides from her main subject and predicate, personalizing her voice for readers and representing the rhythm of a fish biting a hook. The series of phrases in the second sentence emulate the slippery process of thinking as well as the frightening process of presenting such thinking for all to see. The metaphoric connections between fish and thought blur the binaries of animal/human, nature/civilization, leisure/work, the necessity of eating/the narcissism of thinking, and so on. Reversing Audre Lorde's claim that the master's tools will never dismantle the master's house, Woolf's style employs the master's stylistic tools to challenge the master's house.

When these stylistic strategies are juxtaposed against the narrator's subsequent visit to Oxbridge, however, a feminist agenda emerges from this revisionary imitation. After the Beadle chases her off the grass (the gravel was the proper place for women), the narrator claims with ironic understatement that the only problem with the Beadle's action is that he "sent my little fish into hiding" (*Room* 6), an action that occurs despite her leisure and privilege to stroll through the paths at Oxbridge. When situated within this context, Woolf's punctuation, grammar, and trope may be read as exposing a significant result of women's socialization: women doubt their own intellectual powers, their own authority. In this reading, Woolf's style emerges as more than just amusing conventions or stylistic tricks that dress her thoughts (Showalter, *Literature* 295). By rejecting the form/content dichotomy and by foregrounding how stylistic conventions both encourage and restrict us, Woolf's style emerges as an integral component of her mind, her body, her writing, and her life. Thus, language is exposed as an integral component that, along with the personal and the cultural, construct and reflect our realities and ideologies.

Support for revisionary imitation can also be found in Woolf's praise of Mary Carmichael's writing process, which merges the new and the old (*Room* 85). Carmichael's move need not be read as maintaining the status quo but rather as continually converting "the old" into a style of one's own. Further support for a revisionary imitation can be found in Woolf's review of Dorothy Richardson's prose where Woolf defines Richardson's particular "woman's sentence": "It is of a more elastic fibre than the old, capable of stretching to the extreme, of suspending the frailest particles, of enveloping the vaguest shapes. Other writers of the opposite sex have used sentences of this description and stretched them to the extreme. But there is a difference. Miss Richardson has fashioned her sentence consciously. . . . It is a woman's sentence, but only in the sense that it is used to describe a woman's mind by a writer who is neither proud nor afraid of anything that she may discover in the psychology of her sex" ("Dorothy Richardson" 191). It is the ever "new" contextual function of Richardson's sentences, not simply their "old" structures, that determines her style.

The particularity in Woolf's theory of style, or a "woman's sentence," escapes the traps of linguistic, cultural, and biological essentialisms. Such particularity assumes that language is a shared social experience but that women and men occupy different cultural spaces within language; it also implies that within these two cultural spaces, particular women and particular men occupy different psychological spaces. Thus, Woolf's stylistic theory incorporates textual differences as well as cultural and psychological differences. This tripled difference is perpetuated in *A Room of One's Own* where Woolf presents not only a textual argument (that women authors like Mary Carmichael must break both sentence and sequence) but also an interwoven cultural and psychological proposition (that for women to produce good fiction they must be afforded free time and personal space—£500 and a room of one's own—in which to think and write) (88, 4). According to Woolf, the effect of these textual and cultural and psychological strategies is to move writers and audiences to what Kenneth Burke calls "attitude" and "action" (*Rhetoric of Motives* 50).

AUDIENCE

Although Woolf does not theorize about audience in a traditional way, she does dwell on the effects that audiences have on her own texts and writing process. Thus, she exposes questions that all women writers may benefit from exploring. For instance, Woolf claims that writing for an audience excites her.[22] Yet this excitement has both possibilities and limits for her writing process. While contemplating imminent reviews of *To the Lighthouse*, she admits that praise mingled with constructive criticism spurs her ideas and her writing (*Diary* 3: 135). When contemplating the effect of a particular male critic in 1934, however, she hints at his power to invoke writing block. She has stopped writing because if she picked up a pen she would be tempted to answer his criticisms; shaping a text, in this case *The Pargiters*, based on these criticisms would be disastrous, denying her own vision (*Writer's Diary* 221). As illustrated by these and other examples, Woolf's concept of audience focuses on many levels—men and women, general and particular, actual and imagined, personal and impersonal—all of which are very real and most of which have gendered components.

Men in general haunt Woolf as a woman and a writer. She jokes about this fact when the narrator of *A Room of One's Own* asks the young women of Fernham whether or not a man is hiding behind the curtains or in the cupboards, listening to her speech (82, 111). These men in general are more than just individual threats: they represent the power of patriarchy. But ironically, men in general are rarely the audiences that women acknowledge. Instead women internalize patriarchy by constructing the Angel in the House, a creature who is so powerful a "self-audience" for women that she shapes both their private and public behavior: "She was intensely sympathetic. She was immensely charming. She was utterly unselfish. She excelled in the difficult arts of family life. She sacrificed herself daily. If there was a chicken she took the leg; if there was a draught she sat in it—in short she was so constituted that she never had a mind or a wish of her own, but preferred to sympathize always with the minds and wishes of others. Above all—I need not say it—she was pure" ("Professions for Women" 59).

While the Angel's values express a male-identified fantasy about white middle-class women, the implications of these values embody a female reality. As such, the Angel functions rather ironically as a survival technique for women, allowing them a covert agency. This phantom in women's minds enables them subtly yet successfully to exert influence, through men of course, on private and public affairs. The Angel's strategy is mirrored reflection: "Women have served all these centuries as looking-glasses possessing the magic and delicious power of reflecting the figure of man at twice its normal size" (*Room* 35). Although this reflecting function affords women some power, it mostly drains them. What little power they reserve for themselves is negative. They chastise themselves through the male-identified Angel's voice, consciously and unconsciously reinforcing patriarchy's preferred roles for women, the result being low levels of confidence and self-esteem.[23] Patriarchy and specific men, however, benefit from this insidious process. They are freed from having to chastise women overtly as well as from having to suffer any blame, guilt, or responsibility for women's self-chastisement; they are also seemingly freed from any responsibility for women's plights.

Woolf's concept of audience for women writers is not limited to a patriarchal specter of men and reflecting Angel. Sometimes the men in general take on particular faces, which peek over Woolf's shoulder as she reads and writes and as she contemplates reading and writing. These particular faces are sometimes inspiring, sometimes not. For example, when contemplating E. M. Forster's refusal to review *A Room of One's Own*, she imagines him and her other friends saying, "Mrs. Woolf is so accomplished a writer that all she says makes easy reading. . . . [T]his very feminine logic . . . [is] a book to be put in the hands of girls" (*Writer's Diary* 145). Yet in her own voice she posits somewhat contradictory reactions: "[Such responses make] me suspect that there is a shrill feminine tone in it which my intimate friends will dislike. . . . [But] I doubt that I mind very much" (145). Woolf's responses represent a typical behavior pattern of a woman within patriarchy: blaming herself, then deciding not to mind, but minding very much. Woolf's relationship with Leonard Woolf, however, seems more productive for her writing process although he holds tremendous power over her self-confidence. When she anticipates his reaction to *Three Guineas*, she predicts that he will have hesitations because the effect on a reader is always less than the author hopes. Thus, she establishes low expectations so that when she gets his backhanded approval, she may be slightly more positive: "L. gravely approves 3 Gs. Thinks it an extremely clear analysis. On the whole I'm content. One cant expect emotion, for as he says, its not on a par with the novels. Yet I think it may have more practical value" (*Diary* 5: 127). Glad for the approval, she still makes excuses for her work (and possibly for Leonard's review); that is, she establishes a different set of criteria, "practical value" rather than aesthetic excellence, by which she may judge her work more positively than Leonard has. Yet Woolf is honest about her desire for support: as a husband, Lytton Strachey would have inhibited her from writing; Leonard, however critical, has just the opposite effect, or so she says (3: 273). Recognizing the influence of particular men and then positioning herself in the best possible relation to them seems to be a lesson of Woolf's discussion of audience.

But men are only part of women writers' actual and imagined audience. Women in general haunt Woolf, too, but a bit more positively. When discussing her reasons for writing in *The Pargiters*, she claims that she wants to provide young women with a sense of their history so that they can better understand their present positions (9). When discussing her reasons for writing *A Room of One's Own*, she confides in a letter to her friend G. Lowes Dickinson that she hoped to encourage young women who oftentimes get quite depressed (Gordon xiv). When writing for these women, Woolf feels compelled to instruct them about the double binds and false dilemmas that are part of their socialization within patriarchy. So she models a false dilemma that confronted her when writing her conclusion to *A Room of One's Own*: first, she declares her desire to write a peroration for women that will inspire them; then, she discusses the commonsense logic of our culture that encourages women to compete with, not inspire, each other (*Room* 110, 111). Woolf encourages young women to challenge such double binds and false dilemmas by searching for their own truths. Again she models the process by asserting a truth of her own: that she likes women for their "unconventionality . . . subtlety . . . and anonymity" (111). These faceless young women do not intimidate Woolf in the same way as the faceless men, possibly because they are young, more probably because they do not represent the power of patriarchy either in education, professions, or politics.

Women also take on particular faces that haunt Woolf as she writes, providing both limits and possibilities for her writing process. The limits include socialization that constructs the Angel in the House, which Woolf must later kill. Lady Carnavon and Mrs. Popham, for example, reinforce proper social roles and proper social boundaries at a formal dinner party by immediately changing the subject when a young Virginia discusses a risque Platonic passage; her stepbrother George Duckworth later chastises her for her bad manners and informs her that polite society is not accustomed to young women speaking at all ("22 Hyde Park Gate" 152). (As her abuser, he has a vested interest in this proposition being true.) But specific women also encourage Woolf to explore her own visions when writing. Vanessa Bell's emotional praise of *To the Lighthouse* is greatly anticipated and deeply appreciated; Vita Sackville-West inspires *Orlando*; and Ethel Smith bolsters Woolf's confidence with her rhapsodies about *A Room of One's Own* (*Diary* 3: 135–36, 292).

Woolf recognizes that these multiple levels of audience affect not just what is said, but especially what is not said. She praises Jane Austen's talent for conveying both ("Jane Austen" 120). Articulating the unarticulated is important to Woolf. When words fail, she often identifies the space of the unarticulated with dashes and ellipses. She employs ellipses to represent the communication gulf between men and women in *Three Guineas* (4). And she employs them to represent the interpretive gulf between patriarchal consciousness and feminist consciousness in *A Room of One's Own*. Most often these ellipses follow the word *but*: "But . . . she has not a bone in her body"; "But . . . I had said 'but' too often"; "But—I am bored" (100). This punctuation strategy makes visible a space of dissonance, exemplifying the difference between the patriarchal premises that have come before the *but* and the feminist conclusions that are offered after the ellipses. Throughout her corpus, Woolf is concerned with what can(not) be said, what can(not) be assumed, what can(not) be questioned, and what can(not) be concluded. The elliptical pauses, the glances aslant, the hinted implications—all become points of interest in Woolf's material feminist analysis of the textual, the cultural, and the psychological. Yet she chooses her moments and manners of feminist articulation carefully. Sometimes she knowingly resorts to her childhood's Victorian game of manners, which she argues is not all bad: this game allows people to say things at a slant that could not be said directly ("Sketch of the Past" 129).[24]

Inconclusive Musings

Lest Virginia Woolf's feminist theory of rhetoric appear too neat and orderly, let me return to the materialism that permeates this theory. It is a troubled materialism that hovers around the divide between how Woolf talks about language in her materialist feminist critiques and how she talks about language in her Modernist theory of transcendent art. Jane Marcus, Michèle Barrett, and Daniel Ferrer, among others, have discussed this (di)vision.[25] By claiming that Woolf's ideas about women and writing may be appropriated for a feminist theory of rhetoric, I am not presuming to bridge, or erase, this (di)vision. Rather I am attempting to reread it in hopes of asking and evoking questions about gender and writing that can inform rhetoric and composition studies, particularly for teachers trying to conceptualize their own theories of teaching writing and for students trying to come to terms with what it means to write and to be written within our culture.

The following are just a few examples of questions made possible by Virginia Woolf's feminist theory of rhetoric:

1. Does what Walter Beale calls "the high wall of Modernism" built on the foundation of Romanticism work to keep students from writing, from considering themselves writers, from demystifying how language functions in their daily life?

2. How can we make students more aware of the gendered function of ideology in language (in terms of sexual orientation, race, gender, class, etc.)? And, realistically, how much can we expect this consciousness to accomplish?

3. How do we theorize a function of the unconscious in writing classes without turning our classes into encounter groups in which teachers make the students "sick" so that the classroom experience can "cure" them?

4. What is the connection between art and politics, not only for modernists and women writers but for rhetoric and composition scholar/teachers and their students?

5. How does Woolf's concept of agency challenge the concept of identification upon which many traditional rhetorical theories are built? And how is Woolf's challenge to identification different than that offered by poststructuralist theories, which celebrate the death of the author?

Woolf's feminist theory of rhetoric provides us a space for asking questions such as these that may call traditional theories of rhetoric into question. Her theory also gives us a way of thinking about how women's lives, how women's texts, and how women's lives as texts come into play and signify meanings that are not indefinitely deferred nor immediately closed down. Thus, Woolf reminds us that in our postmodern world we can still claim for ourselves a truth, or an ethic such as feminism, even if we cannot claim it as foundational.

Within this realm of socially constructed truths, rhetoric becomes even more important for negotiating our texts, our cultures, and our subjectivities. Its gendered function becomes important for men and women, but especially for women who must demystify the complexities of patriarchy if they are to grow and survive. They must learn not to let their little fishes be sent into hiding either by men who represent the patriarchy as beadle, librarian, or professor or by other women who represent the patriarchy as Angel, Lady, or friend. Moreover, women must learn to value their work as more than just a "good piece of donkeywork" (*Diary* 5: 127).[26] By gaining confidence within the interwoven textual, cultural, and psychological, women not only reflect changes in these material conditions but also construct them.

Woolf outlines her nonviolent strategy for such changes in her letter to the barrister: "we can best help you to prevent war not by repeating your words and following your methods but by finding new words and creating new methods" (*Three Guineas* 143). And she sets boundaries for such changes in her discussion of Mary Carmichael: we have "to devise some entirely new combination of [our] resources . . . so as to absorb the new into the old without disturbing the infinitely intricate and elaborate balance of the whole" (*Room* 85). Extrapolating Woolf's Anglo-American feminist theory of rhetoric and putting it into play with other theories is just one means of implementing this strategy and acknowledging its boundaries.

3

De/Mystifying HerSelf and HerWor(l)ds: MARY DALY

[T]his book is primarily concerned with the
mind/spirit/body pollution inflicted through patriarchal
myth and language at all levels.

—Mary Daly, *Gyn/Ecology*

A s a feminist philosopher, theologian, and political activist,
Mary Daly is deeply concerned with Bathsheba's dilemma;
however, she defines it in slightly different terms than
does Woolf. Daly argues that the patriarchal categories constructed
through language result in "a kind of gang rape" of a woman's
mind and body (*Beyond* 152). In spite of (or perhaps because of)
this jarring image, Daly also argues that a woman need not be
doomed nor determined within these categories but may, instead,
turn language back on itself and construct new categories while
embarking on the journey of radical feminism. Such a journey—
from twice-born Athena to thrice-born Athena,[1] from Righteous
Truth to Sinister Wisdom, from Dutiful Daughter to Revolting
Hag, from Spooking to Sparking to Spinning—has as its goal
"the discovery and creation of a world other than patriarchy"
(*Gyn/Ecology* 1). Daly invokes this multidimensional journeying of
radical feminism for herSelf and Others in her texts. But Daly's
texts do more than just record three decades of an evolving radical
feminist consciousness. Her critiques of myth, language, and ideology may also be read from the site of rhetoric and composition studies to extrapolate an Anglo-American feminist theory of
rhetoric.

Since Daly first began writing in the 1960's, her mythic and
linguistic critiques of patriarchy have gotten progressively more
radical.[2] *The Church and the Second Sex* argues for equality of the

sexes within the Church (6). *Beyond God the Father* argues for
a new, unfolding definition of God that will create a space of
"human becoming" (40). *Gyn/Ecology* argues for a radical feminist
metaethics with which any woman can refute patriarchal history—
for example, Indian suttee, Chinese footbindings, African genital
mutilation, European witchburning, and American gynecology—
and dis-cover her own history as well as its connections with other
women's histories (xlvii). *Pure Lust* argues for an alternative to
phallic lust in the form of a revisionary Pure Lust, which names
the humor, hope, and harmony of women who challenge patriarchy (1–2). *Websters' First Intergalactic Wickedary of the English Language* by Daly and Jane Caputi offers a Metapatriarchal dictionary
that creates new words and exposes sexist assumptions in old words
by playing with etymological and metaphorical meanings (xiv–xv).
As the culmination of all these works, the autobiographical *Outercourse: The Be-Dazzling Voyage* explores intersections of the personal, the philosophical, and the theological in radical feminist
journeying.

Most importantly for rhetoric and composition studies, however, Daly's texts outline particular language strategies through
which she finds her voice(s) and through which she hopes other
women will find theirs. Daly's texts outline these strategies mostly
in prefaces and introductions, forewords and afterwords, not only
naming problems that will be explored but also identifying purposes and methods. In this way, her texts expose and critique
insidious connections between myth, language, and the perpetuation of patriarchy. By examining Daly's critiques, by analyzing
her own specific rhetorical strategies, and by exploring the differences between what she claims to do in her writing and what I
read in her writing, I offer a rendering of her texts from the site
of rhetoric and composition studies that articulates her contributions to this field. My purpose is to extrapolate an Anglo-American
feminist theory of rhetoric that challenges the genderblindness of
more traditional rhetorical histories, theories, and pedagogies.

To this end, I first locate Mary Daly as a rhetorical theorist. I
then examine how her texts may be read as exposing a foreground
rhetoric of patriarchal mystification and its strategies, which may
be categorized into traditional rhetorical canons of invention, arrangement, style, memory, and delivery. In the majority of this

chapter, however, I explore how Daly's texts may be read as conceptualizing a Background rhetoric of radical feminist de/mystification and as modeling its strategies; these Background strategies of Spinning, Dis-ordering, Be-Spelling, Re-membering, and Be-Speaking are a feminist reversal of traditional rhetorical canons and, as such, imply revised concepts of a writing process and a rhetorical triangle. I conclude by posing theoretical and practical questions made possible by Mary Daly's Anglo-American feminist theory of rhetoric.

Locating Mary Daly as a Rhetorical Theorist

Mary Daly does not situate herself or her texts within a predominantly male tradition of Western rhetoric or even within a predominantly male tradition of Western scholarship.[3] While she acknowledges that a woman must enter patriarchal fields if she is ever to move beyond those fields, Daly's texts ultimately challenge such fields as well as their powerful traditions (*Gyn/Ecology* 8). Daly clearly states why such challenges are needed: "Within a culture possessed by the myth of feminine evil, the naming, describing, and theorizing about good and evil has constituted a maze/haze of deception" (2). Daly identifies this maze/haze as patriarchy,[4] as the dominant ideology that cuts across all cultures, that encompasses everything, and that perpetuates itself through the good man speaking well about myth and language. She exhorts women to break through this maze/haze. Yet she rejects anti-intellectualism as a method, for she sees anti-intellectualism as a trap, an understandable but ultimately unproductive reaction against patriarchal education and scholarship that moronizes women (22). Instead, Daly calls for feminist scholarship that will enable feminism(s) to "become sensible" so that women can both think and feel themSelves becoming (23). The feminist scholarship that Daly models celebrates two moves: creating her own ideas through language yet being impeccably scholarly about doing so (*Pure Lust* 412). The purpose of these scholarly moves is the liberation of myth and the liberation of language. Such liberation, Daly believes, has the potential to liberate women into radical feminism. To demonstrate how this theory of liberation locates Daly as a rhetorical theorist, I will critique her radical feminist concepts of Women, myths, and language function.

When talking about the liberation of women, Daly means *all* women. That is, she believes that because patriarchy "is itself the prevailing religion of the entire planet," it oppresses all of us regardless of our cultural location (*Gyn/Ecology* 39). But Daly has been challenged for this seemingly uncomplicated use of the term *women*, and her texts have been attacked as separatist, essentialist, and racist. Because rhetorical theories ever circle around assumed definitions of subjectivity, Daly's claim and her critics' challenges deserve attention before we investigate her feminist theory of rhetoric.

Because Daly's feminism focuses on women's concerns, it is often charged with being a separatist ideology. Daly responds to this charge as follows: "The words *gynocentric be-ing* and *Lesbian* imply separation. This *is* what this book is about, but not in a simple way" (*Gyn/Ecology* xlvi). That is, Daly is not a traditional separatist in terms of denying men the presence of women or women the presence of men, despite complaints that dismiss her as such because she has banned men from some of her classes. Daly interprets these complaints as male identified. Rather, Daly is a radical feminist separatist in her own terms; she encourages women to be present to one another, to identify ourselves in relation to each other instead of in relation to men. Within Daly's Woman-identified feminism, a radical feminist separatist is a be-ing who affirms "the flow of connectedness within each woman" and who works for a "feminist separation from the State of Separation" that is patriarchy (*Pure Lust* 371–72, 373). Consequently, Daly spends little or no time talking about men, not because they cannot be liberated but because she figures plenty of other people will champion their cause (*Beyond* 8, 172–74). From this position, Daly's feminism articulates how women can recognize and refuse their inferior status within patriarchy and achieve their own power within radical feminism. Daly's radical feminist separatist agenda has as its primary goal the transformation of a woman's Self and as its secondary goal the transformation of the social (*Gyn/Ecology* 7). Within this logic, a radical feminist may exist with(in) the same time and space as patriarchy. Following a similar logic, Daly's feminist theory of rhetoric may be located within the rhetorical tradition(s) without being domesticated by it.

Because Daly's radical feminism focuses on women's Selves and on the powers of these Selves, it is often labeled essentialist. This charge is meant to dismiss Daly's intellectual power as naive by forcing her into the category of biological determinist. But Daly refuses such categorizing. She is not an essentialist in the Aristotelian sense; she does not believe that an irreducible essence defines a thing or a Self.[5] Neither is she an essentialist in John Locke's terms; she rejects his real and nominalist distinctions.[6] Instead, Daly redefines essentialism as a radical feminist concept.[7] This essentialism presumes an essence or a radical feminist Self that is always already in process, that is, the "Original core of one's being . . . that participates in Be-ing," which is the "Ultimate/Intimate Reality" or "Final Cause" (*Wickedary* 95, 64). Within this theoretical framework, Daly's radical feminist Self is an essence in motion, a be-ing continually constructed through the interweavings of myth and language, a be-ing participating in Be-ing (*Pure Lust* 160–61).[8] Thus, Daly is an essentialist, but in her own terms.

Because Daly's feminism focuses on the effects of patriarchy on all women, it has been accused of having an unacknowledged Euro-American focus. The most well-known challenge of this kind comes from Audre Lorde. On 6 May, 1979, she wrote a letter to Daly detailing her interpretation of *Gyn/Ecology*; when she received no written reply, Lorde published her letter. In it, Lorde commends Daly for her "good faith toward all women" ("Open Letter" 67). She agrees with Daly that the oppression of women crosses all ethnic and racial boundaries; however, she argues that Daly's focus erases differences within this oppression (70). For example, Lorde concurs with Daly that too little has been written about African genital mutilation but also asks Daly to consider not just the similarities between African genital mutilation, Chinese footbinding, and American gynecology but also the differences: "To imply . . . that all women suffer the same oppression simply because we are women is to lose sight of the many varied tools of patriarchy" (67). Lorde concludes her letter with a thank-you for the insights that Daly has given her and an offering of her own insights as repayment (71). In many ways, Lorde's letter is offered as a gift because she had earlier decided never again to talk with white women about race; for Daly, however, she makes an exception.

In the introduction to the second edition of *Gyn/Ecology*, Daly acknowledges Lorde's letter. Although she implies that Lorde has misunderstood her intent, she apologizes for the pain that any unintended receptions of her book might have caused: "I regret any pain that unintended omissions may have caused others, particularly women of color, as well as myself. The writing of *Gyn/Ecology* was for me an act of Biophilic Bonding with women of all races and classes, under all the varying oppressions of patriarchy" (xxxi). Although willing to apologize for unintended slights, Daly refuses to debate Lorde in published discourse, claiming that such debates hurt women's causes. And while I agree with Daly that women's wrangling over who is more oppressed is probably a counterproductive political move, I do not believe this is what Lorde intended. Feminists may learn and grow from exchanging ideas, that is, from negotiating the very real differences between our intentions and our receptions.

The above challenges to Daly's texts should resonate for all of us as we consider her feminist theory of rhetoric. Although Daly rarely uses the word rhetoric, her critiques of patriarchal myth and language are indubitably rhetorical, for at the intersections of myth, language, and ideology we arrive at rhetoric.[9] When describing the rhetorical functions of such intersections, Daly establishes no easy cause and effect. Instead, she argues that our myths and language must change if patriarchy is to change and that patriarchy must change if our myths and language are to change. This claim does not posit a logical contradiction. Rather, it conceptualizes a complex, active cultural matrix within which a woman may employ language to (un)weave interweavings of patriarchal myth, language, and ideology within herSelf (*Gyn/Ecology* 389–424).

Daly's concerns about women and myth permeate her texts. Although strongly grounded in Western philosophy and Judeo-Christian theology, her texts define myth in the broadest sense of the wor(l)d. She is particularly concerned with how these myths metonymically re-present patriarchy. Her critiques of such re-presentations encompass different cultures,[10] yet the common denominator is that these critiques reimagine myths by dis-covering[11] women's perspectives, something that many traditional myths have either blindly or purposefully ignored. For example, the Neith myth is re-membered as the Libyan Triple Goddess whom the Greeks whitewashed into Athena (*Gyn/Ecology* 75, 88). Athena's myth is dis-covered as a Warrior goddess who must be born not only of Metis's womb, not only of Zeus's head, but also of her own words (13–14). Cinderella's myth is re-called as a young Oriental girl's being subjected to beautifying (read "eroticized") footbindings (151–52). Snow White's myth is un-covered as a young girl's being offered the same poisonous apple of patriarchy that the wicked stepmother has choked on all her life (44, 351). The Virgin Mary's myth is re-visioned as a young girl's being overwhelmed by a loving father's sexual advance (85). And the myth of the Trinity (the Father, Son, and Holy Ghost) is re-cognized as a patriarchal reversal of Trivia, the Triple Goddess who is manifested via Maiden, Mother, and Crone (75–79). Such antipatriarchal conclusions will no doubt disturb those who take less extreme positions. But this disturbing element is precisely why Daly's texts are worth reading. Demaris Wehr echoes this claim in her review of *Pure Lust*: "While such strong denunciations no doubt serve to deter adherents of these beliefs from reading [Daly's] work, I recommend they read [her texts] anyway. Why? Her powerful mind, her creative genius and her uncanny ability to put her finger on deep emotional, psychological and spiritual problems are ignored at our peril" (14). Moreover, Daly's metonymic critiques model a method that may be employed in a variety of contexts.

Of particular interest to rhetoric and composition scholars is the way Daly theorizes a tripled language function: that is, sign, symbol, and metaphor. She acknowledges that language functions as a sign system, with all the potential for free play that such a system entails. Without such play, feminists could not use old words in new ways. But she also insists on language's simultaneous symbolic function, which she believes both historicizes and invokes free play. She compares these functions of sign and symbol as follows: "Symbols, in contrast to mere signs, participate in that to which they point. They open up levels of reality otherwise closed to us and they unlock dimensions and elements of our souls which correspond to these hidden dimensions and elements of

reality. . . . Of course, there can be no One Absolutely Right symbol for all Lusty women, for we belong to different tribes and
have great individual diversity" (*Pure Lust* 25). Daly's problem
with patriarchal symbols is obvious in her definition of them as
"commonly flattened-out, frozen metaphors that have been captured, reduced, and reversed into one-dimensionality" (*Pure Lust*
405–6). Her solution to this problem is radical feminist de/mys-
tification. This de/mystifying process exposes that symbols and
their meanings are not eternally nor universally fixed; hence, they
may be changed. Such a process also affirms the power of symbols for women in general and in particular, a move that enables
Daly's concept of symbol to avoid the gender erasure that often
occurs when people retreat into totalizing linguistic philosophy
(all Americans speak the same language), totalizing feminism (all
women are oppressed by language in the same way), or totalizing
tokenism (a particular woman's problem with language is an exception, an aberration).

Although symbols function as metaphors within Daly's theory
of language, metaphors possess more possibilities than mere symbolic function. More than stylistic dress laid onto thought, metaphors are the innate generative power of language that enables
it to be used, consciously and unconsciously, to subvert the status quo. Daly defines the feminist agenda of this language function as follows: "[M]etaphors evoke action, movement. They
Name/evoke a shock, a clash with the 'going logic' and they introduce a new logic. Metaphors function to Name change, and
therefore they elicit change" (*Pure Lust* 25).[12] In turn, metaphors
generate other metaphors, some of which Daly names metapatriarchal metaphors.[13] Such metaphors rupture the dominant logic(s)
of patriarchy and propel "a woman further into the Wild dimensions of Other-centered consciousness—out of dead circles into
Spiraling/Spinning motion" (405). Daly insists that metapatriarchal metaphors be seen not as fixed symbols, not as fixed abstractions, but as the never ending processual energy and motion
that is radical feminism (407, 327–33) In this way, Daly conceptualizes a gendered language function that not only reflects reality
but also continually (re)constructs it. It is this gendered function
that separates Daly's theory of metaphor from humanist ones.

In Daly's theory the tripled language functions of sign, symbol,

and metaphor occur simultaneously in two dimensions: the foreground and the Background. Daly defines *foreground* as the "male
centered and monodimensional arena where fabrication, objecti-
fication, and alienation take place" (*Wickedary* 76). She defines
Background as "the Realm of Wild Reality; the Homeland of
women's Selves and of all Others" (63). Radical feminism, then,
is a woman's newly created yet remembered journey from foreground to Background. It is a journey *from* the realm of patriarchy
where meanings are frozen and reversed to a realm other than
patriarchy where women may reconnect with unfrozen, a priori
meanings that defy the patriarchal structure of language. Daly
names this radical feminist process of Websters' moving from foreground to Background as Spinning (*Gyn/Ecology* 389–91).

Spinning is a be-ing's participation in the metaphoric drive of
language in order to de/mystify gendered terms, phrases, claims,
and actions. The passage below is a prime example of Daly's Spinning through writing. Through her wild and wicked feminist play
with the word *paradise*, she challenges commonly accepted foreground meanings and discovers radical feminist Background ones:

A primary definition of *paradise* is "pleasure park." The
walls of the Patriarchal Pleasure Park represent the condition of being perpetually parked, locked into the parking
lot of the past. Abasic meaning of park is "game preserve." The fathers' foreground is precisely this: an arena
where the wildness of nature and of women's Selves is domesticated, preserved. It is the place for the preservation
of females who are the "fair game" of the fathers, that
they may be served to these predatory Park Owners, and
service them at their pleasure. Patriarchal Paradise is the
arena of games, the place where the pleas of women are
silenced, where the law is: Please the Patrons. Women
who break through the imprisoning walls of the Playboys'
Playground are entering the process which is our happen-
ings/happiness. This is Paradise beyond the boundaries of
"paradise." Since our passage into this process requires
making breaks in the walls, it means setting free the fair
game, breaking the rules of the games, breaking the
names of the games. Breaking through the foreground

which is the Playboys' Playground means letting out the
bunnies, the bitches, the beavers, the squirrels, the chicks,
the pussycats, the cows, the nags, the foxy ladies, the old
bats and biddies, so that they can at last begin naming
themselves. (*Gyn/Ecology* 7)

Many strategies employed in the above passage represent Daly's
Spinning through writing, which uses language against itself, that
is, uses foreground strategies to expose Background meanings. Toward this end, Daly employs several Ciceronian topoi. Definition
enables her to redefine *paradise*, exposing how the foreground concept traps women and how the Background concept empowers
them. Etymology enables her to unpack lost meanings of *paradise*,
which further enhance her Background definition. Analogy, too,
enables her to expand her definition of *paradise*, comparing it to
a "park" and a "game preserve" in order to expose the penned-in
animal status afforded to women in the foreground. Partition enables her to divide and define *game preserve* so that *game* suggests
women and *preserve* suggests their disempowerment. Finally, effect
enables her to explain how women are silenced, and difference
enables her to demonstrate that women should name themselves.
Likewise, Daly utilizes several figures to construct Background
meanings. Metaphor allows her to expose *paradise* as a "Playboy's
Playground." The alliteration of *ps* and *ss* allows her to construct
a tone that is disdainful of the foreground. Polyptoton allows her
to employ different forms of *preserve* to emphasize the static nature
of the foreground. Paronomasia allows her to unpack *fair game* as
both beautiful women and easy prey, exposing the animal status
of women. Prosonomasia allows her to extend her metaphor and
nickname men as "Playboys" and "Patrons."
    By challenging patriarchal meanings, Daly's paradise passage and
its strategies challenge the genderblindness of traditional logic and
rhetoric. They also exemplify Daly's belief in language play: breaking through foreground meanings is a context-bound possibility,
not simply a utopian desire. Although Daly acknowledges the limitations of such play for transforming the social, her wild and
wicked Spinning is a deadly serious and revolutionary endeavor in
that it possesses the potential to transform the Self.
    Patriarchal scholarship diminishes the process of Spinning by

capturing it in dictionaries and renaming it linguistic etymology. But according to Daly, other records also exist as deep Background feelings and ideas. These feelings and ideas are what Lorde challenges Daly to take even further: "Mary, I ask that you re-member what is dark and ancient and diving within yourself that aids your speaking" (69). It is to these ideas and feelings that Daly looks for inspiration; it is to them that she refers when traditional linguistic scholars accuse her etymologies of being "incorrect" or "far-fetched." She might agree that they are fetched from afar, but such far-fetched truths propel Daly's radical feminism. From this position in motion, Daly would not accuse foreground scholars in their own language of privileging the signified; she would accuse them of perpetuating the static premises of patriarchy. By exposing this play between foreground meanings and Background meanings, Daly unmasks how myth and language intersect in the foreground to perpetuate patriarchy. In other words, she un-covers the dominant rhetoric of patriarchy.

A Rhetoric of Patriarchal Mystification

This dominant foreground rhetoric perpetuates the eighth deadly sin of deception (*Pure Lust* x).[14] The primary function of this deceptive rhetoric is to socialize women into the foreground, reinforcing its powerful ideology through the interweavings of myth and language. As such, this deceptive rhetoric constructs an inverted foreground culture that mystifies by reversing primary and derivative values (Burke, *Rhetoric of Motives* 104). Daly describes this foreground inversion as patriarchy's power to steal women's words and meanings (*Pure Lust* 86). In the following passage she exemplifies this claim: "Women's minds have been mutilated and muted to such a state that 'Free Spirit' has been branded into them as a brand name for girdles and bras rather than as a name of our verb-ing, be-ing Selves. Such brand names brand women 'Morons.' . . . Patriarchy has stolen our cosmos and returned it in the form of *Cosmopolitan* magazine and cosmetics" (*Gyn/Ecology* 5). Such foreground inversions of meaning are commonly perceived not as "mind-binding"[15] but as the "natural order of things" at the interwoven levels of the institutional, the personal, and the textual; as a result, women are discouraged from re-membering and un-covering possible Background meanings. The implications for women are enormous. They suffer not only from plastic and potted passions[16] but also from stifled and stilted speech. Shaped by genteel manners and customs, this speech, or "shallow ver-biage," exists to flatter men and build their confidence; it pays no heed to a woman's repressed ideas and emotions (*Pure Lust* 18). Thus, a rhetoric of patriarchal mystification promotes what Daly calls the Big Lie.

This rhetoric, however, is not happenstance. It is driven by fore-ground methods. Within Western rhetorical traditions, these meth-ods have been categorized into the canons of invention, arrange-ment, style, memory, and delivery. Although Daly does not couch her analysis in terms of the rhetorical traditions, her primary proj-ect may be read as identifying mystifying invention strategies, which she perceives to be particularly responsible for reproducing the continual stasis of the foreground.

The foreground's first mystifying invention strategy, trivializa-tion, makes unimportant that which is important and succeeds when we fall prey to hierarchal, dichotomized thinking; for in-stance, antifeminists wondering why feminists are so concerned with women's problems when many other, more important troubles exist in our world, such as poverty, war, and racism. A second, particularization, focuses on only one aspect of an issue or event and succeeds when we neatly compartmentalize ourselves and our complex social matrix; for example, Anglo-Americans claiming or implying that race is only a concern for African Americans or Asian Americans. A third, spiritualization, is a form of particu-larization that separates mind, spirit, and body, and it succeeds when we ignore material influences on spirituality; that is, when the body is maimed to celebrate the soul. And a fourth, univer-salization, renders particular differences invisible by concentrating on the fictionalized whole, and it succeeds when we erase cate-gories of difference, particularly gender, from our analyses; for example, claiming that we should focus on strategies of empow-erment for all humans, not on particular strategies for Hispanic women (*Beyond* 5).

A fifth strategy, erasure, fosters a foreground forgetting of both mythic and linguistic events. Mythic erasure represses women's lives, stories, and meanings from traditions of history, literature, politics, theology, folklore, philosophy, and so on. Linguistic erasure represses women's words and their presence in grammatical constructions of language (*Gyn/Ecology* 8). Erasures succeed when the foreground remains unquestioned; for example, when literary canons composed predominantly of males are presented as the best that has ever been said and written. A sixth, reversal, inverts the hierarchal values assigned to binary oppositions; it also occurs on both mythic and linguistic levels. Mythic reversals co-opt women's biological and social powers. Theological and mythological examples are Adam's giving birth to Eve and Zeus's giving birth to Athena; a philosophical example is Socrates' adopting conception and birthing as metaphors for his method of dialectic.[17] Linguistic reversals devalue language assigned to women; for example, our witchy connotation of *hag* mystifying its etymological root in *holiness* and our unquestioning use of *bunny, bitch, beaver*, and so on, mystifying our frequent association of animal names with women (14–17, 7). Daly conceptualizes subcategories of reversals: simple inversion (MX missiles as Peacekeepers), reversals that posit the elementary world as the model for natural phenomena (watches explaining a deistic cosmos), reversals that project male qualities onto women and nature (penis envy, predatory birds), and reversals by which patriarchal males appropriate capacities and qualities of women (philosophical midwifery) (*Wickedary* 239–58).

A seventh strategy, false polarization, posits false binary oppositions. Unlike some feminists, Daly does not reject the method of binary oppositions; in fact, she regularly employs them; for instance, foreground and Background. What she does attack, however, is the patriarchal presence assumed by the false positioning of binaries. Such a strategy succeeds when we are afraid to name true positionings. Mythically, we see male-defined sexism (men holding the door open for women) being set up against male-defined feminism (women hating men) (*Gyn/Ecology* 8). The sexism is extremely conservative; the feminism, extremely radical. Such false positionings allow antifeminists to say, Gee, I hold open a door for a woman and she acts like this?—the result being that feminism(s) are easily dismissed. Linguistically, false binaries emerge as man/wife (which denotes differences in power and roles), madonna/whore (which limits women's options), and stud/wimp (which limits men's).

Divide-and-conquer, an eighth strategy, separates the oppressed to keep them from uniting and rebelling. Also occurring at mythic and linguistic levels, this strategy succeeds by turning women against each other, encouraging us to compete with one another rather than critique systemic oppressions. Mythic divide and conquer celebrates a token woman (whom Daly calls "twice-born Athena" or "Daddy's girl") as a positive role model for other women because she has played the game and pulled herself up by her bootstraps; ironically, the token's function is often to fill an unspoken quota and keep other women from attaining the same successful place. Linguistic divide and conquer is a form of particularization. It compartmentalizes our logic so that we separate, for example, logical and emotional appeals, thus effectively hiding (the existence and the validity of) their interconnectedness (*Gyn/Ecology* 8).

A ninth strategy, mummy words, entails using language to deaden the mind. This strategy succeeds when language remains invisible, when it is perceived as a tool that carries meaning rather than as an integral component in the construction of meaning. Daly cites the following examples: *civilization, mystery, custom, forefathers, history*—all of which are usually silent about women's actual social roles (*Wickedary* 243). Tenth, dummy words also imply a strategy of using language to deaden the mind; however, these words appear harmless so as to metaphorically mystify the danger of their referents. Again, this strategy succeeds when we allow language to remain invisible and do not question it. Daly cites these examples: *daughter* used as a radioactive decay product, *breeder* reactor, *air-breathing missile, artificial intelligence* (245). Eleventh, anti-biotic words imply a strategy in which dummy terms are so exaggerated that they deserve a separate category. Like mummies and dummies, anti-biotic words succeed when their language is commonly accepted instead of exposed as the hyperbolic ironies they are. Daly notes the following example: acronyms like MAD (mutual assured destruction), names like *bomblet*, terms like *fallout, nuke, meltdown, deployment, and plutonium*, and code words like *disinformation* (character assassination) and *neutralize* (assassination) (246–47).

The Sado-Ritual Syndrome is the twelfth and most powerful strategy that patriarchy employs to relegate women to foreground stasis. Although the Syndrome occurs transculturally, it manifests itself differently: for example, Chinese footbinding, African and American genital mutilation, Indian widow burning, European witch burning, and so on. According to Daly, such rituals are perpetuated via men's and women's participation in the Sado-Ritual Syndrome's seven moves: obsessing about purity; erasing responsibility for atrocities performed in the name of a transcendent truth; catching on and spreading quickly; using women as scapegoats and "token torturers"; obsessing on order, repetition, and detail; accepting behavior that in other contexts would appear appalling; validating a ritual's existence through academic scholarship (*Gyn/Ecology* 130–35). The socializing function of this Syndrome keeps women from questioning their plight and imagining other possibilities. Because such patriarchal logic is inscribed within our bodies, this Syndrome is a powerful strategy for maintaining the status quo.

Although Daly discusses the remaining rhetorical canons in less detail, they also participate in constructing the foreground's rhetoric of patriarchal mystification. For example, she claims that foreground arguments are *arranged* in a "tidy" order, which she defines as "tracked, tamed, sanitized, routinized" (*Wickedary* 97); furthermore, she names the linear movement of this arrangement strategy "pure thrust" (221). Daly also claims that *styles* of such arguments too often invoke the noun-goddess and passive voice, thus deleting agency and direct action (86, 215). She further claims that such arguments construct a *memory* that allows only enough space for foreground memories; these memories perpetuate the "cock and bull story [of] patriarchal history, any highly respected account of the exploits of cocks and bullies which effectively erases the existence and history of women and all Others" (190). Finally, Daly claims that the *delivery* of these arguments occur either as consciousness razing or as re-covering, that is, covering again (191, 222).

Within a rhetoric of patriarchal mystification, these five canons successfully mystify possible Background meanings by constructing foreground meanings that appear so clear, so precise, so logical, so normal, and so true that none of us think to question them.

None of us can stand outside this rhetoric or its meanings because they are found at all levels of society: "from styles of grammar to style of glamour, from religious myth to dirty jokes, from theological hymns honoring the 'Real Presence' of Christ to commercial cooing of Coca-Cola as 'The Real Thing,' from dogmatic doctrines about the 'Divine Host' to doctored ingredient-labelling of Hostess Cupcakes, from subliminal ads to sublime art. Phallic myth and language generate, legitimate, and mask the material pollution that threatens to terminate all sentient life on this planet" (*Gyn/Ecology* 9). Within the foreground, the only option open to women is reacting, fighting on foreground turf in foreground terms (*Wickedary* 222). But Daly claims that such games cannot be won and that participation in them only further inflicts "mind/spirit/body pollution" upon a woman (*Gyn/Ecology* 9). For this reason, she offers an alternative to this foreground rhetoric of patriarchal mystification.

A Rhetoric of Radical Feminist De/Mystification

This Background rhetoric encourages and enables women to de/mystify foreground meanings and dis-cover Background ones. Such a de/mystifying rhetoric is imperative if women are to unmask the eighth deadly sin of deception, which permeates every word we use (*Gyn/Ecology* 3). Daly describes this de/mystifying rhetoric in *Pure Lust*: "Breaking the bonds/bars of phallocracy requires breaking through to radiant powers of words, so that by releasing words, we can release our Selves" (4). She names the moves of this rhetoric *exorcism* and *ecstasy*, with *exorcism* entailing the (meta)physical dis-possessing of patriarchy and *ecstasy* entailing the (meta)physical giddiness that emerges when women are released from foreground meanings (*Gyn/Ecology* 2; *Wickedary* 75). As such, a rhetoric of radical feminist de/mystification encourages and enables a woman to Spin between the foreground and Background, continually (un)weaving the intersections of patriarchal myth and language in order to create and dis-cover both herSelf and herWor(l)ds.[18]

This Background rhetoric depends upon language, namely, the

possibilities of metaphor that Daly associates with the powers of magical conjuring:

> The Active Potency of the archimage, then, is transformative Power. This faculty, through which she "brings celestial forces to earth," is the power of healing broken connections. One way through which this is communicated is the transmission of Metaphoric words that transverse/pass across the fathers' archetypes, awakening the stifled *archai* with word-waves/wand-waves. The words/wands of Weird women also transverse the archetypes in the sense that they overturn and reverse them, reversing their reversals. For words are weapons, Labryses of Archimagical Amazons. Women participating in the biophilic powers of the Archimage also transverse in the "obsolete" sense of the term, which is "alter, transform," as we change our lives in the process of dis-spelling the archetypes. (*Pure Lust* 90)

This magical conjuring through metaphor manifests itself in many ways. Consider the slight of place that occurs when a woman is shifted from a "thing" noun to a "verbal" noun: instead of being a thing or object, she becomes a Namer or a Speaker, who has the power to "Name away the archetypes that block the ways/words of Metabeing" (86–87). In this way, magical conjuring both ruptures phallogocentric grammar and generates Daly's Elemental Feminist Philosophy. This Philosophy is a kind of be-ing and be-thinking that is grounded in a Metapatriarchal consciousness which presumes reason to be a function of instinct, intuition, and passion as well as mind (*Wickedary* 72).

Magical conjuring through metaphor is crucial to Daly's rhetoric of radical feminist de/mystification. It enables women to overcome both verbal violence and verbicide. While verbal violence degrades a woman semantically (*Gyn/Ecology* 358, 359–62), verbicide carefully kills words in order to rob them of meaning and reduce them to noise (*Wickedary* 233). The danger of verbicide is that it splits a woman from herSelf and creates in her an insecurity that results in amnesia, aphasia, and apraxis (*Pure Lust* 94). But Daly assures us that such states need not be permanent: "The remedy is unrelenting understanding that Stamina is stronger than the verbiage of the re-verberators, and that breathing/speaking forth Elemental words/actions is itself the creation and communication of Stamina, which is the living thread of conversation spun by Fates. . . . Naming our way beyond verbicide (which is deeply connected with gynocide) we are creators of our own fates—becoming Fates" (95). If a woman employs this remedy, she becomes patriarchy's worst fear: a castrator. For magical conjuring through metaphor implies the castration of language and images that construct and reflect patriarchy (*Beyond* 9; *Pure Lust* 166–69). In the process, magical conjuring creates new Elements—new hearing, new contexts, new speech, and new words—whose discursive powers can cast spells on the personal and the cultural.[19]

The first Element that Daly's Background rhetoric must conjure is a new hearing. In the last chapter of *Gyn/Ecology*, Daly concludes that the word was not the beginning, the hearing was (424). With this assertion, she challenges patriarchal obsessions with First Causes. She locates hearing (a human potential), not the Word (God's utterance), as the space where we can analyze Be-ing and Know-ing. This (meta)physical space is where women can question patriarchal ideology through myth and language:

> The essential thing is to hear our *own* words, always giving priorattention to our *own* experience, never letting prefabricated theory have *authority* over us. Then we can be free to listen to the old philosophical language (and all philosophy that does not explicitly repudiate sexism is old, no matter how novel it may seem). If some of this language, when heard in the context of female becoming is still worth hearing, we need not close our ears. But if we choose to speak the same sounds they will be formally and existentially new words, for the new context constitutes them as such. Our process is *our* process. (*Beyond* 189)

Once this hearing is tapped and a radical feminist journey begun, other Elements necessary to Daly's Background rhetoric are also magically conjured. Once a woman hears differently, she must constantly negotiate between foreground and Background contexts.

Because this process cannot be arrested, new hearing continually generates new contexts, that is, new movements between foreground and Background. Even when a woman uses old language, new contexts transform it into new speech (*Beyond* 159). In turn, new speech generates questions as well as answers to these questions (8–9). As such, new speech is essential to Daly's rhetoric of radical feminist de/mystification. Without it, language becomes a trap; women, merely determined parrots. But a woman's employing new speech does not mean that she should imitate male-identified discourse (8). New speech leads to new words, and this process continually unfolds at all semiotic levels—in talk, in texts, in clothing style, in body language, and so on (*Gyn/Ecology* 340; *Wickedary* 86). In this way, Daly's rhetoric of radical feminist de/mystification occurs in the presence of patriarchy.

Like its foreground reversal, Daly's Background rhetoric is not happenstance. It is driven by Background methodicide, which Daly defines as "deicide by means of asking Nonquestions, and Discovering, reporting, and analyzing Nondata" (*Wickedary* 82). Methodicide is not the denial of method but rather the denial of foreground methods and the celebration of Background ones.[20] How does Daly's methodicide translate into practice? It encourages a woman to actively read and write against patriarchal myths and language that construct herSelf and her daily life. Because it occurs in the midst of systemic oppressions, methodocide has its limits; nevertheless, it can be invoked by a Self, whose limited conscious agency may trust its unconscious for assistance.

Methodocidal reading and writing presume that a woman can and should break the silence imposed by patriarchal structures of history, culture, society, and family (*Beyond* 93). Breaking the silence, however, is not a simple talking cure, nor is it without consequences. Instead, it is a never ending process that breaks subject/object categories into intersubjective relations that continually (re)produce meanings beyond the hearing of patriarchal ears (152). It induces "the vertigo of creation," the dizziness associated with Spinning (*Gyn/Ecology* 414–17). Methodocidal reading and writing also presume that patriarchal concepts like "natural" and "objective" must be challenged and that patriarchal arguments must be analyzed to determine how they focus only on certain facts, never questioning the assumptions or implications of these facts while ignoring other facts that may inform a woman's experience (*Beyond* 107).

Daly advocates specific de/mystifying manuevers for methodocidal reading and writing. These manuevers, I argue, construct her Background rhetoric of radical feminist de/mystification. This rhetoric reverses the foreground canons of rhetoric and posits instead interwoven Background Non-canons of Spinning, Dis-ordering, Be-Spelling, Re-membering, and Be-Speaking.

SPINNING

The re-versing of invention, Spinning is the first of Daly's Background Non-canons. Neither *topoi* nor place, Spinning is the major metaphoric motion of Daly's Background rhetoric (*Gyn/Ecology* 424). Daly defines Spinning as "Dis-covering the lost thread of connectedness within the cosmos and repairing this thread in the process" (*Wickedary* 96). In the foreground, however, such Spinning is often deflected and deflated with the following results: "Our creativity is misdirected into misplaced rage against other women. It is traced into soap opera level aspects of 'relationships.' Under therapeutic treatment, it is tracked into psychobabble that closes off deep Memory. When academically trained, it repeats male theories. Groomed for professional excellence, it serves phallic institutions. 'Religious,' it worships a male god" (*Pure Lust* 18). By moving Spinners toward the Background, Spinning exposes patriarchal socialization, reversing the foreground's deflection and deflation of Gyn/Ecological Creation and modeling this reversal for others (*Gyn/Ecology* 404). But such an invention process is not easy: it requires repetitive practice, not just wishful thinking (*Pure Lust* 261). To articulate the methods and possibilities of such an invention process, I have culled Daly's texts to identify different invention strategies, which may be read together as the Non-canon of Spinning that drives Daly's Background rhetoric.

The first type of Spinning is Daly's reversal of the seven-step Sado-Ritual Syndrome. As noted earlier, this Syndrome details how patriarchal rituals obsess on purity, erase responsibility, spread quickly, use women as scapegoats and as token torturers, promote compulsive orderliness and obsessive repetition, make the unacceptable acceptable, and justify themselves through scholarship

(*Gyn/Ecology* 130–35). But radical feminists may turn this Syndrome against itself, employing it as a de/mystifying strategy. Such de/mystifications may occur in interrelated reading and writing moves. In *Gyn/Ecology* Daly uses this Syndrome to read and write against cultural rituals such as widow burning and genital mutilation; in *Pure Lust* she employs this Syndrome to analyze and write against the effect of such atrocities on women's spirituality. This Syndrome could also be used to analyze Miss America pageants, *Cosmopolitan* covergirls, women in academia, and so on. And though Daly discusses this Syndrome in relation to patriarchy's atrocities against women, William Jones finds this analysis useful in demystifying patriarchy's ritualized oppression of African Americans.[21]

The second type of Spinning is Ludic Celebration. Daly defines this strategy as "thinking out of the experience of being; the free play of intuition in New Space" (*Wickedary* 143). Ludic celebration begins with Laughing Out Loud, a strategy of "cracking the hypocritical hierarchs' house of mirrors [and] defusing their power of deluding Others" (142). This strategy not only breaks foreground logics but moves the Laugher into Background logics. Daly describes three types of Laughing Out Loud or Be-Laughing: Nixing, Hexing, and X-ing. Nixing is the re-fusal of absence and the assertion of presence (264). Hexing is the casting of Spells or Be-Wishing that breaks patriarchal boundaries (267–68). And X-ing is the naming of strange coincidences and synchronicities that are important to women's lives (269). These Ludic Celebrations are all "intertwined, interwoven wondrous workings/wordings that are Dis-covered and passed on" so that women can "keep a Silly Sense of Humor and regain a Sinful Sense of Direction" (263, 272).

A third type of Spinning is Be-Musing, "be-ing a Muse for oneSelf and for Other Muses [while] refusing Musing to a-Musing scribblers" (*Wickedary* 65). In other words, a woman should refuse to serve as muses for others who drain her energy; instead, she should re-fuse herSelf and other Others who share her desire to de/mystify foreground meanings and un-cover Background ones. Such a move is neither simple nor easy, for it flies in the face of powerful socialization that asks women to be kind, nurturing, and supportive. But such a total woman, Daly argues, is really a "totalled woman" (232). Hence, Be-musing enables a woman to rec-ognize her totalled foreground self as a false identity that covers her Background Self (95). Once Be-Musing occurs, the foreground self dis-covers the Background Self in a move that Daly names Realizing Presence.

A fourth type of Spinning, Realizing Presence refers to the Self's "active potency/power to create and to transform, to render pre-sent in time and space" (*Pure Lust* 149). Despite her definition of Self as "the Original core," Daly is not a traditional humanist (*Wickedary* 95); such a position is much too patriarchal for her. The key distinction between Daly's Self and a humanist self lies in her definition of *Be-ing* as the "Ultimate/Intimate Reality, the constantly Unfolding Verb of Verbs which is intransitive, having no object that limits its dynamism" (64). As a part of this constant unfolding process of Be-ing, Daly's Self as be-ing is neither static nor unaffected by context. Instead, her Self as be-ing continually spins between foreground and Background, and "this Active Voic-ing . . . Spooks the spookers" (*Gyn/Ecology* 340). Daly's Self ex-ists as an active though not autonomous agent who is continually (re)constructed by patriarchal myth and language. While being (re)constructed, this Self may turn language on itself in order to unweave patriarchal ideology. Such a process frees the Background Self from foreground selflessness. Thus, Daly's Self is an agent who chooses herSelf and defines herSelf in relation to her own experiences, not only in relation to children or men (3–4).

Realizing Presence reverses two common foreground states: the presence of absence and the absence of Presence (*Pure Lust* 149). The former refers to the lack of meaning in male-identified myths and ideologies, which manifests itself as mental and spiritual "bloat"; the latter refers to a missing substance and purpose, the absence of Self (147). Daly acknowledges that questions of pres-ence and absence have dominated philosophical debates for centu-ries. Yet she also acknowledges that such questions have played out tragically in popular culture: the result is that a woman is robbed of her sense of Self and, hence, her confidence and ability to act. To reverse this phenomenon, Daly encourages us to Sin Big; because one etymology of the word *sin* is "to be," to Sin Big means to question foreground assumptions and refuse false ones, including the death of the author/speaker/writer/Spinner (151).

The desired result is Realizing Presence, which can make a woman aware of herSelf, let her dis-cover Background meanings, and enable her to own the original power of her words (162).

Closely related is a fifth kind of Spinning, Realizing reason.[22] Daly defines this process as "both dis-covering and participating in the unfolding, the Self-creation, of reason," not as a transcendent truth but as an ongoing (meta)physical process; and she cites this strategy's most common manifestation in the repetition, the litany, of the sentence, "I just didn't realize . . . " (*Pure Lust* 162). Bonnie Mann gives an example of Realizing reason when discussing how she uses *Gyn/Ecology* in her work with battered women; one woman named Barbara, when she first heard Daly's work read aloud, exclaimed, "Oh my god! I'm a radical feminist!" (xli).[23] In this instant, Barbara Realized reason by making connections between her particular experiences and those of other women.

Daly warns us that establishing particularization and universalization as a binary opposition creates a false opposition (*Pure Lust* 322–25). Yet she posits them as active, interwoven principles of Realizing reason. The particular enables women to celebrate our diversity while the general provides structures within which such diversity flourishes. Respecting both the particular and the general, and not getting trapped in the general, is a great concern of Daly's:

> Not only are there ethnic, national, class and racial differences that shape our perspectives, but there are also individual and cross-cultural differences of temperament, virtue, talent, taste and of conditions within which these can or cannot find expression. There is, then, an extremely rich, complex Diversity among women and within each individual. But there is also above, beyond, beneath all this a Cosmic Commonality, a tapestry of connectedness which women as Websters/Fates are constantly weaving. The weaving of this tapestry is the Realizing of a dream, which Adrienne Rich has Named "The Dream of a Common Language" (26–27).

In Daly's theory, this common language creates a space that is continually unfolding, a space in which logics of the general and particular can exist.

By refusing stasis, Realizing reason assumes the unstoppable play of language between foreground and Background. As such, it breaks the logic of the foreground, exposing not only the existence of Background logic but also the multiplicity of this logic: "The expression 'Realizing reason' is doubled-edged. It is even multiple edged" (*Pure Lust* 162–63). Thus, Realizing reason is not the reification of a static logos within a determined cosmos, nor is it the celebration of an unknowable chaos within an unknowable cosmos; rather, it is the ongoing discovery and creating of logic(s) other than patriarchy (*Gyn/Ecology* 160–69). A particular strategy for Realizing reason is Be-Shrewing or "being a Shrewd Shrew," which reverses Aristotelian syllogistic logic (*Wickedary* 65): "*Shrewdness* was understood by Aristotle as 'a faculty of hitting upon the middle term [connecting link] instantaneously.' As he explained: It would be exemplified by a man who saw that the moon has her bright side always turned towards the sun, and quickly grasped the cause of this, namely that she borrows her light from him [*sic*]; or observed somebody in conversation with a man of wealth and divined that he was borrowing money, or that the friendship of these people sprang from a common enemy" (*Pure Lust* 267). Aristotle's syllogism is based on commonly accepted first principles and middle terms, what most people call common sense. Daly's shrewdness, however, is dependent on women's posing different first principles, different middle terms, different senses, and different contexts (269).

Daly's gendered challenge to Aristotle's logical syllogism has implications for the rhetorical enthymeme. In terms of individual socialization, Daly's challenge exposes how common assumptions privilege the power of the center. For example, such outsiders as women, minorities, and lower-class white males are encouraged to accept the economic structure of capitalism because they, too, may one day benefit from it; the odds of its happening, however, are never discussed. Conversely, Daly's challenge exposes how a focus on difference subverts the power of the center. Suppose the above-mentioned outsiders have no aspirations to climb a capitalistic ladder but rather prefer to pursue radical politics; as such, they might be accused of constituting clear and present dangers to our way of life. Nevertheless, they would exemplify how different principles and different senses may tear holes in the dominant ideology.

Daly's gendered challenge to Aristotle's enthymeme reveals the difficulty of communication between center and margins. Suppose a nonfeminist disagrees with a feminist claim, for example, that military women should fly jets in combat because they are as well-trained and capable as men. The nonfeminist could refute the major premise (i.e., ability and training are necessary for flying jets in combat) by invoking biological differences between men and women and by claiming that such differences affect either ability or training; or the nonfeminist could concede the major premise but supply a different middle term (e.g., combat necessitates special considerations for women in addition to their ability and training). Either way, the feminist claim is dismissed, and communication is closed down with a simple *because* clause. To move beyond such closure, the major premises, middle terms, and their underlying premises must be teased out; then they must be reimagined, articulated, questioned, and negotiated.

Context is the determining factor for deciding whether or not Be-Shrewing should be acted upon. Sometimes it is too draining, too time-consuming, too futile. Juanita Comfort speaks of picking her battles carefully, of choosing *not* to lay out the logic needed to educate a white professor who had refused to consider seriously the contributions of women within a certain literary period. Sometimes, however, Be-Shrewing is imperative. Deneen Shepherd speaks of carving a space for herself within academic discourse, challenging feminists (particularly, white feminists) to reconsider the place of personal narrative, the place of oral tradition as ways of knowing and being within academic discourse. As both Comfort and Shepherd make clear, deciding whether or not Be-Shrewing should be acted upon steals time. If the decision is no, time has still been spent considering the possibilities. If the decision is yes, even more time must be taken to remap premises, reconfigure logical stances, and painstakingly lay out claims and reasons. So the question is not whether Be-Shrewing costs time, but how much. Hence, Be-Shrewing slows political action.

A sixth kind of Spinning is Feminist Naming. Daly defines this strategy as "Truth-telling," or the "Original summoning of words for the Self, the world and ultimate reality" (*Wickedary* 83). Feminist Naming enables a woman to uncover Background meanings as she sees, feels, thinks, intuits them: "[It is a] deliberate confrontation with [the] language structure of our heritage [that] transcends the split between nonrational sounds of 'tongues' and the merely rational semantic games of linguistic analysis, for it is a break out of the deafening noise of sexist language that has kept us from hearing our own word" (*Beyond* 167).[24] Eight methods of Feminist Naming are outlined in *Gyn/Ecology*: (1) making up words—for example, *gyn/ecology*, (2) unmasking deceptive words—for instance, *recover*, which actually means to cover again, (3) unmasking hidden reversals—such as *glamour*'s referring to a witch's power, not merely a cosmetic trick, (4) inviting readers to see and hear words differently—for example, *de-light* or *re-verse*, (5) tracing etymologies—as in *text* and *textile*, which have the same root although they have evolved in different gendered directions, (6) considering multiple meanings of words—such as *spinster*, referring to an unmarried woman and to a radical feminist Spinner, (7) rejecting inauthentic words that obscure women's lives and their oppression—for instance, *chairperson*, and (8) listening to one's intuition and making personal decisions—such as Daly's decision not to use *herstory* (24). Despite its power, Feminist Naming does have limits. Sometimes we only know our truths by their absence, by a felt sense that has no name. Sometimes, even if we do have names for our truths, the common sense of the dominant culture dismisses them as unimportant.

Because Feminist Naming is synonymous with Truth-telling, Daly does not validate prevaricating as Quintilian does in his famous discussion about why good men tell lies (12.33–45). In Daly's theory, lying has three possible results: silencing the Self, assuming a privileged position over others (as in lying to them for their own good), or perpetuating the Big Lie of patriarchy. Not lying is an important political step for Daly, not only for establishing her own Background Self but also for directly challenging her readers' daily identification with commonly accepted foreground myths and languages. To promote Truth-telling, Daly tells the truth about it: not lying has consequences (*Gyn/Ecology* 1–36). Nevertheless, Feminist Naming as Truth-telling serves several important (meta)physical functions. It enables a woman to confront false naming as a patriarchal tool of social control (*Beyond* 126). It enables her to conceptualize and articulate herSelf and the Background realm (*Pure Lust* xii). And it enables her to reimagine deity as Be-ing. This latter move is imperative if the first two are to occur. For Feminist Naming is participating in Be-ing, "naming *toward* God [instead of] fixing names *upon* God, which [deafen] us to our potential for self-naming" (*Beyond* 33). Thus, Truth-telling takes on processual motion that lying tries to halt.

Daly's first Non-canon begins with exposing the Sado-Ritual Syndrome and culminates in the Play of Feminist Naming, which in turn generates more Syndrome exposures. And so goes radical feminist Spinning, proceeding in a Dis-ordering way.

DIS-ORDERING

The re-versing of arrangement, Dis-ordering is the second of Daly's Background Non-canons. Daly defines Dis-ordering by tracing its etymology to *order*, which derives from Latin terms that mean to warp and to weave; this warping and weaving is associated with "Tidal Weaving and Reweaving; breaking through the tidy order/orders of Boredom" (*Wickedary* 118). By playing with this warping and weaving metaphor, Daly refuses a fixed or formulaic foreground arrangement. Like Socrates, she offers no tidy introductions, narrations, proofs, refutations, or conclusions. Unlike Socrates, however, she describes Background Dis-ordering as Tidal, composed of gendered cosmic rhythms and interconnectedness (97). As such, Dis-ordering resembles a freewriting that de/mystifies patriarchal myth and language.

Daly's weaving metaphor implies that Dis-ordering is a process of constructing texts that is grounded in the particular space and time of composing, whether that composing be reading or writing. This weaving metaphor also implies that Dis-ordering emerges as patterns that are simultaneously crafted and functional. Such claims are supported by her definition of *weaving* as an "Original activity of Websters: creating tapestries of Crone-centered creation; constructing a context which sustains Sisters on the Otherworld Journey"; and a "mode of Travelling: wending one's way through and around the baffles of blockocracy; crisscrossing and connecting with other Voyagers" (*Wickedary* 99–100). This definition simultaneously posits Dis-ordering as a process ("activity"), a product ("tapestries"), a space ("context"), a time ("Travelling"), and a recognition of intersubjectivity ("crisscrossing and connecting"). This definition challenges foreground arrangement patterns, whether classical schemes or their much diminished twentieth-century receptions like the five paragraph theme.

As demonstrated by Daly's own textual practice, the implications of Dis-ordering are multiple. First, it celebrates intertextuality. In many cases, Daly's forewords and afterwords are written years after the text's original publication; thus, they talk to and about the texts that follow, breaking down boundaries between time and space, reaffirming and rejecting earlier metaphors, methods, and claims. Likewise, subsequent books are conversations with and about her earlier texts. Second, Daly's Dis-ordering can break patriarchal logic for writers and readers. By jolting them with her claims and language play, she invites them to read and write differently, with more gender awareness. She is realistic, however, about the extent to which she can control the reception of her texts, as evidenced by the patriarchal reviews that she predicts for *The Church and the Second Sex*.[25] Third, if Dis-ordering does not break patriarchal logic(s) for all her readers, at the very least it will alleviate Boredom, "the official/officious state produced by bores" (*Wickedary* 186). Fourth, Dis-ordering re-fuses Spinning, generating ideas by taking writers and readers to a new space and time. For some, this new place is the Background; for others, it is a heightened awareness, or a vehement reaffirmation, of the foreground. Fifth, Dis-ordering merges subject and object, process and product, celebrating the journey while recognizing that each tapestry/text must be completed and used if only as a pattern for further Spinning. In these ways, Dis-ordering is neither a glib response to patriarchy nor a mere antiformalism.[26] Rather, it embodies radical feminist journeys and invites others to join (*Gyn/Ecology* 23).

As discussed thus far, Spinning in a Dis-ordering fashion concentrates primarily on the voyager's attempt to de/mystify the foreground and discover her Background Self. But when Be-Spelling enters into play with Daly's first two Non-canons, it discloses how Spinning in a Dis-ordering fashion is not just done in a vacuum but encompasses innocent bystanders, enchanting those who happen to get caught up in the whirl.

BE-SPELLING

The re-versing of style, Be-Spelling is the third of Daly's Background Non-canons. A casting of charms and enchantment through language, Be-Spelling is listed in the *Wickedary* as the "ontological Shape-Shifting of words which awakens latent powers of be-ing in the Spell-speaker, in the hearer, and in the words themselves" (65). This definition reveals Be-Spelling's rhetorical functions, both communicative and socializing; the power of Be-Spelling is centered at the intersection of speaker, hearer, and language where it assumes a potency unrealizable at any one of the three points individually. That power may be channelled in "overthrowing dronedom/clonedom," that is, in throwing "the old order out of order" (19).

Be-Spelling functions at both conscious and unconscious levels, as exemplified by Daly's descriptions of her own textual practices. Her unconscious magical conjuring of metaphorical language is especially powerful for evoking an alliterative, incantatory quality in her prose: "[The words] seem to want to break the bonds of conventional usage, to break the silence imposed upon their own Backgrounds. They become palpable, powerful, and it seems that they are tired of allowing me to 'use' *them* and cry out for a role reversal. I become their mouthpiece, and if I am not always accurate in conveying their meanings, that is probably because I haven't yet learned to listen closely enough, in the realm of the labyrinthine inner ear" (*Gyn/Ecology* 25). At other times, Daly's conscious magical conjuring is especially powerful for constructing, reflecting, and reinforcing her messages. In forewords, afterwords, introductions, explanatory notes, and prefaces, she discusses seven conscious Be-Spelling choices: spelling, grammar, word choice, pronoun usage, capitalization, punctuation, and sources. But whether unconscious or conscious, Be-Spelling choices do not culminate in static stylistic rules that all feminists should follow. Rather, these choices embody visual ruptures in texts that force writers and readers to become aware of, and reflect on, the foreground function of language. As such, these choices pose questions that each writer and reader must answer. Such a questioning process is necessary, Daly argues, if we are to recognize the ideological assumptions built into our foreground language practices.

To demonstrate Be-Spelling through her own writing, Daly cites seven particular strategies that expose links between words and magical conjuring. First, her Spellings are links that "open gateways, summon spirits, brew brainstorms, and Be-Speak Other worlds" (*Wickedary* 13). Such Spellings invoke Dis-Spelling, "unspelling/respelling the possessed words of phallocentric language [in order to release] the Original Magical Powers of Words" (118). Daly proposes three basic Spelling strategies: changing spellings so that words are seen differently (e.g., *Gyn/Ecology* instead of *gynecology*), changing contexts of spellings so that words are heard differently (e.g., the radical feminist un-covering of *spinster* as one who Spins), and spinning off so that words heard differently are written differently and thus seen differently (e.g., words in the *Wickedary*) (14–18). The reasons for conjuring such Spellings are simple: patriarchal language and scholarship cannot convey women's Background energy (*Pure Lust* 30). These Spelling strategies challenge the foreground assumption that correct spelling is indicative of intelligence yet extraneous to meaning; simultaneously, they expose the Background assumption that Spelling not only reflects but constructs a reader's and writer's Self.

Second, grammar is also a link between words and magical conjuring. Background grammar is the "harmonious interplay among the primal sounds of words; concordance of words Sounding and Resounding together in complex compositions, as they communicate manifold meanings" (*Wickedary* 77). Linking *grammar* etymologically to *glamour*, Daly repudiates foreground meanings that reduce *grammar* to dull, dry, static studies and *glamour* to painted, airbrushed magazine covers. Instead, she uncovers their Background meanings of Be-Witching, or "breaking the rules/roles of boring bewitchingness" (66). When juxtaposed to Background Be-Witching, foreground grammar and glamour are exposed not as objective descriptions of language and beauty but as means of social control (24, 128). For example, Daly argues that foreground grammar deletes agency: passive voice mystifies accountability by erasing who or what performs an action; unattributed adjectives in such expressions as "*undesirable* behavior" suppress the agent's identity (i.e., *who* finds the behavior undesirable); and generic nouns such as *people* and *they* allow particular perpetrators to hide behind the general (*Gyn/Ecology* 324–26). In addition to deleting agency, Daly argues that foreground grammar deletes possibilities. That is, foreground grammar posits static categories and rigid rules of syntax, which Background grammar challenges with active verbs, active adjectives, and specific Naming that spooks the passive. Hence, Daly encourages a Spinning woman to play with the categories and rules of grammar, to practice Sin-tactics by making connections between seemingly unconnected information. Sin-tactics is a crucial strategy of Daly's Be-Spelling, enabling a Spinning woman to break patriarchal logic(s), rhetoric(s), silence(s), and taboo(s) (*Wickedary* 30).

Closely associated with Daly's concerns about spelling and grammar is her third Be-Spelling strategy, diction. She carefully deliberates over word choice not because words are politically correct but because they construct and reflect our be-ing in particular spaces and times. Words must be written and read both to expose old meanings in the foreground and to construct new meanings, New Words, in the Background: for example, what Daly calls *discrimination* in 1968 she might call *oppression* in 1975 (*Church* 14–15). Changes in time and space create different places in which people have different perspectives and words have different functions, hence Daly's interest in etymologies and Meta-etymologies (*Wickedary* xxiii). She employs them not only to expose Cronelogical meanings for Feminist Naming but also to invoke Be-Spelling enchantments, which she hopes will spark Spinning in herSelf and her readers (*Gyn/Ecology* 24). Thus, diction embodies more than a polite reflection of class status and educational achievement; in Daly's theory, it embodies a metaphoric, generative function.

Fourth, although pronoun usage is a type of word choice, Daly singles it out for individual mention as a Be-Spelling strategy. Pronouns pose particular problems because they perpetuate the dilemma of subject/object relations. Daly invokes her concept of intersubjectivity to resolve this dilemma theoretically and particular pronoun strategies to resolve it linguistically. When considering third-person pronouns, Daly not only rejects the generic *he* but more interestingly questions the use of *they* when referring to women: *they* is an "objective" subject position that allows a woman to separate herself from other women. When contemplating first-person pronouns, Daly offers no easier choices: *I* conceals the writer's sex as does *we* (*Gyn/Ecology* 18–19). To solve this problem in the *Wickedary*, Daly and Caputi stipulate that we includes not only the coauthors but also other Background journeyers (xxii). Despite these strategies, Daly admits that no easy solutions or hard and fast rules exist: in the final analysis, context should determine pronoun selection (*Pure Lust* 31).

Fifth, Daly claims that her Be-Spelling strategy of capitalization reflects her meanings, not foreground ones or standard usage; yet she also discloses that the previous claim is not always true (*Wickedary* xxi). Nevertheless, patterns do emerge. Daly unfolds her capitalization logic as follows: "I consistently capitalize *Spinster*, just as one normally capitalizes *Amazon*. I capitalize *Lesbian* when the word is used in its woman-identified (correct) sense, but use the lower case when referring to the male-distorted version reflected in the media. *Self* is capitalized when I am referring to the authentic center of woman's process, while the imposed/internalized 'self,' the shell of the Self, is in lower case" (*Gyn/Ecology* 25–26). Daly uses capital letters to distinguish *Wickedary* usage from standard usage, to emphasize foreground fabrications, to laugh at foreground seriousness, and to name Background meanings (xxi–xxii). Thus, her capitalization identifies for herSelf and her readers the differences between foreground and Background; it also forces readers to see and hear words in a different way.

Sixth, Daly's Be-Spelling strategy of punctuation is surprisingly standard. She puts quotations and dialogue in quotation marks; she emphasizes words being defined with italics; she ends sentences with periods and question marks; and she indicates possession with apostrophes. Her most subversive punctuation strategy involves the hyphen and the slash. With these marks, Daly regularly separates prefix and root, root and suffix as in *un-cover* or *re-cover*, *gyn/ecology* or *a/mazing*. In terms of signifieds, such strategies uncover foreground reversals; for instance, *un-cover* suggests that there was once a cover-up. These strategies also create Background meanings; for example, *Gyn/Ecology* suggests that women need to be saved. In terms of signifiers, however, such strategies provide a visual break in the language, a crossing out or slashing of foreground signifieds.

Daly's seventh Be-Spelling strategy, her use of sources, is an important political statement. As "the rebuttal of the rite of right re-search," Daly's feminist scholarship challenges patriarchal scholarship (*Gyn/Ecology* 23). To reverse standard foreground practices, Daly transvalues sources: her primary sources are women's experiences; her secondary sources, men's texts from a variety of fields (27; *Pure Lust* 31). Unlike some feminists, Daly does not avoid using men's texts nor apologize for doing so; however, neither is she a disciple of these texts. Whether using them as proof or as springboards for thought, Daly is always aware of women's contributions to these texts (*Gyn/Ecology* 27). Because of this awareness, Daly's sources invoke fleeting shadows in prefaces and dedications as well as forgotten episodes in women's history. In this way, her citation process is Woman identified.

As a feminist reversal of style, all of these Be-Spelling strategies are important to Daly's rhetoric of radical feminist de/mystification. The purpose of these strategies is to remind writers and readers of Virginia Woolf's claim that meanings do not reside in books and dictionaries but live in minds (*Wickedary* 27). And within such minds, much is created and much is Re-membered.

RE-MEMBERING

The re-versing of memory, Re-membering is the fourth of Daly's Background Non-canons. It is Daly's answer to the Nietzschean question of how to create a memory for the human animal (*Gyn/Ecology* 109; *Pure Lust* 169–78). Crucial to Daly's radical feminist journeys between foreground and Background, Re-membering entails "Re-calling the Original intuition of integrity; healing the dismembered Self" (*Wickedary* 92–93). More than rote memorization, Re-memberings unpack foreground mystifications and reassemble them as Background de/mystifications. In this way, Re-memberings reverse foreground dismemberments of ourSelves and our wor(l)ds and posit new Background definitions. But such a defining process is not linear, with a neat beginning, middle, and end; instead, it folds back on itself in a never ending recursive motion. By citing specific texts to exemplify these definitions, Daly demonstrates how foreground memories and Background memories may exist simultaneously while taking their meanings from their immediate contexts.

So important is Re-membering to Daly's rhetoric of radical feminist de/mystification that she conceptualizes seven different types. The first, Memory, is "the power to Re-member; the power to transcend the categories of tidy time, to connect with the sources of instinctive, ecstatic knowledge" (*Wickedary* 79); it puts fragmented members together into a web in which reason and instinct, seriousness and ecstasy construct a fuller knowledge than that which exists in the foreground. The second, Gynocentric Memory, is both the "Memory of a Gynocratic world that pre-existed patriarchy" and the "Crone-logical Memory: history that records/Re-calls events of central importance to women" (136). Merging history and prehistory, this memory is woman centered in its attempt to uncover the gaps, the white spaces, and the off-the-page spaces in (pre)history. The third, Elemental Memory, is the "faculty that Re-members knowledge, emotions, and experiences beyond the fabricated elementary 'recollections' of the foreground" (80). Here Daly plays with foreground *elementary* and Background *Elemental*, defining the former as a lack of connection with the earth and the latter as the presences of this connection (73). Within an Elemental Memory, humans do not have dominion over the earth; instead, they understand their interconnectedness with the earth as well as the truths this interconnectedness bestows. The fourth, Tidal Memory, is the "Memory of the Deep Background, characterized by Tidal Rhythms of Re-membering"; because Daly posits *Elemental* as a synonym for *Tidal*, tidal memory can be read as a kind of Elemental Memory (97).

The fifth type of Re-membering, E-motional Memory, is an "Elementary Memory, stirring deep Passion, generating Movement out of the Fixed State" (*Wickedary* 80). Neither static nor rational, E-motional Memory rides the rhythms of emotions and constructs a space for emotion and body language within Background logic(s) and rhetoric(s). By validating commonplace and commonsense meanings in a woman's life, E-motional Memory posits these meanings as valid proof. The sixth, Memory of the Future, is "active participation in Tidal Time; action that affects/effects the Future" (80). This memory makes both past and future possible in the present for individual be-ings and cultures. It also foregrounds the rhythmic, associative nature of memory and breaks down the affect/effect (subject/verb) dichotomy. Finally, the seventh, Metamemory, is "Deep, Ecstatic Memory of participation in Being that eludes the categories and grids of patriarchal consciousness . . . Memory beyond civilization" (81). Driven by Meta-etymologies and Meta-metaphors, Metamemory enables a woman to think beyond the foreground and Re-member her interconnectedness nature, other people, and the cosmos. Thus, a woman Re-members herSelf as a be-ing, a member of the ecological web that participates in Being.

Taken together, these Re-memberings do not question the process of categorizing; however, they do question the desire for static categories in patriarchal logic. As fluid Background categories, these Re-memberings blur boundaries and generate possibilities. Because these memories and their meanings are deeply rooted in our everyday words, Daly argues that we may discover them by analyzing not only language function, nor only language use, but also the manner and context in which language functions and is used (*Pure Lust* 152). Hence, Re-membering enables Be-Speaking, both verbal and textual.

BE-SPEAKING

The re-versing of delivery, Be-Speaking is the fifth of Daly's Background Non-canons. Daly defines Be-Speaking as "bringing about a psychic and/or material change by means of words; speaking into be-ing" (*Wickedary* 65). As such, Be-Speaking becomes more than a list of simple tips for effective body language and enunciation; it becomes an integral gesture in the construction of power and knowledge that is rhetoric. According to Daly, this reversal of delivery has multiple possibilities within our culture, possibilities that include writing, painting, pottery, social work, marches, and scholarship as well as speaking (*Pure Lust* 120). Within these multiple possibilities, each woman may contribute her particular talents, interests, and experiences.

Daly names three interwoven strategies—Raging, Be-Wildering, and Be-Thinking—as the main motions of "speaking into be-ing." Raging is not a developmental stage that must be resolved in order to progress to the next one; rather, it is a transforming force that presumes E-motion, especially anger, possesses the potential to unbind minds (*Gyn/Ecology* xxxi). Raging reverses foreground repressed rage and enables us to keep women's loss of power within patriarchy constantly in the forefront of our thinking and acting. Although Raging can be misdirected, it can also be productively channeled into other Be-Speaking strategies, such as Be-Wildering and Be-thinking.

Be-Wildering takes the Self as well as Others farther into the Background when they follow the Call of the Wild (*Wickedary* 66). Once this Call is discovered and Re-membered, Be-Wildering emerges as an exploratory gesture that challenges foreground logic and invites others to embark on radical feminist journeys by staying on the question. Be-Wildering does not pose simple questions nor provide easy answers. Rather, it enables us to tease out the blur-rings of foreground categories as well as to question the categories themselves. Its purpose is to demonstrate that different ways of thinking/speaking/writing are neither craziness, nor wrong tracks, nor the sum total of raging hormones.

Because Raging and Be-Wildering are rhetorical strategies that lead to Background logic(s), they presume Be-Thinking, or think-ing one's way farther into the Background with a warped logic (*Wickedary* 65). By urging women to Re-call Original Questions, Daly challenges the foreground's obsession with first causes; more-over, she exposes that questions should concern Final Causes, not first causes. Simply put, Final Causes are "the beginning, not the end of becoming"; as such, they provide the space of agency or Be-Speaking (76). Thus, Be-Speaking invokes the mental, spiritual, and bodily be-comings of radical feminism.

With the process of Be-Speaking, we arrive back at Spinning. This movement exposes the interwoven nature of Daly's Non-can-ons. Because her rhetoric of radical feminist de/mystification is pre-dominantly a generative rhetoric, Spinning occurs throughout all the Non-canons; that is, Spinning is both a cause and effect of Dis-ordering, Be-Spelling, Re-membering, and Be-Speaking. Daly's Non-canons are not linear motions, nor compartmentalized catego-ries, nor simple causes and effects. Instead, Daly's Non-canons par-ticipate in continual be-ing—blurring, overlapping, and/or chang-ing at particular moments of composing. For this reason, Daly's Background rhetoric of radical feminist de/mystification is a rever-sal of, not a counterpart to, the foreground rhetoric of patriarchal mystification. For Daly's Background rhetoric presumes a different mindset, a different process of seeing and hearing, a different set of assumptions about myth and language, and a different reading of their ideological implications for ourSelves and our wor(l)ds. Hence, her Background rhetoric posits her radical feminist concept of writing process.

DALY'S RADICAL FEMINIST HAG-OGRAPHY

Radical feminist writing processes must be articulated, Daly argues, because feminist processes "must become sensible (in actions, speech, works of all kinds) in order to become" (*Gyn/Ecology* 23). Rather than beginning from a general premise of that which *should* be, Daly begins with her own feminist writing process, which presumes a metaphoric language function that enables the writer to break through foreground meanings into the Background. Daly names her feminist writing process "creative Hag-ography" and attributes it with several powers. It enables women to generate new Background thoughts and actions about women. It un-covers old thoughts and actions about women that have been denigrated or hidden over time. And it rebuts patriarchal methods of research in order to challenge the nature and value of foreground knowledge (23). Through these powers, Daly's radical feminist writing process participates in changing the personal, the textual, and the cultural. But this process requires the strength to stop repeating the same old patterns: that is, to Spin new ideas and ethics by reversing the old ones, to Dis-order old logics, to Be-spell our audiences, to Re-member ourSelves, and to Be-speak all of the above, not necessarily in that order (23). In turn, Daly invites other women and feminists to adapt their own versions of writing process for their own ends.

A particular kind of writer emerges through Daly's feminist writing process: the "Cosmic Writer is any Lusty woman who speaks the Words of her own being" and who, when such action is taken, is spurred to write more, Name more, and speak more (*Pure Lust* 120, 173). Even though Daly acknowledges limitations in posing literacy as a solution to patriarchal oppression, she believes that most women have the power to articulate our own particular experiences, Naming them verbally if not in writing (174).[27] And even though she recognizes that the resulting consciousness will not erase nor even reform the social, she does be-lieve that such a feminist literacy enables a Self to Be-Speak its way out of foreground meanings into Background ones (121). In this way, foreground speaking gives way to Background Speaking. Moreover, Daly insists that such Speaking cannot be seen as a one time experience but rather must be accepted as a continual journey. As such, this Naming/Wording/Speaking discovers, creates, and translates the radical feminist journey of weaving the self into the Self, a process that manifests itself throughout the body and onto the page (173).

For Daly, such weaving culminates not only in a radical feminist Self but also in a living text with radical feminist voices of its own. Daly describes her concept of text as follows: "It is by no means my contention that the task of feminist writers, or of any writer, is literally to 'transcribe' books that exist elsewhere. How-ever, the intuition of a library and a community of scholars in another dimension seems to me inspired. For in true acts of cre-ation one does participate in Other dimensions. Moreover, it is true that as we go about our work 'here' we are making our way 'there.' For in honest acts of creation deep Be-ing is disclosed. Such acts are carriers/Metaphors of Metabeing" (*Pure Lust* 120). This definition is in no way Platonic. "Other dimensions" refers not to Plato's transcendent and immutable forms of being, but rather to Daly's transcendent-and-immanent, always mutable pro-cess of be-ing within Be-ing. Thus, Daly's text is not a static reflec-tion of a static truth, or a patriarchal essentialism. Instead, it is a constructed web of words that, in turn, constructs the Self as a text who reads and writes other texts. This constantly interchang-ing process constructs a new space in a new time, which is one of Daly's definitions of radical feminism.

Although Daly's ideal audience is receptive to this new space and new time, her Background rhetoric with its Background cate-gories—Non-canons, writing process, writer, and text—leave her open to a plethora of criticism from unreceptive audiences, whether feminist or otherwise, whether academic or otherwise.[28] For ex-ample, poststructuralist (feminist) critics might argue that, by pos-iting a priori meanings, Daly naively privileges the signified over the signifier. Materialist (feminist) critics might argue that, by pos-iting a transcendent Be-ing in which Websters may participate,

Daly naively assumes that patriarchal ideology and its power structures can be transcended by autonomous agents. Psychoanalytic (feminist) critics might argue that, by positing a material and spiritual Self who uses language for her own ends, Daly naively privileges consciousness. And African American critics might argue that, by positing gender as the dominant category of analysis, Daly naively dismisses the power differentials of race. Mary Daly, however, is anything but naive: she simply refuses to play within patriarchal logics and rhetorics. Instead, she Spins such criticisms to expose the gaps in them.

Daly recognizes such criticisms and models strategies for exposing their "logic" in a playful afterword to *Pure Lust*. In this "Non-Chapter Thirteen: Cat/egorical Appendix," Daly narrates an academic journal representative's attempt to interview her, but instead of speaking for herSelf, Daly gives voice to her familiar, a feline named Ms. Wild Eyes whom the representative reluctantly agrees to interview in Daly's stead. The purpose of the interview is to identify, locate, or fix Daly's theory for the journal's constituency. The irony, of course, is that in attempting to fix Daly, the representative fixes himself. Using him to parody male-identified poststructuralist theories of language, Daly demonstrates that sexism is more deeply embedded in academia than are theoretical convictions about language (*Pure Lust* 412–15). For example, by preferring to talk with Dr. Daly instead of with her familiar, the representative seems to privilege autonomous agency, not heteroglossic discourse. By wanting to come straight to the point, he seems to desire clarity and presence, not play and absence, in language. By obsessing about her feminist invention process, he seems to prefer empirically-based theories of knowledge, not constructionist ones. By accusing her of insulting people (read "men"), he seems to promote a conspiracy of silence within the academy, not political action. By accusing her of biological determinism, that is, by interpreting be-ing and Be-ing as static concepts, he seems to defend the categories of phallogocentric culture, not their overlaps or gaps. By refusing her redefinition of Sin, he seems to champion fixed meanings, not multiple ones. And by ignoring her degrees in theology and philosophy and by trying to confine her to literature, he seems to reinforce a dichotomy between truth and fiction, not their blurrings. When at the end of the interview he still professes perplexity about Doctor Daly's work, Wild Eyes further confuses him with her own Background cat/egorical imperative: "What did you expect? Fuzzy foreground abstractions? We can't discuss metapatriarchal metapatterning Metaphor with just anyone . . . " (415).

While admittedly manipulating this representative as well as her "audience" in this NonChapter, Daly de/mystifies the rhetoric of patriarchal mystification as espoused by the journal representative so that the charges leveled against her are exposed as unconscious desires of academia. By refusing to participate in this rhetoric and its desires,[29] that is, by declining to debate the representative on his foreground turf and in his foreground terms, she forces him to be responsible for his own understanding of her Background turf and terms. If he so chooses, they have the possibility of communicating; if he does not, at least Daly has created her own Background space and time where her Self and be-ing are not dependent upon his language or logic. Daly's refusal to participate in his foreground rhetoric of patriarchal mystification is not simply the luxury permitted an Anglo-American, tenured professor; neither is her construction of a Background rhetoric of radical feminist de/mystification a universal theory. Rather, it is, for Daly, a means of Self-survival that allows her, and perhaps others, to flourish within the presence of patriarchy.

Inconclusive Musings

Mary Daly's Anglo-American feminist theory of rhetoric conceptualizes both the existence and strategies of a foreground rhetoric of patriarchal mystification and a Background rhetoric of radical feminist de/mystification with its accompanying concept of Hagography. The key to escaping from foreground rhetorics into Background ones is the socially transformative power of language. In Daly's theory, language may be employed to Spin ourSelves and our wor(l)ds, Dis-ordering and Be-Spelling so that we may Remember Background meanings and Be-Speak them for ourSelves and for others.

But because no theory can explain and predict the actions and attitudes of every particular individual in every corner of the world, Mary Daly's feminist theory of rhetoric—being, among other things, white, middle-class, American, and lesbian—cannot but mystify as it demystifies. Because Daly's Anglo-American feminist theory of rhetoric cannot provide a totalizing theory, it should not be read as *the* answer to all women's problems; neither should it be dismissed out of hand. For Daly's feminist theory of rhetoric poses questions and possible answers about a multitude of our concerns: women and agency, the play of language, the construction of knowledge, the existence of de/mystified meanings, the conception of be-ing/Be-ing as a verb, the categories of foreground logic, the multeity of meanings, and the distinctions between truth and fiction, to name only a few. All these issues can subsequently inform feminist composition pedagogies.

Specifically, Daly's Anglo-American feminist theory of rhetoric invites continued conversations about the intersections of feminism with rhetoric and composition studies:

1. How does Daly's concept of Spinning, or Gyn/Ecological Creation, challenge Aristotle's concept of inventive topoi and multicultural concerns about invention?

2. How does Daly's concept of agency, which assumes a material and spiritual dimension, complicate the social constructionist theories of rhetoric and writing pedagogy that focus primarily on the material?

3. How does Daly's concept of conjuring through metaphorical language complicate Nietzsche's and subsequent deconstructionist theories of metonymic language function? And what are the implications for reading and writing pedagogy?

4. How does Daly's critique of patriarchal logic and its penchant for stable categories create a space in which Plato's and Descartes's charges against rhetoric may be refuted?

5. How does Daly's theologically grounded feminist theory of rhetoric, which focuses on both the word and The

Word, challenge Kenneth Burke's rhetorical theory of logology and Logology?[30]

Chances are, most readers will not easily identify with Mary
Daly's metaethics or her rhetorical strategies; on the other hand,
they will not soon forget her powerful prose either. But whether
or not we agree with her conclusions, whether or not we adopt
her strategies, once we read Mary Daly, we are never quite the
same (un)gendered readers or writers again. Throughout her texts,
her goal is simple but not easily achieved: "Virginia Woolf knew
of the need for a feminist tradition when she wrote of her hope
for the eventual arrival of Shakespeare's sister. I hope for the arrival
also of the sisters of Plato, of Aristotle, of Kant, of Nietzsche:
sisters who will not merely 'equal them,' but do something different, something immeasurably more" (*Church* 51). Mary Daly may
not exactly be the Judith Shakespeare that Virginia Woolf imagines
in *A Room of One's Own*, and she may have Spun beyond desiring
to be Nietzsche's sister. Perhaps she can instead be read as the
thrice-born Athena imagined in *Gyn/Ecology*, who is born into
a particular culture not only through her mother's womb, not
only through her father's brow, but also through her own words.
Therein, I argue, lies the importance of Mary Daly's Anglo-American feminist theory of rhetoric: it conceptualizes a revisionary language theory and praxis through which a woman may participate
in de/mystifying herSelf and herWor(l)ds.

4

Re-Visioning the Borderlands:
ADRIENNE RICH

> We need to support each other in rejecting the limitations
> of a tradition—a manner of reading, of speaking, of writ-
> ing, of criticizing—which was never really designed to in-
> clude us at all.
>   —Adrienne Rich, "Toward a More Feminist Criticism"

Adrienne Rich explores Bathsheba's dilemma in both her poetry and prose, articulating this dilemma as follows: "I think it has been a peculiar confusion to the girl or woman who tried to write because she is peculiarly susceptible to language. She goes to poetry or fiction looking for her way of being in the world . . . and over and over in the 'words' masculine persuasive force' she comes up against something that negates everything she is about" ("When We Dead Awaken" 39). By claiming that words have a "masculine pervasive force," Rich assumes that language use and language function are gendered; as such, language plays an integral role in constructing a woman's subjectivity. By claiming that a woman has "*her* way of being in the world," Rich also implies that factors other than language—for example, a woman's situated experiences with/in her body and culture—come into play; nevertheless, it is through language that we assign value to these other factors.

Not content just to name Bathsheba's dilemma, Rich also analyzes its implications and poses alternatives. Rich argues that in reaction to the negation a woman encounters in language, she is often caught between conflicting desires of retreating into the dream of a common language or asserting the politics of her location. The former may be read as the desire for commonality; the latter, as a recognition of differences in daily political realities.

107

To move a woman from desire to political action, Rich offers this advice: instead of futilely stagnating within Bathsheba's dilemma, a woman should refuse stasis and take action via re-vision. Such re-visionary action requires two steps: first, each subject must acknowledge her own evolving subjectivity; then, she must acknowledge her location as a subject within a specific community.[1] This doubled action enables a woman to critique the possibilities and limits of her personal agency within a patriarchal system; such action enables a woman to dis-cover and re-vise her life, her history, and her futures; only then does the dream of a common language emerge not as a retreat but as a celebration of the differences among us. But in order for this doubled action to succeed, a woman must also re-vise her language.

In keeping with Rich's re-visionary spirit, I reread her writings about women, language, and culture to construct an Anglo-American feminist theory of rhetoric. As in previous chapters, my purpose is to offer a feminist theory that challenges the genderblindness of traditional rhetorical history, theory, and pedagogy. To do so, I first locate Rich as a rhetorical theorist; that is, I examine how her concept of re-vision posits interrelated theories of women's agency and language function. Second, I reread two of Rich's metaphors, the dream of a common language and a politics of location, as possible language moves. In this rereading, Rich's dream of a common language does not posit a space where women (and men) can meet on common ground; rather, it conceptualizes women's silences within patriarchy as well as the reasons for these silences. Also in this reading, Rich's politics of location does not posit a static essentialism; rather, it conceptualizes a space of feminist agency as well as strategies for articulating women's silences. Third, I conclude by posing questions made possible by Rich's Anglo-American feminist theory of rhetoric.

Locating Adrienne Rich as a Rhetorical Theorist

Adrienne Rich does not locate her work within the tradition of Western rhetorical theory. Instead, she defines herself as "a writer, a teacher, an editor-publisher, a pamphleteer, a lecturer, a some-times-activist," and, most of all, a poet (*Blood* vii). Her poetry collections brilliantly explore and model the connections between language, textuality, particular women, and culture(s). And it is her interest in poetry that led her to prose: after her first essays about poetry, she began writing more about the cultural context of her poems and about her evolving feminism. Because Rich's texts encompass a wide range of subjects in a wide range of fo-rums, their feminist influence has been widespread.[2]

Most noted as a poet, Rich captures important personal and cultural moments in her poetry. For example, *A Change of World* (1951) hints at the static position expected of women in patriar-chy. *The Diamond Cutters and Other Poems* (1955) explores an artist's or a woman's need for distance if she is to hold onto her sense of the ideal. *Snapshots of a Daughter-in-Law* (1963) expresses disenchantment with a white, middle-class woman's position in marriage and articulates the "craziness" that can accompany this disenchantment. *Necessities of Life* (1966) examines a woman's re-entry into life, coming to terms with nature, darkness, and death. *Leaflets* (1969) deals with women, words, and broken relationships. *The Will to Change* (1971) reimagines women's roles and pursues the role of language in constructing a woman's subjectivity. *Diving into the Wreck* (1973) considers the consequences of re-vising a woman's life by reimagining women's personal and collective his-tories and myths. *The Dream of a Common Language* (1978) con-templates the communication gaps between women and between women and men. And *Your Native Land, Your Life* (1986), *Time's Power* (1989), and *An Atlas of the Difficult World* (1991) all ques-tion the functions of memory, location, and aging. In "When We Dead Awaken: Writing as Re-Vision," Rich provides the best analysis of how the textual strategies of her poetry may be read as a theory of women writing; in this essay, she explains how her evolving poetic style emerges in tandem with her evolving feminist consciousness.

Rich's collections of essays also investigate these issues. *Of Woman Born* (1976) conceptualizes women's place within patriar-chy by exploring motherhood as both a relationship and an insti-tution. *On Lies, Secrets, and Silence* (1979) articulates the patriar-chal constraints on women's speaking and writing by examining

Rich's own growth as a lesbian-feminist poet, her recovery of other women writers, her experiences with open admissions and pedagogy, her attempts to come to terms with racism, and, of course, her concept of women writing. *Blood, Bread, and Poetry* (1986) models the concept of a politics of location by considering other women's histories, Rich's Jewish heritage, her heterosexuality and lesbianism, as well as the limitations of Anglo-American feminisms for other ethnic groups. And *What Is Found There* (1993) explores the interweavings of poetry and politics in daily life, questioning what it might mean to *"write, and read, as if your life depended on it"* in the last decade of the twentieth century in the United States, where poetry and politics have been split at the root in the public's mind ("As If Your Life" 32).[3]

In both poetry and prose, Rich focuses on the possibilities of and for women, all the while using the word *women* very carefully. Because Rich's feminist theory is centered on the term *women*, I unpack this term to clarify its potential for women in Rich's feminism. I then demonstrate and critique how Rich's feminism posits a re-visionary agency that is driven, in part, by language. In this way, I locate Rich as a rhetorical theorist.

Rich's use of the word *women* quite obviously emphasizes gender concerns. She admits that for a period of time she could not separate her feelings toward men as individuals from her anger toward patriarchy as a system. Ultimately, however, her definition of radical feminism does not preclude men: "I believe that feminism must imply an imaginative identification with all women (and with the ghostly woman in all men) and that the feminist must, because she can, extend this act of the imagination as far as possible" ("Anti-Feminist" 71).[4] Thus, like her persona in "From an Old House in America," Rich does not hate men; after all, she has three sons. She simply chooses to focus on women, particularly on all the relationships possible between women (5.1–2). When employing this feminism to analyze her own experiences and observations, Rich draws two conclusions. First, for *all* people to survive, a radical feminist agenda is needed to transform patriarchy; thus, she posits an inclusive feminism with the potential to transform the social. Second, women must participate in this social transformation if it is to become a reality; thus, she posits the possibility of evolving subjectivity ("Anti-Feminist" 84). Rich's first conclusion refutes charges of separatism;[5] the second, charges of a static biological essentialism. Although she does recognize separatism as a philosophical and strategic choice for other feminists (*Blood* viii),[6] Rich does not employ the term *women* to construct a feminism based either on separatism or biological determinism.

Rich's use of the word *women* not only recognizes the complexities of gender but also the complexities of race. In her essay "The Distance between Language and Violence," she describes the method and effect of racism being inscribed on her white skin:

> I still try to claim I wasn't brought up to hate. But hate isn't the half of it. I grew up in the vast encircling presumption of whiteness—that primary quality of being which knows itself, its passions, only against an otherness that has to be dehumanized. I grew up in white silence that was utterly obsessional. Race was the theme whatever the topic.
>
> In the case of my kin the word sprayed on the overpass [Niggers] was unspeakable, part of a taboo vocabulary. *That* word was the language of "rednecks." My parents said "colored," "Negro," more often "They," even sometimes, in French, "*les autres.*"
>
> Such language could dissociate itself from lynching, from violence, from such a thing as hatred. (181)

To fight this socialization, Rich recognizes that she still needs to do antiracist work; therefore, she embraces a feminism that provides "a political and spiritual base from which [she can] move to examine rather than try to hide [her] own racism" ("Disobedience" 84). Rich also challenges her readers to make such recognitions and to do the ensuing antiracist work. One effective starting point for such recognition and for such work is asking ourselves the following question: "Who is *we*?" ("Notes" 231).

But gender and race are not the only categories that Rich foregrounds; moreover, she does not present such sociopolitical categories as neatly divided entities. Instead, they intersect, overlap, intertwine, circle back on one another, and blur. For example, when writing a letter to her friend Arturo about the blurrings of art and politics, she defines their friendship as the intersections of many social categories: "We're both different generations, cultures, genders; we're both gay, both disabled, both writers"; yet she also defines the friendship as the result of "laughter, good food, and anger" ("Dearest Arturo" 22). The intersections of social categories are especially important to Rich, though. For they not only define each person; they also delineate the logics of each person and, hence, the (im)possibilities of interpersonal communication. Rich is very aware of this phenomenon, for twice in her letter she asks Arturo: *"Does this make sense to you?"* (23, 27).

Rich's process of trying to make sense to Arturo presumes the possibility of agency arising from, among, and through all these social categories. In feminist circles, agency has become a hotly debated concept, not *whether* it exists but rather *where* and *how* it exists.[7] Like Joan Hartman and Ellen Messer-Davidow, Rich assumes that agency is possible for a woman if it is defined as capability, not intentionality. Defined in terms of capability, agency implies complex intersections of subjectivity and systems, not just a subject's willingness to act but also the systemic spaces within which such acting may or may not be possible (Giddens 9–10). This sense of agency assumes that subjects and systems "are mutually constitutive" (Hartman 13). As such, Rich's agency does not presume an autonomous will that can single-handedly overcome structural oppression; neither does it presume a human subject relegated only to discursive positions. What it does presume is the possibility for doing, and the possibility of doing always raises questions of power.

Rich's agency opens up a space for change in which a woman may assert her power by recognizing and refusing subjective and structural oppressions. But such power is limited. Constraints may appear in the personal, the cultural, and the textual. Yet because these constraints are neither universal nor ahistorical, a woman should not reject her agency. For claiming her agency provides her (and other women around her) with an alternative to feeling alone, sad, and discouraged, to wondering if indeed she has a place in the world. Instead, it encourages her to participate in constructing her own life and history ("Twenty-One" 15.13–15). As one Rich persona claims, clinging "to circumstances" could absolve her of all responsibility for her own life, but such clinging would also take away choice and result in her giving herself away ("Sources 22" 20–28).

Although Rich's concept of agency implies questions of power, Rich notes that power is a troublesome concept for women and feminists: "It has been long associated for us with the use of force, with rape, with the stockpiling of weapons, with the ruthless accrual of wealth and the hoarding of resources, with the power that acts only in its own interest, despising and exploiting the powerless—including women and children" ("What Does" 5). Nevertheless, women and feminists cannot hide from the existence and the effects of patriarchal power; consequently, we must redefine our power, not as a force bestowed upon us by others but as a force continuously achieved through resisting and refusing patriarchal power. Such a redefined concept of power has the potential to shift the power base from an elite group to all people; thus, it not only influences a woman but also the textual and the cultural, which she writes and which writes her.

The means through which a woman taps this agency and power is re-vision. Rich's re-vision means "seeing again," rereading history, literature, philosophy, politics, and so on, to uncover women's erasures and foreground women's roles. This seeing again emerges as a woman's means of personal and cultural survival. Because it is a search for identity, Rich's re-vision foregrounds the personal. Because it is a refusal to participate in patriarchy, it exposes how the personal intertwines the cultural. And because it encourages a woman to reread women's texts in order to recognize how their logics and styles are shaped by patriarchal structures, Rich's re-vision of the personal and the cultural also has a textual dimension ('When We Dead Awaken" 35, 39). Given the interconnectedness of these three areas, re-vision possesses the rhetorical potential to affect all of life: what we consider knowledge, who we consider expert and capable of making decisions, who has access to knowledge and its tools as well as who deserves housing, food, health care, and literacy ("What Does" 5).

The textual dimension of Rich's re-vision is of particular interest to rhetoric and composition scholars who study how language intersects with the personal and the cultural to construct our particular subjectivities and our community's values. To understand the textual dimension of Rich's re-vision, we must first understand how she defines language: "Language is as real, as tangible in our lives as streets, pipelines, telephone switchboards, microwaves, radioactivity, cloning laboratories, nuclear power stations. We might hypothetically possess ourselves of every technological resource on the North American continent, but as long as our language is inadequate, our vision remains formless, our thinking and feeling are still running in old cycles, our process may be 'revolutionary' but not transformative" ("Power and Danger" 247–48). By interweaving its materiality and its transformative potential, Rich's language function enables a woman both to participate in patriarchy and to transform it.

To take advantage of language's transformative potential, a woman must recognize Rich's three interwoven language functions: communicative, socializing, and imaginative. Recognizing the communicative function is crucial for women and feminists because the survival of any revolutionary group depends on the effectiveness of its communications network ("Toward More" 85). Recognizing the socializing function is important for women and feminists in that words can spur us into action or paralyze us, affecting how we live, how we think, where we speak, and who hears us. As such, this socializing function shapes feminists' particular subjectivities and worlds (90–91). Recognizing the imaginative function of language is even more critical for women and feminists because, if a woman's material existence is to be transformed, her consciousness must be able to break through the rhetoric of patriarchy. Based on these three language functions, a woman's speaking and writing emerge as forums wherein she may not only discover and state her ideas but may also help mold both her reader's evolving subjectivity and her own. Like Woolf, Rich believes these language functions presume an intellectual freedom ("When We Dead Awaken" 43), and like Daly, she believes these language functions presume a woman's being open to the active, transformative power of metaphor.

Because metaphors rely on the "encounter between the thing to be named and that foreign entity from which the name is borrowed," they inevitably presume differences (Ricoeur 24). But these differences are often mystified by a focus on similarities. Rich defines her concept of metaphors by employing metaphors. For example, one Rich persona claims that metaphors are a final attempt to communicate, to move people via images, patterns, and stories ("Valediction" 12). If the metaphoric focus is shifted from common ground to differences, then the possibilities of communication without common ground can be theorized; such a move may prove necessary, not just theoretically appealing, given the diversity of our world. Playing with Wittgenstein's metaphor comparing language to a city, another Rich persona likens a woman's use of metaphor to her driving her car to the edge of the city limits ("Images" 1–3). Pushing the city limits may signify a logical reaction to a particular situation, such as the desperation, anger, and desire for escape that erupts when other strategies have failed, or it may signify a thrill, a pleasure, a simple joie de vivre. Both metaphoric definitions put a woman in the driver's seat, so to speak, enabling her to communicate and to set her own limits for communication. Such power seemingly gives her unlimited license to control herself and her worlds. But speaking is not driving, and concentrating on the metaphoric associations with driving limits the ways a woman can think about speaking, about agency, and about her place in the cultural, especially if she cannot afford a car.

Thus, Rich exposes the limits to metaphor's transformative powers through metonymies: that is, a woman communicating and a woman driving are both part of larger structures. The woman communicating speaks from within a general symbolic position that women occupy; this position is always speaking through a particular woman even when she is speaking against it. The woman driving is constrained by the make of her car as well as by the laws that govern the road. Despite a woman's desire to control language so that she can, in turn, control herself and her world, she is never totally autonomous. Given Rich's metaphoric and metonymic language functions, a woman has both endless possibilities and limits ("North American Time" 6.1–4). To pursue the possibilities, she must negotiate the limits; she must recognize that language "cannot do everything," that textual critiques must be intersected with the personal and the cultural if a realistic understanding of agency is to emerge ("Cartographies" 7.1–2).

Rich models the textual dimension of her re-vision by rereading Woolf's *A Room of One's Own*: "I was astonished at the sense of effort, of pains taken, of dogged tentativeness, in the tone of that essay. . . . It is the tone of a woman almost in touch with her anger, who is determined not to appear angry, who is *willing* herself to be calm, detached, and even charming in a roomful of men where things have been said which are attacks on her very integrity" ("When We Dead Awaken" 37). Whether or not we agree with her interpretation, Rich's rereading and rewriting model how a woman may conceptualize strategies that have silenced women in the past and how she may discover other strategies that may be employed in empowering reading and writing moves. Thus, Rich's re-visionary rereading and rewriting not only exposes how language (re)constructs patriarchal values and power but also constructs a space from which a woman's power may emerge. Yet Rich also reminds us that re-vision has consequences.

One consequence is that monsters haunt a re-visioning woman's sleep ("Snapshots" 3.1). The nightmarish monsters may be patriarchal constructions, such as the bitch goddess, the medusa, or the "nature" of Woman. Such monsters can paralyze a woman, forcing her to try to fulfill patriarchy's expectations of her simply to avoid becoming, or being seen as, a monster ("Toward More" 90). Yet these monsters may also be reinterpreted in ways that motivate women into action, like Cixous's laughing Medusa. Although the latter move seems the more productive one, it too has consequences: as one Rich persona claims, it does not mean being anesthetized; it means mustering the strength and courage to make "powerful" and "womanly" choices ("Sources 24" 9).

A second consequence of re-vision is that the myths, lore, theories, rituals, and languages that are so dear to us are suddenly exposed as gendered and sexist, as well as racist, classist, homophobic, and so on; as such, they are exposed as being as harmful as they are helpful to a woman's evolving subjectivity. For example, the fairy tale "Beauty and the Beast" establishes for women the impossible goal of purity and the Anglo-European criterion of beauty. Most real-life women can only fall short when compared to Beauty; only a few come close. If feminists are serious about promoting an agenda that builds confidence in most women and makes success possible for them, then we must re-vise our myths, lore, theories, rituals, and languages. Because such re-visions force us to confront the dark side of all that we have cherished, they can be painful ("Twenty-One" 5.1–4). And it is to this pain that the persona in "Education of a Novelist" refers when she claims that she rebelled from "sentimentality" not because it was untrue but "because it was cruel" (2.1–3).

A third consequence of re-vision is that those with vested interests in maintaining patriarchal myths, lore, theories, and the like will fight feminist re-visions. What this claim means is that those with vested interests will fight a *woman* who is doing such re-visioning. Why? Because, as the persona says in "From an Old House in America," such a woman endangers the status quo (16.1–2). As a result, a re-visioning woman faces opposition at work, at home, and especially within herself; for the ideologies of the status quo are as deeply etched within her body as within those who fight her ("Turning" 1.13). If not careful, she is likely to find herself like the caged lioness—penned in, forever looking at open country through steel bars, paying "penance" for crossing into a strange land before hunters captured her ("The Lioness" 16–22, 32–35).

Yet not all consequences of re-vision involve such perils. In her own attempt to come to terms with the cruelty, pain, and ideological battles that surround re-vision, Rich writes poetry and prose in her own words to construct her own feminist theory and consciousness. But because theory has long been associated with patriarchal traditions, Rich feels compelled to critique her definitions of theory as well as to articulate her methodologies of theory building. First, she refutes patriarchy's dichotomy between theory and concrete experience; she argues that this dichotomy results in "abstractions severed from the doings of living people, [which are] fed back to people as slogans" ("Notes" 213). Because this dichotomy seemingly separates mind from body and action from ideology, it allows people to deny that systemic oppressions exist (e.g., "I treat women fairly, so I don't see what the problem is"); it allows people to disavow responsibility for their own actions (e.g., "I didn't mean anything by hiring a man instead of a woman"); and it allows people to excuse others' actions (e.g., "He was only joking when he cracked that women want to be raped."). Thus, the theory/experience dichotomy marginalizes anyone outside the "we" of the speaker: women are marginalized by men; the poor are marginalized by the rich; minorities are marginalized by Anglo-Americans; minority feminists are marginalized by Anglo-American feminists; lower-class feminists are marginalized by middle-class feminists; and lesbians are marginalized by heterosexuals. Hence, the dichotomy of theory and experience constructs a logic that promulgates sexism and other *isms*.

To transcend this dichotomy and its implications, Rich argues that the concepts of theory and experience must be reimagined ("Notes" 210). Instead of perceiving existing theories as foundational truths based on foundational premises, a woman must recognize that theories are constructed truths based on commonly accepted patriarchal premises, which may or may not be true.[8] To counter such theories, a woman must articulate her experiences living within the boundaries of patriarchy and then must generalize from these concrete experiences (213); she may also articulate the experiences that she hopes to achieve and then generalize about those concrete experiences.[9] Either way, Rich posits a definition of feminist theory and methodology that assumes an interconnectedness of theory and a woman's material existence. The purpose of such a theory and methodology is not simply to expose the injustices suffered by a woman in a patriarchal society but to offer alternatives to this victim status. For as one Rich persona claims, when a woman writes her body, she articulates not a repetitive pattern of victimization but a strategy for how survivors have saved, and are saving, themselves ("For a Friend" 10–11; "Compulsory Heterosexuality" 26). In this manner, a survivor demonstrates that the source of her pain can become the source of her power ("Power" 17) and that her power may leave her not only blue and bruised but laughing ("Demon Lover" 98).

Such a purpose is only achieved by questioning everything, including our theories. We must test our theories with each new experience to see if they fit our experiences. If so, we should affirm our theories for that moment; if not, we should reevaluate them. Moreover, we must test our theories against others' experiences so as to ascertain the possibilities and limits of our theories. Throughout these testing processes, we should heed Rich's warning about theory: "if it doesn't smell of the earth, it isn't good for the earth" ("Notes" 214). Because nothing should be exempted from such a testing process, not even our most cherished notions, I critique Rich's dream of a common language to explore the (im)possibilities of women's silences within this dream; I then critique her politics of location to explore the (im)possibilities of women's reading and writing, speaking and listening.

The Dream of a Common Language, or the (Im)Possibilities of Women's Silences

Patriarchy makes possible Rich's dream of a common language. That is, without the assumed gap between women and men that is the founding condition of patriarchy and without the socialized gap between women that is the result of patriarchy, the dream of a common language need not have emerged. Rich expands her definition of patriarchy[10] in the following passage: "[Patriarchy is] not simply the tracing of descent through the father . . . , but any kind of group organization in which males hold dominant power and determine what parts females shall and shall not play, and in which capabilities assigned to women are relegated generally to the mystical and aesthetic and excluded from the practical and political realms. (It is characteristic of patriarchal thinking that these realms are regarded as separate and mutually exclusive.)" ("Anti-Feminist" 101). She further defines its effects: "At the core of the patriarchy is the individual family unit with its division of roles, its values of private ownership, monogamous marriage, emotional possessiveness, the 'illegitimacy' of a child born outside legal marriage, the unpaid domestic services of the wife, obedience to authority, judgment and punishment for disobedience. Within this family children learn the characters, sexual and otherwise, that they are to assume, in their turn, as adults" (101). The patriarchal patterns of this familial socialization are repeated and reinforced in classrooms, in workplaces, and in culture at large. By discussing both particular subjects and the value of their socially constructed roles, Rich demonstrates that patriarchy functions particularly and generally to merge the material and the abstract, while simultaneously mystifying that connection.

Rich's description of patriarchy exposes that women and men occupy different symbolic positions. One Rich persona presumes that these different positions result in a gap between women and men ("In the Evening" 7); another persona describes this gap as an "irreducible, incomplete connection" that we are born into ("From an Old House" 5.11). As such, this gap precedes us and shapes not only our subjectivity but also our relationships. When this gap is juxtaposed with the metaphor of patriarchy, the different symbolic positions become clearer: men are located within the center; women, within the borders.[11] The center is the position of power, whose occupants feel comfortable within the dominant logics, rhetorics, and ideologies. The border is the position of marginalization, whose occupants know the dominant logics, rhetorics, and ideologies but do not necessarily feel comfortable within them. The center serves the normalizing function of maintaining the status quo, yet the border possesses power, too. Although mystified under the name "female," the power of the border is identified by Rich as follows: its occupants "embody and impersonate the qualities lacking in [the center's] institutions— concern for the quality of life, for means rather than for pure goal, a connection with the natural and the extrasensory order" ("Anti-Feminist" 80). In other words, the border fills the center's cracks and gaps. Ironically, this move infiltrates the center, preventing it from collapse while calling it into question. Thus, by examining the border and its blurrings with the center, we can expose how the powers of the center and the border are constantly shifting.

As discussed previously, Rich's most common images for women's position in patriarchy are borders and their blurred edges.[12] In "Contradictions" the persona advises readers who fetishize clean edges to search for truths in the blurred ones (29.10–12). In "Turning" the persona laments that her feet drag the borders of two lands—one where choices are made for her, another that is yet "unnameable" (1.9–10; 5.13). And in "For a Friend in Travail" the persona contemplates edges between waking and sleeping, life and death, West and non-West (12–24). Rich's border image conjures up associative images of guides, maps, geography, location, demography, travel, different cultures, and so on, all of which reinforce her image of radical feminism as a continuing journey (*On Lies* 17–18). From a rhetorical perspective, her border image suggests that rhetorical situations of radical feminists be conceptualized as borderlands between writer and readers, past and present, men and women, different interpretations, and different truths. Rich's auxiliary image, blurred edges, locates the making of meaning in the intersections of writers and readers, past and present, men and women, and so on. Although blurred edges tend to frighten people who desire certainty in life and in theory, Rich explores the power of these edges to generate new insights ("Contradictions" 29.11–12).

Movement between the center and the borders, however, is limited. In Rich's theory, a man may move into women's spaces. That is, he may choose to locate himself on the border, recognize the ghostly woman within, and earn a position of trust. Although this move entails his partially relinquishing the privilege of the center, it does allow him to partake of the power of the margins ("Three Conversations" 120). But when a woman tries to move into the center, she enters a Burkean parlor where she must do more than earn a position of trust; she must contend with structural problems that her male counterparts do not. Because of her awkward and sometimes dangerous position within the center, a woman often feels as if she is speaking in a language that is dead to her, without the power to name or to construct her own reality ("Invisibility" 199). Within this space, a woman is expected to act as if she is grateful, as if she is enjoying herself, even when in fact she feels relegated to an "autistic" state of "Non-being" that traps her in logics and arguments that do not reflect the rhythms and meanings of her previous locations ("From an Old House" 6.3–8; "Transcendental Etude" 66–76). Within the center, these rhythms and meanings become "not merely unspoken, but *unspeakable*" ("It Is the Lesbian" 199). In this way, a woman is prevented from taking full advantage of the center's power, and even if she can take advantage of this power by acting like a man, she risks losing "the eye of the outsider" ("What Does" 3). If she loses this eye, she risks losing herself in the universal and reinforcing patriarchal patterns. Thus, Rich encourages a woman to focus on the blurred edges and to consider how she may reread or reconfigure them to construct her own source of power.

Given that women and men occupy different spaces within the symbolic and given that an irreducible gap exists between these spaces, Rich argues that a woman may often feel as if she is speaking "the oppressor's language" ("Burning" 2.17–18). Based on a woman's desire to deny or bridge this symbolic gap, she sometimes retreats into what Rich names the "dream of a common language" ("Origins" 1.12).[13] At first glance, this dream appears to be the obvious solution to Bathsheba's dilemma because it appears to create common ground for women (and men) within the symbolic. At second glance, the dream of a common language seems to be a dangerous fantasy, for as long as the marginalized dwell within this dream, they downplay their differences and unwittingly perpetuate their own marginalizations. Many women have discovered that this dream is indeed a dream and that their waking reality frequently finds them relegated to an uneasy silence, a position perhaps most common in privileged Anglo-American women.[14] At third glance, the dream of a common language still appears as a dangerous fantasy; however, it may also be examined to identify powers that a woman may garner within its constraints. Though reinforced by different institutionalized rituals, a woman's silences need not be read as simple passivity. Indeed, her silences may take many forms and serve many functions, which Rich describes.

According to Rich, one form of silence is stasis. As the persona in "An Unsaid Word" knows, the most difficult thing for a woman to do is remain standing silently and unchanged until her man returns to her (4–7). This Stepford-wife syndrome is well documented: a man leaves the house, works at his job, grows, changes, matures; meanwhile the woman in his life is expected to remain constant—always young, always attractive, always stable, always comfortable, always secure. A woman may react to this imposed silence with guilt and resentment. She feels guilty as she grows older, gains knowledge, and desires to speak; simultaneously, she resents the men and other women who expect such a silent stasis from her. In reaction, she may sulk or speak too loudly or act too brashly, thus reinforcing age-old stereotypes about emotional women. But instead of tracing the cause of such emotional outbursts to the symbolic gap between men and women and then trying to negotiate it, patriarchy promotes a commonsense logic that traces these outbursts to biology, that is, to essential female hormones that cannot be changed. In this manner, mystifications about a woman's "nature" dominate our commonsense assumptions and continually marginalize women. Only through questioning such mystifications may these commonsense assumptions be re-vised.

While static silences may signify a woman's lack of self-reflectivity or self-knowledge, a second kind of silence may signify the presence of plans with histories and forms of their own ("Cartographies" 3.12–13). Rich identifies six different reasons why a woman might choose silence. A woman may remain silent because she refuses to hurt herself or others (4.4–5). This silence is frequently based on familial "loyalty," whether valid or misplaced, that emerges within families, romantic relationships, friendships, and workplaces ("Woman Dead" 8.9–10).[15] A woman may also remain silent because she recognizes that her "answers" will not work for others ("Cartographies" 6.8–9). This silence may result from a sad resignation; it may also demonstrate a respect for difference. Sometimes a woman remains silent because she understands that answering back is not really an answer for her situation. This silence may indicate that a woman needs to ask her own questions as well as set her own agendas. It may also indicate that she is repressing her emotions and playing within the logics of the dominant discourses; for instance, a battered persona tells herself that if she just remains within these logics, then "they" (including her brother-in-law who happens to be a psychiatrist) cannot "get" her ("Contradictions" 4.11–14). Another reason a woman remains silent may be that she realizes that language alone cannot solve her problems ("Cartographies" 7.12). This silence acknowledges that people and events are influenced not just by personal agency but also by bodily and intuitive experiences as well as cultural structures. Also, a woman may remain silent because she needs the space and time to listen to herself and her surroundings, letting her truths incubate before they emerge ("Contradictions" 8.20). This silence recognizes the importance of listening in constructing truth as well as the importance of context in speaking and writing ("Transcendental Etude" 98–99). Finally, a woman may remain silent, like Emily Dickinson, not because she is ill but because she wants to entertain and explain herself in her own time and in her own terms ("I Am in Danger" 22–24).

A third category of silence is a woman's lying to herself or others in order to silence her own truths.[16] Rich defines *truth* as follows: "There is no 'the truth,' 'a truth'—truth is not one thing, or even a system. It is an increasing complexity" ("Women and Honor" 187). The problem with lying is that these words cannot be taken back; they enter a woman's body and repeat themselves. After a while, she cannot remember which lies she told consciously and which she believed. Resembling Quintilian's good man speaking well who lies to promote the proper ends, Rich's good woman speaking well lies because she is afraid of her own truths and desires to ensure her status quo, that is, her position of propriety within patriarchal values and institutions. A woman lying pretends to thrive within the dream of a common language but is actually lonely within her web of lies. Nevertheless, she continues to weave them. Yet according to Rich, the irony of a woman's lying is that it inadvertently splits the dream of a common language. That is, lying constitutes a potent force in a woman's unconscious that creates cracks and gaps in a woman's consciousness, and whether or not a woman consciously desires to know them, her truths will inadvertently emerge to fill these cracks and gaps ("Women and Honor" 187, 191, 198; "Cartographies" 1.2–6, 1.9–12, 2.7–10).

Rich argues that all silences are driven by a few conscious or unconscious strategies. A cultivated blindness—such as gender-blindness, raceblindness, classblindness—enables a woman to deny that problems exist inside and outside her own little world. Reductiveness enables a woman to depict her oppressions as less complex than they actually are so that she may explain them away with simple analyses. Caricature enables her to exaggerate her oppressions so that she may laugh them off. Distortion enables her to focus selectively on her oppressions so that she may hide or repress the truths she cannot yet confront. Trivialization enables her to ignore important implications of her oppressions so that she may feel in control of them and, thus, dismiss them (*On Lies* 14). Finally, abstraction enables a woman to retreat from concrete experiences, driving a wedge between theory and praxis so as to release a thinker from the responsibility of taking action ("Cartographies" 4.4). Such moves are not hard to understand, given that patriarchal socialization imposes these very mindsets upon us and given that we cannot control the consequences of challenging such socializations. But the implications of such moves do raise questions of ethics. Individually, a woman's potential as an evolving subject may be diminished or erased. Collectively, women's histories and traditions may be diminished or erased.[17] As a result, conceptualizing strategies for enduring or ending silences becomes a project that every woman must repeat generation after generation.

From a rhetorical perspective, Rich's strategies of silence have implications for the canon of memory. Her concept of memory moves beyond the simplistic, though helpful, mnemonic strategies advocated by traditional rhetorical theories. Her memory lives within a person's body, not as static images but as feelings, ideas, and actions. It functions there, consciously and unconsciously, as a "smoky mirror" that reflects the world differently from different angles and at different times ("Eastern War" 10.25). Moreover, it not only reflects the world; it also reflects the face of the observer ("Through Corralitos" 3.10–12). Such a concept of memory and history calls into question the more traditional conceptions, their necessary conditions, and their politics. It also highlights the influence on memory of a feminist consciousness located within a specific cultural space and time.

Rich worries that the late twentieth century has produced a shift in particular and collective memories. Young people seem not to read, not to "know how to talk, to tell stories, to sing, to listen and remember, to argue, to pierce an opponent's argument, to use metaphor and imagery and inspired exaggeration in speech . . . " (*On Lies* 12–13). This lack of knowledge invokes and reinforces passivity, a willingness to accept the status quo despite its problems. In such a situation, the dream of a common language thrives. But the persona in "Origins and History of Consciousness" demonstrates the possibility of awakening from this dream, comparing it to an escape from "drowning" (2.7–14). For this reason, radical feminism is so important to Rich: it makes possible a politics and ethics that wakens people by "turning Otherness into a keen lens of empathy" ("If Not with Others" 203). Rich's proposal to understand Otherness as a politics of location embodies one way for women not only to awaken from the dream of a common language and but also to articulate its accompanying silences. Such a politics of location offers one solution for Bathsheba's dilemma. To weigh the possibilities of this solution, I explore Rich's politics of location as a means of conceptualizing spaces for an agency that drives her Anglo-American feminist theory of rhetoric.

A Politics of Location, or the (Im)Possibilities of Women Reading and Writing, Speaking and Listening

Rich's concept of a politics of location names both physical and theoretical spaces. It takes as its first premise a woman's body, not patriarchal theory or commonsense assumptions. It assumes women's bodies to be the grounds for feminist theory, not the objects to which theories should be applied. Because a politics of location interweaves the theoretical and the concrete, it provides a site of agency from which a woman may read and write, speak and listen; and from this site complex truths emerge, not authoritative ones ("Toward More" 94). Unlike many patriarchal theories that masquerade as universal, univocal, and disinterested, Rich's politics of location admits its situatedness, its multivocal contradictions, and its interests. Such a location is not a simple identity politics that assumes fixed categories and easy classifications that emerge from the entity itself; such is the description of an Aristotelian essentialism. Rather, Rich's standpoint theory assumes that categories overlap, that boundaries blur, and that the categories as well as their definitions change from year to year, day to day, essay to essay, poem to poem. Therefore, its epistemologies and ideologies challenge patriarchy at intertwined local and global levels.[18]

Rich's concept of a politics of location has a local dimension from which a woman may re-vision her own identity. Rich models her concept and emphasizes its particularity by exploring her own location within patriarchy: "I need to understand how a place on the map is also a place in history within which as a woman, a Jew, a lesbian, a feminist I am created and trying to create" ("Notes" 212). But the identity that emerges from her exploration is complex and contradictory: "The middle-class white girl taught to trade obedience for privilege. The Jewish lesbian raised to be a heterosexual gentile. The woman who first heard oppression named and analyzed in the Black Civil Rights movement. The woman with three sons, the feminist who hates male violence. The woman limping with a cane, the woman who has stopped bleeding are also accountable. The poet knows that beautiful language can lie, that the oppressor's language sometimes sounds beautiful. The woman trying, as part of her resistance, to clean up her act" ("Split at the Root" 123). Every woman has an equally complex identity. The question for each woman becomes, can she be honest enough with herself to make such identifications? The next question becomes, how can she respect and negotiate the contradictions within her, between herself and others, and among different cultures?

Rich's politics of location also has a global dimension from which a woman may re-vision her world. But one woman's politics of location does not speak to all women, let alone all people. Neither does one feminism's politics of location. For example, Rich claims that Anglo-American radical feminisms have suffered too long from a generic white, middle-class, heterosexual identity and that this identity has mostly been concerned with how white, middle-class, heterosexual women find themselves located both within and against white patriarchy (*Blood* x). Rich argues that such an identity cannot explain all the experiences of African Americans or Native Americans, in spite of Anglo-Americans' good intentions; indeed, Rich argues that such an identity is reductive because it downplays the celebration of difference.[19] To counter this reductiveness and prevent stagnation within Anglo-American radical feminisms, Rich urges these feminisms to pursue a concept of difference that resists fragmentation and reveals how women are shaped by their local and global politics of location ("Resisting" 151). For example, Rich believes that Anglo-American radical feminism must imagine a world where all women are recognized and respected as particular members of particular groups. To implement such change, Rich proposes that the concepts that are central to other ethnic feminisms be incorporated into Anglo-American radical feminisms. For example, bell hooks calls for radical, nonessentialist revisions of identity politics that will enable African Americans "to explore the marginal locations as spaces where we can best become whatever we want to be while remaining committed to liberatory black liberation struggle" ("Radical

Black Subjectivity" 20). Likewise, Rich would encourage Anglo-American feminists to reconsider identity politics. Rich's purpose is not to whitewash such reconsiderations but to continually question the positions of Anglo-American feminisms and to demonstrate a solidarity of difference among many feminisms. In addition to identity politics, Rich also encourages white feminists to rethink concepts of simultaneous oppressions, ideology grounded in concrete experience, and the refusal to be bribed into silence or inaction in return for a room of one's own ("North American Tunnel Vision" 165).

As described, Rich's concept of a politics of location has three important implications. First, it assumes that subjects possess complex identities that are positioned among fluid categories and blurred boundaries. As a result, totalizing theories are not possible; neither are stable ones. Thus, Anglo-American radical feminisms must admit their limits (*Blood* xii). Second, if the categories of identity are put into play, then the politics of feminisms must be put into play. For such a move to occur, it must overcome some feminists' deeply entrenched desire for closure, which arises from fears that such open-endedness may result in the death of their politics.[20] Yet such a move need not force us to reject politics nor to embrace a "happy pluralism" (Scott, "Deconstructing Equality" 145). Instead, it continually challenges us to critique our categories, question our truths based on these categories, and revise our actions based on these assumed truths. Third, because Rich's politics of location allows the signifier to stay in play while simultaneously allowing spaces for political action, it opens a space of agency where a woman can act from her situatedness without being essentialized by it. In this space, the body and the body's location in the world shape the questions and answers of contemporary feminisms, as well as the subsequent value placed on the personal, the cultural, and the textual.

Rich's politics of location and its agency enable women to move beyond dreaming the dream of a common language and embracing its accompanying silences. Although Rich recognizes possibilities within silence, she also recognizes that a woman has other options: she may try to bridge the gap between women (and men) with truth telling, or she may try to background the gap by speaking and writing for herself and, perhaps, for other women. Rich celebrates the second option as the most productive for developing a strong voice and womanly sense. Yet even though a woman may use her politics of location as a site from which to articulate her silences, Rich reminds us that "[b]reaking our silences, telling our tales, is not enough" ("Resisting" 145). We must also consciously consider our ethics, namely, what to do with our stories and when to take action. For Rich, one such action is writing.

Rich's writing to promote a feminist agenda presumes feminist writing processes. Although Rich does not posit nor define the term *feminist writing process*, she does posit and define the term *feminist history*. By switching terms in her definition, I offer the following as Rich's working definition of feminist writing processes:

> As differentiated from women's [writing process], feminist [writing process] does not perpetuate the mainstream by simply invoking women to make the mainstream appear more inclusive. It is not simply contributory; it demands that we turn the questions upside down, that we ask women's questions where they have not been asked before. Feminist [writing process] is not [writing] about women only; it looks afresh at what men have done and how they have behaved, not only toward women but toward each other and the natural world. But the central perspective and preoccupation *is female*, and this implies a vast shift in values and priorities. ("Resisting" 146–47)

This definition of feminist writing processes assumes that their topics are limitless, their focus is woman centered, and their goal is transforming patriarchy. As such, feminist writing processes imply interwoven feminist canons of invention, arrangement, and style.

Based on re-vision, Rich's feminist invention strategies assume that a speaker/writer attempts to make sense of patriarchy by analyzing sex and gender issues. To do so, a speaker/writer must be prepared to do the following: "To question everything. To remember what it has been forbidden even to mention. To come together telling our stories, to look afresh at, and then to describe for ourselves. . . . To do this kind of work takes a capacity for constant active presence, a naturalist's attention to minute phenomena, for reading between the lines, watching closely for symbolic arrangements, decoding difficult and complex messages left for us by women of the past. It is work, in short, that is opposed by, and stands in opposition to, the entire twentieth-century white male capitalist culture" (*On Lies* 14). Questioning, remembering, telling stories, describing, reading between lines, analyzing the symbolic, and deconstructing women's texts—all are invention strategies that women may adapt to their own ends for particular situations. Other strategies include educated guesses, or intuitive rememberings based on the facts at hand ("Resisting" 148), and disobedience, or breaking the rules of logic, invention, style, and so on ("Disobedience" 78).

Questioning everything undergirds Rich's feminism. Once a woman grants that everything is to be questioned, her project becomes teasing out the starting points for questioning, the places where breaks in the dominant ideology can emerge or are emerging. Rich describes these places as follows: "There is a peculiar tension between an old idea system from which the energy is gone but which has the heaped-up force of custom, tradition, money, and institutions behind it, and an emerging cluster of ideas alive with energy but as yet swirling, decentralized, anarchic, constantly under attack, yet expressing itself powerfully through action" (*Of Woman Born* ix). There is no set formula for detecting these tensions, nor for instructing a woman how to act once she finds one. Thus, such questioning assumes the burden that each woman will need to ask her own questions and find her own answers, hopefully inspired by women before and around her. There is, however, one question that every woman has in common: how to discover the "language" with which to speak to the "spirits" that haunt a "place" ("Toward the Solstice" 40–42).

Remembering, telling stories, and describing serve similar functions. These invention strategies foreground the concrete experiences of a woman living within patriarchy and imagining other kinds of living. In the process, they enable each woman to remember, or put together, the fragmented pieces of her life, to offer readings of her experiences that present her truths; they also conceptualize the patriarchal structures in which a woman's experiences occur. As a result, *the unspeakable* is challenged, *the speakable* is expanded, a woman's experiences may amass new values, a woman may come to voice, and a woman may take action based on this voice. But remembering, telling, and describing should not be romanticized; these actions may be painful and, taken to an extreme, politically inexpedient. For certain stories are extremely difficult to remember or tell or describe; furthermore, any attempt to revel in a victim status by continually recounting the same stories can prevent a woman from acting. Thus, a woman should question not only her stories and her resulting actions but also her method of remembering, storytelling, and describing.

Reading between the lines means acknowledging women's position within the symbolic and analyzing the edges that blur. Rich encourages a woman to read the absences, the gaps, the blank spaces in literature, history, science, politics, and the like, as well as in her own life; for meanings exist there as well. Such action may take the form of analyzing symbolic actions—that is, constructing texts through speech and writing—in order to reveal strategies that work for a woman as well as those that do not. It may also take the form of deconstructing women's texts, both past and present, reading them straight on and at a slant to determine what information they provide us. When no lines exist to read between, the best a woman can do is make educated guesses, intuitive rememberings based on the facts at hand ("Resisting" 148). Ironically, patriarchy views such strategies as hypotheses in science but as bad scholarship in feminist studies.

Disobedience undergirds all of Rich's invention strategies. Rich believes that, within patriarchal logic, obedience means not questioning the laws of the fathers and that, conversely, disobedience means questioning. Rich encourages every woman to be disobedient—to question government laws, her father, her mother, her husband, her socialized conscience ("Disobedience" 78).[21] From a patriarchal perspective, such disobedience is potentially dangerous for both the woman and the status quo, yet from Rich's radical feminist perspective, this disobedience can also be potentially liberating for a woman. For Rich redefines disobedience as questioning the patriarchy in order to break its logics, rhetorics, and ideologies. When the neat compartmentalizations of patriarchy collapse, new feminist logics, rhetorics, and ideologies emerge. Within this new framework, to question is to believe, and disobedience becomes a means to self-survival.

These invention strategies based on Rich's politics of location emerge at both general and particular levels.[22] Because women occupy a symbolic space that is different than men's, they must interpret Rich's invention strategies in ways that enable them, as outsiders, to communicate within dominant ideologies. As Rich asserts in "When We Dead Awaken," this dilemma is unique to women: "No male writer has written primarily or even largely for women, or with the sense of women's criticism as a consideration when he chooses his materials, his themes, his language. But . . . every woman writer has written for men even when, like Virginia Woolf, she was supposed to be addressing women" (37–38). But to avoid the trap of thinking her theory and her strategies may be employed by all women in the same way, Rich constantly emphasizes that *woman* is not monolithic. It presumes differences based on token positions, class issues, racial tensions, and so on, and these differences affect how feminist invention strategies are employed by groups of women as well as by a particular woman.

Because each woman's politics of location is unique, each woman will particularize Rich's invention strategies to address her own attitudes and agendas. Thus, feminist invention strategies are closely linked with each woman writer's evolving subjectivity. Rich demonstrates this fact by analyzing her own writing in "When We Dead Awaken," explaining that her re-visionary invention strategies interweave with her emerging feminist consciousness. Like the persona in "Transcendental Etude," Rich cannot begin with uncomplicated invention strategies and move developmentally to more complicated ones, nor can she begin with uncomplicated experiences as subjects and move developmentally to more complex ones; instead, Rich is thrust into the uncomplicated and the complicated all at once, with only a few stolen moments for listening and reflecting (43–61). In the midst of this chaos, Rich's feminist invention strategies become doubly important as means to speak both with herself and with other women.

At all levels, Rich's invention strategies shape but do not determine what a woman sees and how she values what she sees. Thus, they affect what she deems to be important questions as well as what dreams she will dream and what dreams will dream her ("Atlas" 2.22–24; "Nights and Days" 7–8). Rich's feminist invention strategies, therefore, are neither simple nor without consequences. A woman employs Rich's strategies to find languages and images for a consciousness that has not yet been conceptualized, or if it has been conceptualized, there is no record of it, no tradition; as a result, each woman must create new languages and images on her own ("When We Dead Awaken" 30). But all that work is no guarantee of success. Rich warns that everything a writer composes may be used against her and her loved ones, for words released into the public domain take on meanings far broader than a writer ever intends ("North American Time" 2.1–5, 14–16). That is why people are sometimes ostracized, institutionalized, banished, or even killed for reading, writing, speaking, or even listening ("Contradictions" 27.14–18). But as the persona in "Contradictions" claims, the worst thing that can happen to a woman is not to know who she is or where she has been. Despite their risks, speaking, reading, and writing help her attain such knowledge.

Rich's feminist invention strategies have implications for her concept of text. Because her strategies expose patriarchal oppressions, they construct texts that differ from patriarchal ones. But the differences emerge contextually, rather than as an essential formalism. For example, the persona in "Transcendental Etude" tells the story of a woman artist who walks away from an argument and goes into her kitchen to create her own composition from the materials around her—yarn, velvet, shells, milkweed, petunia, cat whiskers, and bird feathers (148–64). By implication, Rich's feminist text emerges in the same way. It emerges from the stories, observations, and analyses of her life and of other women's lives. Thus, Rich weaves together her writing process and product, which have "nothing to do with eternity, / the striving for greatness, brilliance— / only with the musing of a mind / one with her body . . . / with no mere will to mastery" ("Transcendental Etude" 165–68, 171). In five brief lines, Rich's persona opens up textual spaces for musing as well as theorizing; for body as well as mind; for discovery, not mastery; for the particular moment, not the ahistorical universal; and for all of their blurrings. These textual spaces create a site where a woman may change discourse through her textual strategies.

To Rich, changing discourse entails conceptualizing textual strategies that have silenced a woman in the past and discovering other textual strategies that may be employed in the present and future to empower a woman. As one Rich persona confides, she constantly looks for "new forms" and for "old forms in new places"; her search is complicated because she both "know[s] and do[es] not know what [she is] searching for" ("Paula Becker" 20–24). Yet a common form, or pattern, emerges in Rich's essays: first, Rich locates herself within the present, citing her own politics of location as well as the chosen topic and the occasion for writing; next, she remembers stories from her own life and the lives of others, stories that are somehow associated with the conjunction of her politics, topic, and occasion; then, she rereads these stories to explain the present, weaving them together to build a powerful, womanly argument. The purpose of this pattern is not to arrive at a neat conclusion or to assert Rich's conclusions as the one and only truth; rather, the purpose is to discover new starting points, new questions that will trigger other questions and other essays in herself and in her readers.

Although Rich does not stipulate specific textual strategies that will apply to every particular woman in every situation, she does model how contextual considerations of form, content, and authorial consciousness (not authorial control) interweave within her texts. Her poetic choices—for example, breaks between stanzas, spaces in the middle of lines, line endings, first person personae, womanly voices, woman-centered images and metaphors, punctuation and italics, and words—demonstrate this interweaving, emerging as reflections and constructive elements of her feminist consciousness. For example, the persona in "Natural Resources" claims that she will never use the terms *humanism* or *androgyny* again because they do not speak to her current experiences (13.1–8). And the persona in "Diving into the Wreck" experiments with language, using words as "maps," in the hope of creating new words and new myths that celebrate the power of women buried in the wreck (54, 92–94). Rich's prose choices also capture and construct her feminist consciousness. For example, in "Power and Danger" Rich claims that common words must be continually critiqued:

[They] are having to be sifted through, rejected, laid
aside for a long time, or turned to the light for new colors and flashed of meaning: *power, love, control, violence, po-*

litical, personal, private, friendship, community, sexual, work, pain, pleasure, self, integrity . . . When we become acutely, disturbingly aware of the language we are using and that is using us, we begin to grasp a material resource that women have never before collectively attempted to repossess (though we were its inventors, and though individual writers like Dickinson, Woolf, Stein, H. D., have approached language as a transforming power). (247)

And in her *Blood, Bread, and Poetry* essays, Rich employs such critique via her reflective intelligence, her poetic sensibility, her inductive reasoning, and her personal truths, which are addressed to her readers.

With all of her textual strategies, Rich encourages other women writers to assert power within the textual, and according to Rich, asserting such power entails invoking both unconscious and conscious processes. Describing her own writing process, Rich acknowledges that she has become more and more "willing to let the unconscious offer its materials, to listen to more than the one voice of a single idea" ("Poetry and Experience" 89). Yet in both her poetry and prose, Rich employs her unique style as purposely and as honestly as possible, even when (perhaps especially when) dealing with intimate and painful topics. Rich believes that if discourse can change, so too can people's minds and so too can their "intolerable" truths and their "intolerable" realities within patriarchy (*Blood* xi).[23]

Because Rich defines truths as ever-increasing complexities, she does not conceptualize the assertion of agency through langauge in terms of simple cause and effect. Consciously changing discourse will not magically change a person or a culture. But a woman's reading or writing or speaking or listening differently is a start, a beginning, an action that is within each woman's power. Such actions, however, cannot be prescribed; they must reflect a woman's particular experiences within her culture, whether that means renaming her experiences, telling new and forbidden stories, articulating a different kind of logic, or speaking an unspeakable rhetoric. If such action is not taken, inaction "keeps our actions reactive, repetitive" and perpetuates "abstract thinking, narrow tribal loyalties, every kind of self-righteousness, the arrogance of believing ourselves at the center" ("Notes" 223). In other words, inaction guarantees the status quo.

Because such actions must occur within the symbolic, a woman cannot escape the languages, logics, and rhetorics of patriarchy. Consequently, a woman's style is influenced by patriarchy. As an early poet, Rich's style was shaped by male mentors.[24] For a while she learned her lessons well, as indicated by W. H. Auden's introduction to *A Change of World* in which he describes her poems as nothing less than ladylike: "[t]he poems a reader will encounter in this book are neatly and modestly dressed, speak quietly but do not mumble, respect their elders but are not cowed by them, and do not tell fibs" (126–27). As a feminist poet, however, Rich's style is shaped by her desire to tell herself and other women the truths about her life and, perhaps, about their lives—that is, the truth of blood, bread, and poetry. But negotiating the tensions between these two roles is never easy. Rich describes herself as trapped for forty years "in a continuous tension between the world the Fathers had taught me to see, and had rewarded me for seeing, and the flashes of insight that came through the eye of the outsider" ("What Does" 3). Unfortunately for Rich, this "eye of the outsider" too often felt like the eye of madness.

To re-vision this madness within a feminist logic, Rich creates powerful art and powerful politics. According to Rich, art is commonsensically perceived by the white male capitalist culture of North America as transcending life or as representing the best of its possibilities; ironically, or perhaps not so ironically, art simultaneously functions as a commodity that can be purchased by the highest bidder. Likewise, artists are commonly romanticized as necessarily distanced from politics and ennobled only if starving. From her feminist location, however, Rich re-vises this patriarchal concept of art, positing instead a feminist definition of art "not . . . as a commodity, but as part of a long conversation with the elders and the future" ("Blood" 187). Rich's art is available to everyone in different forms, at different levels, and in different degrees. As she states in the preface to her 1993 collection of essays, "I have never believed that poetry is an escape from history, and I do not think it is more, or less, necessary than food, shelter, health, education, decent working conditions. It is as necessary"

(*What Is Found* xiv). Patriarchy mystifies this power of art by labeling the aesthetic feminine and by separating it from the common sphere of daily life; such impulses account for traditional separations of logic, rhetoric, and poetics. Like the Nicaraguan poet/revolutionaries in "Notes," Rich works to re-vise this patriarchal definition of art in hopes of exposing the aesthetic as socially constructed and potentially empowering for a woman.

According to Rich, politics are commonly perceived within patriarchy as mean, narrow, manipulative machinations that people perform to enhance their own powers; as such, it is loathed by the populace and antithetical to art. Rich disagrees with this postulation. Instead, she articulates a feminist concept of politics more in line with the old Greek notion of *polis* except, of course, that Rich foregrounds those who occupy the marginalized spaces of this polis—the poor, slaves, women, and children. Given this feminist focus, Rich defines politics as beliefs in action that are women centered, honest, honorable, positional, uncertain at best, and in need of constant critique ("Women and Honor" 193). For Rich, creating art with words is one means of articulating her feminist politics; in such a manner, Rich intersects art and politics.

In patriarchy, however, art and politics too often emerge as binary opposites, the result being that people separate themselves from the imaginative function of art and dismiss politics as something in which they would rather not participate. But Rich writes against such logic, arguing that "[e]very group that lives under the naming and imagemaking power of a dominant culture is at risk from this mental fragmentation and needs an art which can resist it" ("Blood" 175). Thus, Rich writes in part to expose the interweavings of art and politics, the political dimension of art.[25] According to Rich, such a resistant art is "political in terms of who was allowed to make it, what brought it into being, why and how it entered the canon, and why we are still discussing it" ("Toward More" 95). Does Rich's position imply that art and politics are identical? No, but they do inform one another. Indeed, they cannot escape one another. Their commonality lies in that "both are creative processes requiring many false starts and strange gorounds, many hard choices" (*Blood* xi).

By assuming these intersections of art and politics, Rich is able to ask the following questions about the function of a writer, that is, a writer who cannot help but participate in politics: "What happens to the heart of the artist, here in North America? What toll is taken of art when it is separated from the social fabric? How is art curbed, how are we made to feel useless and helpless, in a system which so depends on our alienation?" ("Blood" 185). Rich asks these questions not so much to discover conclusive answers as to foreground the effects of a politics of location on art. Rich examines her own experiences as a writer in an attempt to make her art/politics philosophy sensible to herself and to her readers:

> To write directly and overtly as a woman, out of a
> woman's body and experience, to take women's existence
> seriously as theme and source for art, was something I
> had been hungering to do, needing to do, all my writing
> life. It placed me nakedly face to face with both terror
> and anger; it did indeed *imply the breakdown of the world
> as I had always known it, the end of safety*, to paraphrase
> [James] Baldwin again. But it released tremendous energy
> in me, as in many other women, to have that way of writ-
> ing affirmed and validated in a growing political commu-
> nity. I felt for the first time the closing of the gap be-
> tween poet and woman. (182)

But despite her personal success of closing the gap between poet and woman, this gap remains open in the cultural: "I have felt released to a large degree from the old separation of art from politics. But the presence of that separation 'out there' in North American life is one of many impoverishing forces of capitalist patriarchy." (184). Negotiating this tension takes a toll on the artist. While nonartists are being denied access to the imagination, artists are being denied access to the blood and bread of daily life. Thus, this tension has an impact on the art produced and on the art's audiences.

Rich does not conceptualize a theory of audience, per se. She does, however, assume certain audiences, such as herself, other women, and other feminists. She writes to figure things out for herself and to communicate her ideas. When contemplating her communicative function, Rich is haunted by two readers: those who will not mistake her meanings and those who believe she knows all the answers for everything ("Contradictions" 20.15–16, 29.1). The former erase her sense of alienation, while the latter place her upon a pedestal. Rich desires the former but not the latter. Yet she speaks directly to the latter, imploring them to think for themselves and to share, not take, her meanings. While Rich recognizes that she cannot control readers' receptions of her poetry or prose, that she may in fact find her work being used against her, she still offers readers advice about how to read her texts and how to live their lives: look for meanings not in static categories but in blurred edges.

For both writers and readers, Rich's feminist re-visioning of the art/politics dichotomy has consequences. Patriarchy's stories, its images, its aesthetic, and its criticisms become political; thus, they are open to debate, negotiation, and re-vision. Likewise, a woman's stories, her images, her sense of aesthetic, and her criticisms become political; thus, her experiences become viable cultural currency in her re-visioning. As a result, a woman may debate canon issues; she may negotiate the interweavings of her mind, spirit, and body; and she may tap into the transformative re-visioning function of language. Within this logic, Rich's Anglo-American feminist theory of rhetoric emerges as one re-vision that a woman can employ to empower herself and, perhaps, other women. For the power of this rhetorical theory, based on a politics of location, is that it can provide a woman a place of strength from which to merge art and politics. From this place, she can dream the dream of a common language—a dream that results not in silence but in personal and cultural change, with respect for the differences among us.

Inconclusive Musings

Adrienne Rich's feminist theory of rhetoric conceptualizes the silences that may haunt the dream of a common language, as well as the reading, writing, listening, and speaking that may emerge from a feminist politics of location. Rhetoric and composition scholars may employ Rich's theory as presented or put it into play with their own concerns. Either way, questions will emerge. The following are some such possibilities:

1. How does Rich's theory of lying reaffirm or call into question Quintilian's?

2. How do Rich's three functions of language—communicative, socializing, and imaginative—challenge James Britton's or other composition theorists' categories of language?

3. How does Rich's theorizing Anglo-American women's silences challenge the assumed presence of voice in many Western rhetorical theories? Moreover, how are such silences (not) manifested for women in other cultures?

4. How does Rich's theorizing about her own white privilege model means of critiquing issues of race in more traditional rhetorical theories?

5. How does Rich's gendered theory of agency call into question the agency of traditional rhetorical theories that posit a goal of producing good citizens?

By contemplating such questions and by unpacking them for classroom praxis, rhetoric and composition teachers can make students more conscious of the gendered functions of language so that they, in turn, can analyze it and calculate its effects.

As a writer and activist, Rich may not be the sister of Shakespeare that Virginia Woolf imagines in *A Room of One's Own* nor the sister of Nietzsche that Mary Daly imagines in *The Church and the Second Sex*. Instead, Rich may be more like the real-life sister of astronomer William Herschel who is celebrated in Rich's "Planetarium" for being an astronomer in her own right. Caroline Herschel used her scientific talents to discover new places in space—eight comets, to be exact. In like manner, Rich employs her language talents to discover " 'new space' within language and on the borders of patriarchy" ("When We Dead Awaken" 49).[26] As such, Adrienne Rich's Anglo-American feminist theory of rhetoric models methods for re-visioning the borderlands in rhetoric and composition history, theory, and pedagogy.

5

Educating Bathsheba and Everyone Else: Quest(ion)ing Pedagogical Possibilities of Anglo-American Feminist Theories of Rhetoric(s)

> What are the possibilities of doing feminist . . . pedagogy in the classroom?
>
> —Magda Lewis,
> "Interrupting Patriarchy"

Just as Bathsheba's dilemma necessitates feminist theories of rhetoric, so too does it necessitate feminist composition pedagogies: that is, just as Bathsheba must become aware of her dilemma and learn to negotiate it, so too must everyone else become aware of it. With this claim in mind, I began this project, envisioning the final chapter as a detailed freshman composition syllabus with detailed explanations about how to employ it. But when I finally reached this chapter and tried to make my plan visible on the computer screen, it eluded me. Why? Certainly not for lack of syllabi. I have plenty of them. And certainly not for lack of detailed instructions. I have conducted too many workshops for that. Still, as I kept writing toward my desired end, this chapter kept getting longer and longer, and my desire kept postponing itself. For a couple of weeks I thought I was suffering from writing block or burnout. But I finally realized that my syllabus and instructions were so embedded in my particular beliefs and my particular institution that they might be only mildly interesting to readers who had never taught before and perhaps less so to those who had.

So I decided instead that my writing strategy should echo the teaching strategy that I employ each time I offer a composition seminar for beginning teaching assistants. In such courses, I inform them that my goal is to encourage their learning to read, write, talk, listen, and think like a teacher. In other words, I ask them to make the imaginary, yet very real shift from student to teacher and to theorize about pedagogy in order to discover that it can be both an exciting intellectual endeavor and an exciting praxis. In this way, I hope to invoke the interconnectedness of theory and praxis, not as a transparent exchange but as a complex inter-action that informs not just their first semester of teaching but the rest of all our teaching lives. I ask them to imagine pedagogy as more than that which monetarily supports their research and to consider how theorizing about students as subjects can intersect with their study of theories, literatures, and rhetoric and compo-sition, as well as with their daily lives. Thus, this final chapter is my attempt to articulate what I ask of my students: how to read, write, talk, listen, and think like a teacher, or in my case, like an Anglo-American feminist teacher of composition, who functions within personal, textual, and cultural limits and possibilities.

I begin this chapter not with a syllabus but with a question, Magda Lewis's question—"What are the possibilities of doing feminist . . . pedagogy in the classroom?"—not so much to answer it as to see where it may lead (186). Such a beginning attempts to model possibilities of feminist pedagogies, which should also ask questions not so much to answer them as to see where they may lead. Such quest(ion)ing does not defer action—political, in-tellectual, or otherwise; instead this quest(ion)ing foregrounds the positionings that actually emerge during quest(ion)ing. Such po-sitionings are too frequently mystified by our culture's common-sense tendency to fetishize answers and solutions as fixed positions, a tendency arising, no doubt, because fixed answers and solutions are so elusive that they become our greatest desires. But when we separate questions from answers and problems from solutions, we denigrate the importance of questions and problems, give too much credence to the answers and solutions, and totally obfuscate the interconnectedness of the two. This commonsense, compart-mentalized logic insidiously affects pedagogy: it posits fixed an-swers and solutions as knowledge, and this knowledge too often presumes a genderblind mastery, which also signifies other blind-nesses as well.

To challenge this mastery pedagogy, I explore Woolf's, Daly's, and Rich's Anglo-American feminist theories of rhetoric in order to articulate possibilities for feminist composition pedagogies, which are needed to educate Bathsheba as well as everyone else. Although I locate these theories as Anglo-American and feminist, I do not similarly locate all the resulting pedagogies that may emerge from teachers who read these theories. To do so would presume that the theories set up a deterministic grid of feminist pedagogy; such a presumption not only narrows possible receptions of these theories but also denies possible agencies of readers. While my hope is that many different teachers will contemplate how these theories may inform specific courses and specific syllabi for particular students at particular institutions, my focus in this chapter is more narrowly construed, concentrating on the possibilities of these theories for feminist composition pedagogies. With this goal in mind, I first stipulate definitions of *patriarchal pedagogies* and *feminist pedagogies*; then, I explore possibilities for feminist composition pedagogies, which are inspired by Woolf's, Daly's, and Rich's Anglo-American feminist theories of rhetoric; finally, I offer some inconclusive musings.

Defining Patriarchal Pedagogies, or the Genderblindness of Mastering Mastery

In his *Institutio Oratoria* Quintilian exposes a patriarchal dimension of pedagogy when he names the teacher *master* and encourages this master to, above all, act like a parent, a paternal parent (2.2). In "The Old Rhetoric" Roland Barthes outlines the goal of such patriarchal pedagogy: when "conquered at last, [it] represent[s] a good 'object relation' with the world, a real mastery of the world and of men" (26). As such, the process of this pedagogy is mastering; the product, mastery. Yet the near impossibility of mastering mastery frustrates teachers and students alike because it sets most of us up for failure. This mastery metaphor especially frustrates feminist teachers and women students. For Quintilian's and Barthes's terms—*master, men,* and *student*—signify an obvious male identification,[1] yet they are commonly employed as if they were universal. This universality not only erases the implied binary pairings of these terms, such as master/slave, men/women, and student/nonstudent; it also mystifies gender and other differences in pedagogical conversations.

If patriarchal theories of mastery are invoked to explain the function of gender and of other differences in such pedagogical conversations, these theories usually only reinforce stereotypes and perpetuate, among other things, genderblindness. Consider, for example, Hegel's master/slave dialectic. Its play of domination and submission may be read as occurring within subjects, but it may also be read as occurring among them; thus, what "began with the insight that desire is intersubjective ends with the recognition that it is political" (Davis 370). By substituting the terms in this master/slave dialectic with teacher/student, we can explain certain tensions within teachers and students as well as among them. Yet the terms are still presented as monolithic, unmarked categories. If we split *teacher* in terms of man/woman and consider this new pairing in relation to the master/slave dialectic, we can explain certain gender tensions in and among teachers; likewise, if we split *student* in terms of man/woman and consider this new pairing in relation to the master/slave dialectic, we can explain certain gender tensions in and among students.[2] If we put these two terms in play, we can also explain certain gender tensions between teachers and students, and these tensions, in turn, should be put into play with other social categories such as age, race, and so on. Although gendered tensions cannot explain the totality of classroom dynamics, they can expose long-overlooked ones. Yet as long as *woman* occupies the subordinate binary position, the gender differences exposed only reinforce centuries-old notions of women's inferiority and subordination. Hence, while appearing to have potential for exposing gender differences, Hegel's master/slave theory actually fosters genderblindness, unless the binary is exploded.

Consider, too, Nietzsche's concepts of possessor/possessed in terms of men and women: "the man is the master because he takes, but the woman is the master because she gives" (Nye 223).[3] Within this theoretical framework, male mastery pedagogies are centered in the head and do not acknowledge visceral, intuitive reactions of the body as valid knowledge. Dismissing such intuitive reactions as low-order evolutionary responses erases potential agencies of the body. Likewise, female mastery pedagogies are located in the emotions and do not acknowledge the rigorous intellectual tasks of which students, particularly women students, are capable. Dismissing such intellectual tasks as "patriarchal" erases potential agencies of the intellect.[4] The common denominator of Nietzsche's male and female masteries is that they both compartmentalize thinking and feeling, head and body; thus, they both reinforce genderblind stereotypes. This binary, too, must be exploded.

The claim that patriarchal pedagogies emerge from a mastery position that perpetuates genderblindness is echoed in Virginia Woolf's, Mary Daly's, and Adrienne Rich's definitions of patriarchal education. For example, Woolf claims that this education always presumes "sides": "it is necessary for one side to beat another side, and of the utmost importance to walk up a platform and receive from the hands of the Headmaster himself a highly ornamental pot" (*Room* 106).[5] This description of pots, Headmasters, and sides pinpoints mastery power dynamics. The pot presented by the Headmaster functions as public validation of a student's accomplishments; private validation, though celebrated in our culture's most valued philosophical and theological texts, is not rewarded within this system. The term *Headmaster* is telling in itself, reducing knowledge to that which is known in the head and implying that learning is mastery; hence, the head masters the body as well as its surroundings and creates an abstraction whose spiderweb connection to material things is severed. Moreover, where there are sides, there are winners and losers; there are also those who are not even allowed to participate in the game. According to Woolf, winners in 1929 are the processions of the sons of educated men who fill the pulpits, classrooms, benches, and so forth, reinforcing a patriarchal culture. Losers in 1929 are the processions of the sons of educated men who fail or achieve only modest success. And nonplayers in 1929 are all women and minority men who are glimpsed, like the women Woolf describes, "whisking away into the background, concealing . . . a wink, a laugh, perhaps a tear" (*Room* 45). As Woolf also argues, this educational logic reflects and reinforces the genderblindness that mastery dynamics in Western culture have been perpetuating since long before the age of Creon (*Three Guineas* 141).[6] She further argues that this logic and its accompanying rhetoric threaten to destroy us all.

Fifty years later, Mary Daly echoes Woolf's description of patriarchal education as the processions of the sons of educated men (*Gyn/Ecology* 35). For Daly, the basis of patriarchal pedagogy is mastering elementary school, which she defines less as a grade level than as a perspective. Elementary school is where and when "elementary subjects (e.g., ill-logic, women-erasing history, manly grammar, psychology, foolosophy, and the-ology) are taught" (*Wickedary* 197).[7] Continued education results not so much in women's and men's promotion to higher grades as in their mastering the academy's patriarchal state of mind, that is, *academentia*, which Daly defines as the "irreversible deterioration of faculties of intellectuals" (184). Thus, elementary school and higher education socialize women into the attitudes and actions of what Daly names the patriarchal foreground. In this foreground, the twice-born Athena reigns as the male-identified daughter, erasing knowledge of her mother's womb as well as her own origins in Africa while mimicking the logic of her father's forehead. But women's feeling overwhelmed within logics that do not explain our own experiences and ideas, women's feeling voiceless and dislocated in time and space without our own traditions, and women's feeling trapped within male-identified languages and male-identified disciplines—all create gaps in the seemingly seamless foregound/forehead. When filled with women's voices, such gaps threaten to interrupt the processions of the sons of educated men.

Adrienne Rich also echoes Woolf's and Daly's questioning of patriarchal education, not just in terms of women's marginalization but also in terms of the mastery structure of the university ("Toward a Woman" 131–32). Rich identifies two particular problems that women may face in patriarchal education, particularly in higher education. First, male-centered courses and programs pretend to be universal while actually erasing contributions of women; such genderblindness eradicates role models for women and reinforces ideas of female inferiority for both women and men. Second, the "hierarchal image, the structure of relationships, even the style of discourse, including assumptions about theory and practice, ends and means, process and goal"—all of these control women and Woman by allowing us mostly marginal spaces (136). Like Woolf and Daly, Rich claims that the genderblindness of patriarchal pedagogies have adverse effects on both women and men, undermining and exploiting women and pushing men "further into the cul-de-sac of one-sided masculinity" (140). From these gendered positions, patriarchal pedagogies (re)inscribe the power positions of the social matrix onto particular men and women:

> [T]he function of educational institutions is the preparation of certain kinds of people to occupy certain places in the work force, and in the division of private from public life. . . . White males are primarily guided toward and trained for the upper-level professional class; white males, some white females, and a very small group of men and women of color toward the middle-level professional class. People of color and poor white females receive the lowest levels of education and are shunted as cheap labor toward lower-paying, unskilled, and service jobs, and, of course, into the armed forces, which actually advertise themselves as educational institutions ("Soul" 191).

And within these gendered positions, women students frequently fall into the trap of dutiful daughter: "[l]ike the father's favorite daughter in the patriarchal family, the promising woman student comes to identify with her male-scholar-teacher more strongly than with her sisters" ("Toward a Woman" 139). Such positions are dangerous when they fool both the scholar and his favorite daughter into believing that they see from the center, which is not really a center at all. As a result, although their actions may be productive, they may also be genderblind, raceblind, classblind, and so on. Furthermore, the problem of such blindnesses is not only with "them." As Rich reminds us in many of her texts, all of us have been so deeply "educated" by patriarchal structures that we must constantly fight such blindnesses if we are to ease the tensions that plague us and our culture.

As described by Woolf, Daly, and Rich, patriarchal pedagogies assume certain theoretical underpinnings. Carmen Luke and Jennifer Gore associate these underpinnings with Enlightenment concepts of self and knowledge (ix).[8] For example, patriarchal pedagogies often construct students and teachers as selves who are autonomous and unified, ungendered and unraced; critiques of these pedagogical assumptions may expose such autonomy as economically limited, such unity as fragmented, such genderblindness as male identified, and such raceblindness as white identified. Likewise, patriarchal pedagogies often posit bodies of knowledge as autonomous and universal, ungendered and unraced; however, anyone familiar with the contemporary canon wars can expose such autonomy as class biased, such universality as culturally biased, such genderblindness as male identified, and such raceblindness as white identified.

As a result, many different challenges have emerged to expose, revise, and overturn such patriarchal pedagogies. The need for such challenges is articulated by Johnnella Butler, who argues that patriarchal pedagogies, whether traditional or leftist,[9] result in the following cultural "ills," the main points of which are listed below.

1. A lack of a sense of human commonality and communality.
2. A distorted sense of the value of the aesthetics, ideals, history, and heritage of the Anglo, upper-middle to upper class white American.
3. A distortion of American history and culture through the distortion of the meaning of race and ethnicity in American social and scholarly contexts.
4. A distorted and limited treatment of gender differences and similarities.
5. A distortion of American class realities.
6. A limitation and restriction of education to a static state.
7. A gross limitation of human potential.

(10–12)

One goal that I set for myself in this project is to think my way beyond, or sideways from, the teaching metaphors of mastery and genderblindness, whether these metaphors appear in patriarchal pedagogies, critical pedagogies, or other feminist pedagogies. Perhaps attempting to move beyond these metaphors and address the aforementioned ills may seem a utopian fantasy to some readers. So be it. What Woolf, Daly, and Rich have taught me is that, even if subjects have only limited agencies, their first steps are important in constructing contexts in which the impossible may eventually become the possible and sometimes even the probable: just as women writing make possible women writers, so too do students writing about, and from the position of, gender make possible student writers who are more aware of how gender intersects with other categories of difference within the complex social matrix in which we live and learn.

Defining Feminist Pedagogies, or Treating the Ills of Patriarchal Education

I begin my discussion of feminist pedagogies with Patti Lather's appropriation of David Lusted's definition of pedagogy: "I take *pedagogy* to mean that which addresses 'the transformation of consciousness that takes place in the intersection of three agencies— the teacher, the learner, and the knowledge they produce together'" (121).[10] As useful as this definition is, it still obscures gender as well as the ills of patriarchal education. To expose gender so as to "treat" these ills, feminist pedagogies have arisen—first focusing on gender alone, then focusing on a complicated social matrix in which gender functions as a key category that intersects with race, class, sexual orientation, and so on (Luke and Gore 7–10).[11] The reasons behind this changing focus are simple: feminist pedagogies that focus only on gender or only on race mislead teachers and students about our own identities, agencies, and locations within the complex social matrix; radical transformative feminist pedagogics, however, expose the complex social matrix as well as our particular locations within this matrix (Johnnella Butler 17). The driving assumption behind both pedagogical moves, however, is that awareness may become the first step toward action, which may, in turn, become the first step toward individual and collective change. This assumption also informs the feminist pedagogies promoted by Virginia Woolf, Mary Daly, and Adrienne Rich.

Although Woolf bemoans the state of women's colleges in the

first chapter of *A Room of One's Own*, she outlines her hopes for them in *Three Guineas*. Specifically, she advises administrators of women's colleges to take advantage of their colleges' positions as "young and poor" and to be "adventurous"—all in the hopes of creating new educational structures in which to unweave the insidious interweavings of sexism, capitalism, and fascism that she believes lead to war (33). According to Woolf, the buildings of women's colleges should be constructed "of some cheap, easily combustible material which does not hoard dust and perpetuate traditions" (33). Their curricula should include only that which can be easily taught and learned by the poor: "the arts of human intercourse; the art of understanding other people's lives and minds, and the little arts of talk, of dress, of cookery that are allied with them" (34). Their goals should foster holistic, not specialized, knowledge—a knowledge that combines the powers of mind and body. Their teachers should be "drawn from the good livers as well as from the good thinkers" (34). And finally, their theoretical grounding should be in the four great teachers of women: poverty, chastity, derision, and freedom from unreal loyalties (79). Such a definition of feminist pedagogy foregrounds the intersubjectivity of students, teachers, and institutions, thus implying an interconnectedness of pedagogical strategies and topics, of education and life.

Daly's feminist pedagogy insists upon pedagogical Spinning, which encourages women to trespass into male-dominated fields with the intent of refusing foreground knowledge and seeking Background knowing. Playing with Plato's famous myth of the cave, Daly claims that "Amazing expeditions into the male-controlled 'fields' are necessary in order to leave the fathers' caves and live in the sun" (*Gyn/Ecology* 8). The quest(ion)ing of such expeditions challenges the masters, their mastery, and their language; as such, it possesses the potential to lead students into what Daly calls the radical feminist Background. Daly's pedagogy offers students, especially women students, the possibility of committing Roboticide (*Wickedary* 160) and becoming Nag-Gnostics or "Elemental Feminist Philosopher[s]" (147) who are capable of Sinthesis, that is, proposing "Wicked proposition[s] or argument[s]" (164). All Nag-Gnostics are Searchers and, like Daly, some are Word Witches (160, 182). But becoming a Nag-Gnostic is neither simple nor easy. Rather, it entails embracing Studied Unlearning, which Daly defines as follows: "[T]he intellectual project/process of a Nag-Gnostic Crone who studies a traditional discipline to the point of knowing it backwards and forwards, shifts her angle of vision, opens her Third Eye, and analyzes the field from a Cronelogical perspective; true truancy, requiring study/training and untiring untraining; unnarrowing, harrowing process of Feminist Searchers" (169–70). Because this Studied Unlearning combines project and process, it presumes the merger of pedagogical strategy and topics. Its main pedagogical strategy is Flight of Ideas, otherwise known as "a Wandering from subject to subject, Dis-covering deep Elemental connections" (125), which Daly names Syn-Crone-icities (170). Among those topics deemed Nag-noteworthy for study are the following: Gnomic writing, which "expresses Earthly Reality" (130); Hagocracy, "the history of women who are on the Journey of radical be-ing" (138); and Philosophia, "the wisdom formulated by women; love for the wisdom of women; desire and passion for understanding: an intellectual urge toward love of life" (154). Daly's Flight of Ideas about the above topics does not culminate in a static truth but rather in an Unstable State, the "blissful condition of Nags who have broken loose from the stable-world of phallo-institutions" (175), a state where Volcanic Wisdom and Foresight are possible (176, 126).

Like Woolf and Daly, Rich has constructed her own definition of feminist pedagogy. In "The Soul of a Women's College," she encourages women's colleges to define themselves in terms of their particular historical moment, their goals being to encourage women to respect themselves as well as others and to encourage women to work for "a world in which social and sexual and cultural differences will be respected, where the white, male, Western perspective will be one of many, and not the predominant one" (196). To achieve these goals, Rich advocates a pedagogy that interweaves style and content ("Toward a Woman" 143) and in which teachers are drawn from women activists who are scholars and artists and who will engage students both inside and outside the classroom ("Soul" 197). This interaction should emerge through antihierarchical teaching strategies "more dialogic, more exploratory, less given to pseudo-objectivity, than the traditional mode" ("Toward a Woman" 143). Such dialogues should occur in multicultural core courses of "women's history, thought, political roles, labor, art"; in disciplinary courses that foreground the influence of women upon the discipline as well as the influence of the discipline upon women; and additional courses that provide women with skills for surviving in the world, courses in "old and new ways of resolving conflict, of coalition building, of collective participation," or in other words, courses in rhetoric ("Soul" 196, 197). Moreover, institutions should provide child care, encourage part-time students more, provide women's services to all women in the community, and research issues relevant to local communities ("Toward a Woman" 145–53). As Rich notes, such change should occur "not merely for changing institutions but for human redefinition; not merely for equal rights but for a new kind of being" (155).

Other feminist theorists have constructed their own definitions of *feminist pedagogies* in an attempt to merge structural concerns with particular students' concerns or, in more popular terms, in an attempt to merge the political and the personal in the classroom in hopes that awareness will promote action and change. For example, Cynthia Caywood and Gillian Overing champion feminist pedagogies that promote a classroom equity, with *equity* meaning the construction of "new standards which accommodate and nurture differences" (xi). Maxine Greene endorses feminist pedagogies that employ poststructuralist moves to rethink the "construction of knowledge and the life of meaning" (x); Patti Lather posits one such (post)critical pedagogy: "In translating critical theory into a pedagogical agenda, (post)critical foregrounds movement beyond the sedimented discursive configurations of essentialized, romanticized subjects with authentic needs and real identities, who require generalized emancipation from generalized social oppression via the mediations of liberatory pedagogues capable of exposing the 'real' to those caught up in the distorting meaning systems of late capitalism" (131). To expose the complexities of this material "real," bell hooks advocates feminist classrooms that are more confrontational than nurturing, places "where there is a sense of struggle, where there is visible acknowledgement of the union of theory and practice, where we work together as teachers and students to overcome the estrangement and alienation that have become so much the norm in the contemporary university" ("Toward a Revolutionary" 51). And echoing hooks's calls for conflicts, Susan Jarratt further advocates sophistic pedagogy in the feminist classroom, because students and teachers must learn to negotiate our truths "not only through self-discovery but in the heat of argument" ("Feminism and Composition" 121).[12]

With echoes of the aforementioned definitions resounding in my mind, I pose yet another definition of *feminist pedagogies*, one that is informed by all of the above claims.[13] That is, I define feminist pedagogies as follows: the situated knowing-being-doing-learning that, first, presumes gender as a key, but not the sole, category within the social matrix and that, second, emerges through interwoven learning strategies and course topics; such strategies and topics are driven by teachers' (un)conscious feminist assumptions, influenced by students' particular subjectivities, circumscribed by institutional values, and affected by particular historical moments and cultural locations. The purpose of such pedagogies is not simply to provide more favorable learning environments for women, although such a move is extremely important. The purpose is also to foster feminist literacies in all students, to make them more aware of how gender intersects with other differences within our complex social matrix and of how these intersections construct our subjectivities as well as our cultural values, our epistemologies, and our communicative possibilities. Such feminist literacies demand gender awareness from students but not political commitment; thus, students may leave a class more informed, yet not feminist. Simply put: good evaluations should not depend upon a student's adhering to a strict party line.

My definition of feminist pedagogies assumes several different theoretical underpinnings. To begin, it echoes Rich's claim that feminist pedagogies enable us to conceptualize and theorize about "women as students and students as women,"[14] taking into account all the complexities that the term *women* implies ("Taking Women Students Seriously" 237). At the 1993 Woolf conference, Vara Neverow argued a similar position: if we read *A Room of One's Own*, replacing the word *student* for *woman*, then we can achieve greater understanding of teacher-student dynamics. For example, if the Oxbridge beadle sends the narrator's little fish (her thought) into hiding, so too may master teachers send students' little fishes into hiding. Of course, "women as students" is not synonymous with "students as women": the former assumes questions and problems that women encounter in genderblind classrooms;[15] the latter, questions and problems that all students with all their differences encounter in mastery classrooms. Because the mastery power dynamic subordinates both women and students, this double focus foregrounds common, as well as less common, strategies of oppression; at the same time, it exposes *women* and *students* as marked categories, not essential beings. In addition, reading "students as women" reinforces the pertinence of reading feminist tracts for pedagogical purposes.

By focusing on interwoven strategies *and* topics, my definition interrupts the strategy-versus-content pedagogy debate.[16] Such interruptions expose that neither strategies nor topics have innate, fixed feminist values. Although certain strategies and topics may construct favorable conditions from which a feminist classroom may emerge, there is nothing innately feminist in collaborative groupwork, in sitting in a circle, or in reading or writing about women.[17] Indeed, without careful consideration of classroom dynamics, a teacher may unknowingly dominate students' collaborative work via heavy-handed discussions or teacher-centered directions; such an unreflective teacher may also unknowingly perpetuate age-old stereotypes when teaching women's writing or writings about women and gender.

Given the dangers of unreflective teaching, my definition demands that feminist teachers reflect on our pedagogical strategies and topics so as to articulate our own ideological assumptions for ourselves. For instance, feminist teachers must consider the symbolic positions of women and men when deciding how to treat students. Should men and women students be treated equally? What does *equally* mean? Should women and men students be treated according to their particular needs and differences? Who determines these needs and differences? And how? Likewise, feminist teachers must decide how to include gender in a course. Should it be the topic of the course? Should it be a category by which another topic, for instance, war, is critiqued? Should it be presented in conjunction with race or sexual orientation or religious preference or geographical location? Should it inform everything from planning syllabi to discussing readings to writing final exams? Only by reflecting on our own assumptions can feminist teachers accept responsibility for our institutional powers and simultaneously provide ourselves with theoretical frameworks with which to explain and predict classroom dynamics. At the same time, feminist teachers must keep the following caveat in mind: there are limits to consciousness. Despite all our reflecting and foregrounding assumptions, we cannot articulate our unconscious. And despite all our planning, we cannot totally control how our students receive us.

Given that teachers cannot blithely control students' receptions, my definition demands that feminist teachers articulate our assumptions for our students. Such a move cannot promote total identification between teachers and students, given inevitable power dynamics within a classroom; however, such a move may make pedagogy visible to students and partially demystify it. For example, feminist teachers should not just assign women to be group leaders but should also discuss gendered group dynamics; likewise, we should not just assign writings by and about women but also discuss gendered canonical issues. The purpose of such demystification is to foster critical thinking, reading, speaking, and writing in students—not to produce teacher clones. In the process, students may appreciate the importance not only of *what* they learn but also of *how* they learn, thus recognizing that the former is inextricably woven into the latter.

Given the limitations of teachers' consciousness, my definition also demands that feminist teachers listen to our students and afford them the opportunity to critique our assumptions, whether in class discussions, student-teacher conferences, or anonymous freewritings. By listening, we may become more aware of our flawed logics, our mistaken pedagogical strategies, and our own unconscious assumptions. For students are often quite adept at reading their teachers. In fact, when beginning teaching assistants say that their students cannot read, they may not recognize that the text their students read best is their teacher. Students benefit, too, when teachers listen to them. Such listening opens up spaces for students to become (in)directly involved in some pedagogical decisions of the class, such as the selection of writing topics, reading assignments, grading criteria, classroom activities. In the process, students may further develop their voices, gain confidence in their voices, and recognize the complex gendered socialization that influences their voices. At the same time, they may recognize how these voices can(not) be employed in the presence of an authority figure.

Because the classroom dialogues do not occur in a vacuum, my definition demands that feminist teachers attend to our classes' particular historical moments and cultural locations. To do so, we must not privilege our own information and experiences that we bring to the class; we must also respect the information and experiences that students bring. For instance, students have experienced several years of pedagogies that reinforced patriarchal values; as a result, their resistance to feminist classroom praxis can be as much visceral as intellectual. But feminist teachers can use students' ideas and experiences, indeed their resistance, to help us all think critically about gender's function in the complex social matrix, as when we narrate and critique our gender-based experiences. At the same time, feminist teachers must acknowledge the possibilities and limitations of institutional structures within which pedagogy occurs. Such moves allow feminist teachers to construct pedagogies that both acknowledge the four walls of a particular institution's classroom yet also expand beyond these walls. Such moves also challenge dichotomies of theory/practice, school/real world, and public/private that drive patriarchal rhetorics and inform too many teachers' and students' concepts of education.

Perhaps my definition's most risky move is assuming that heightened awareness may lead to individual and collective action that, in turn, may lead to individual and collective change. For as we all know, a huge gap exists between conscious knowledge and action—whether we are talking about students' awareness of grammar rules and their (in)ability to write well, whether we are talking about our own feminisms and our pedagogies, whether we are talking about students' and teachers' awareness of social ills and our (in)ability and (un)willingness to change them. Although these gaps can never be closed, neither should they be ignored. This desire is what manifests itself when teachers say, If I can just help one student to (x), or If my students can just help one another to (x). How the (x) function is filled, of course, depends on the political persuasion of the teacher. For example, conservatives want to help students recognize that people have autonomous wills and, thus, are totally accountable for their actions; liberals want to help students recognize that structural oppressions limit individuals' agencies and, thus, limit their accountability for their actions; radicals want to help students see that structures must be totally restructured if oppressions are to be reduced or eradicated; and feminists want, among other things, to help students understand the blindnesses—gender, racial, and otherwise—that often underpin the above desires.[18] As Susan Jarratt notes, the politicized move from awareness, to action, to change does not imply an awareness of fixed truths or final courses of action (*Sophists* 111–12). Instead, what is understood about the move from awareness to action is that students and teachers have to repeat it again and again, given different times and different spaces. Lather puts it more succinctly: "positions of resistance can never be established once and for all" (121).

Some readers may find my definition of, and assumptions about, feminist pedagogy too teacher centered. Granted, my definition assumes that the ways in which teachers present strategies and topics, the ways in which we encourage students to engage these strategies and topics, and the ways in which we evaluate students' performances all combine to determine whether or not feminist pedagogies exist. I would disagree, however, about its being too teacher centered and would agree with Jennifer Gore, who argues that "discourses of critical and feminist pedagogy . . . need to provide better guidance for the actions of the teachers they hope to empower or they hope will empower students" (68).[19] Thus, I argue that, especially in student-centered classrooms, teachers have the responsibility to recognize multiple power differentials, certainly not to abuse them and definitely not to erase them (such a move is impossible); rather, their responsibility is to rethink the traditional mastery classroom dynamics and to ask students to rethink them as well. Perhaps a model for this process is the way Woolf encourages women to rethink language use: accept what works, discard what does not, and create what will ("Men and Women" 195). If teachers are not willing to rethink their pedagogy in their classrooms and in their institutions, productive change never occurs.

Finally, my definition employs the plural form of *pedagogy* purposely because, much as I might like to do so, I cannot outline one pedagogy that guarantees every teacher a feminist classroom. As any trainer of teachers knows, given the same syllabus, the same class plan, and the same grading criteria, twenty different teachers with twenty different groups of students will teach twenty different courses. The most I can offer here are some pedagogical possibilities of Woolf's, Daly's, and Rich's Anglo-American feminist theories of rhetoric and an invitation to readers to consider further how these theories and their pedagogical possibilities may or may not inform their own pedagogies.

Pedagogical Possibilities of Anglo-American Feminist Theories of Rhetoric, or What's Feminism Got to Do with It?

How may Woolf's, Daly's, and Rich's Anglo-American feminist theories of rhetoric inform feminist composition pedagogies? These theories do not posit one writing process as an ahistorical structure that empowers all women and all feminists. They do not offer a set syllabus, a set of textbooks, a sequence of papers, or a list of teaching strategies that guarantees a feminist classroom. And as Marjorie Curry Woods suggests, they need not reject everything rhetorical that has come before (24). What they do provide, however, is a set of feminist assumptions that may drive composition teachers' pedagogies, pedagogies whose purpose is to empower both teachers and students by giving us access to our limited, intersecting, and evolving agencies.[20] Situated as these feminist theories of rhetoric are within feminist epistemologies and ideologies, they offer common and particular theoretical threads that may, in turn, offer possibilities for teachers who want to weave particular feminist composition pedagogies.

Common theoretical threads run throughout Woolf's, Daly's, and Rich's theories. For instance, by focusing on women, these theories pose possibilities for recognizing, validating, and addressing Bathsheba's dilemma. In this way, they reject the genderblindness of traditional theories, which means that they expose differences between men and women as well as differences among men and among women. Pedagogically, exposure makes gender visible in classroom discussions, whether as a category of analysis or as a position of speaking and writing. Specifically, composition teachers and students may invoke gender in relation to other differences to analyze assigned readings, cultural events, or student papers; to critique conferences, group work, or class discussions; and to continue questioning our own deeply held beliefs about gender functions. Likewise, teachers and students may articulate our own gendered positions and consider how these positions inform the previous activities.

By insisting on the interconnectedness of theory and praxis, these feminist theories of rhetoric reaffirm the possibilities of pedagogy. When this interconnectedness is ignored, theory and pedagogy as well as teaching and research is compartmentalized. Within the academy, faculty and administrators too often translate this compartmentalization into the ghettoization of pedagogy (i.e., busy work for those who do not know) and the valorization of theory and research (i.e., significant work for those who can and do know).[21] Outside the academy, the general public too often translates this compartmentalization into confused notions of the university and its work. They may consider theory to be "ivory tower" musings unless directly applicable to technology or business, and they may want to know how pedagogy will lead them and their children to profitable, practical work and experience. So the pedagogical imperative for composition teachers is to make visible for themselves and their students the tenuous, spiderweb connections between theory and praxis in rhetoric and composition studies: that is, because rhetoric and composition theories emerge from praxis, they function most productively as a means of *informing* praxis and *informing* subsequent theorizing; they do not function productively as a grid of ideas *applied* to praxis as a means of forcing students, teachers, discourse, classroom dynamics, and so on, into specific attitudes or actions. Promoting this concept in a composition class may mean not just employing theory to design courses but utilizing classroom experiences to redefine theory. It may also mean articulating the category *student* to students. An interesting lesson in subjectivity, as well as an interesting writing assignment, entails letting students know how they are being defined by different writing theorists—for example, cognitivists, neo-Platonists, neo-Aristotelians, or whatever our own particular positions may be—and then having them critique these positions, comparing them against their own perceptions of themselves. Students may then critique their conclusions in terms of gender to prevent, for example, erasures of Woman and women in assigned readings, writings, and discussions. Such moves can help students recognize that writing is not just waiting for the muse to visit and that judgments about writing are not just the product of an individual teacher's "subjective" criteria or an institution's "objective" grading criteria.

By intersecting the personal, the cultural, and the textual, these theories offer possibilities for challenging the social/psychological split that haunts the expressivist/epistemic debates in composition studies. By positing the personal as a fluid yet committed, gendered subjectivity, these theories escape the traps of essentialism and separatism while celebrating women; they also refuse subjects' relegation to mere discursive positions while offering means for real-life, historical change via limited agency. By naming the cultural *patriarchy*, these theories demystify men's and women's gendered symbolic language positions and cultural power, and by exposing how gender intersects with other differences within a patriarchal structure, these theories reveal the particularity of gendered subjects' symbolic language positions as well as their cultural power. By insisting on the materiality of the textual, these theories render language visible, making visible that which has been invisible since at least Descartes; moreover, by celebrating the imaginative function of material language, these theories expose the power of language to deconstruct and reconstruct ourselves, our cultures, and our texts. Consequently, by intersecting the personal, the cultural, and the textual, these theories promote feminist pedagogies that ask teachers and students to consider our reading and writing processes on an individual basis, expose our locations in a larger social matrix, and foreground the function and use of language in perpetuating and revising both our subjectivities and the social matrix. Consequently, teachers and students emerge as active, though limited, players in the process of empowerment, which is no longer seen as that which is done *by* teachers *to* students but rather as something that both teachers and students must constantly pursue and question.

By revealing that particular subjects have particular locations, these theories entertain the possibility that subjects may have their own logics and their own rhetorics, circumscribed of course by their cultures, with each rhetoric possessing particular concepts of invention, arrangement, revision, memory, and so on. Such a claim challenges phallogocentric notions of one logic and one rhetoric as ahistorical, acultural structures that forever repeat themselves. In the classroom, teachers and students may test this claim. For example, we may employ Aristotelian appeals to rhetorically analyze the Declaration of Independence and Navajo chants, yet at the same time we should ask what questions are not answered by the Aristotelian framework. In this way, we critique not only the assigned readings but also the means of analysis. In addition, teachers and students can explore definitions of subjectivity that are assumed in the Navajo chants and then critique Aristotle's theory and the Declaration of Independence in terms of the Navajo theory of subjectivity. Such pedagogical suggestions not only familiarize students with traditional ideas that still permeate our culture but also teach students to question, to revise, to recognize, and to critique the differences that emerge from, and within, these traditional ideas. Such a move enables teachers and students to acknowledge the importance of different cultural positionings in any kind of analysis or revision, whether that analysis or revision occurs via reading or writing. Such a move is especially important, for as Audre Lorde claims: "it is not those differences between us that are separating us. It is rather our refusal to recognize those differences, and to examine the distortions which result from our misnaming them and their effects upon human behavior and expectation" ("Age" 115).

By positing truthtelling as an imperative of these different logics and different rhetorics, Woolf's, Daly's, and Rich's feminist theories of rhetoric celebrate the possibilities not of *the* truth but of women's truths, truths that have too frequently been silenced in the past and that are too frequently silenced in the present. To articulate such silences, these theories break the dichotomies of narrative/argument and fact/fiction; that is, they open spaces for narrative arguments and argumentative narratives and call into question the distinction between patriarchal fact and fiction. In the process, these theories expose a doubled function, breaking the above dichotomies yet simultaneously insisting on the importance of historical locations. This doubled function exposes the myth of linear time by revealing how the past is always folding itself into the present and how, in one form or another, the past is always with us. For example, this doubled function reveals how (lack of) traditions adversely affect women and minorities, how rhetorical situations are not positivistic, and how current claims are drenched in past experiences and assumptions. Pedagogically, students and teachers may explore this assumption by asserting claims on any issue from abortion to xenophobia and then unpacking these claims to determine what voices or influences from the past (parents, traditions, lore, capitalism, etc.) are informing these claims as well as what voices or influences (gender, race, age, etc.) remain silent in these claims. Such pedagogical strategies force teachers and students to tell the "truth" not only of our beliefs but also of our assumptions.

Finally, by articulating their authors' feminist writing processes, these feminist theories of rhetoric emphasize the particularity as well as the gendered components of writing processes. As such, these theories offer possible models for teachers and students to analyze and then imitate, revise, and reject. Teachers and students may consider Woolf's, Daly's, and Rich's writing processes and resulting styles in terms of their feminist politics; then we may discuss whether imitating these processes and styles would be fruitful for our own thinking and writing endeavors. We may also follow these feminists' lead, articulating our own writing processes and speculating about our politics' impact on our processes as well as about our processes' impact on our styles. While functioning as models, these feminist theories of rhetoric also open up new spaces in rhetorical history, theory, and pedagogy. And it is in these new spaces that we may locate Woolf's, Daly's, and Rich's particular pedagogical possibilities.

Woolf's Anglo-American feminist theory of rhetoric reminds feminist composition teachers that we can challenge our students and ourselves with the following reading and writing possibilities:

> 1. to create new words and new methods (of invention, writing, etc.) and to critique not just the implications of these new words and methods but also the pedagogical strategy itself (*Three Guineas* 143);[22]

> 2. to define our own Angel in the House and consider its impact on our writing; or alternatively, to argue that we have no Angel and consider the impact of this fact on our writing ("Professions for Women" 58–60);

3. to consider the concept of "a woman's sentence," determining whether or not we believe it exists and how we think it could or could not be employed ("Dorothy Richardson" 191);

4. to use the four great teachers of women—poverty, chastity, derision, and freedom from unreal loyalties—as topoi to analyze assigned texts and to generate our own texts (*Three Guineas* 79);

5. to analyze how the separation and blurrings of fact/fiction or truth/fiction affects our writing in academia and elsewhere (*Room* 4);

6. to recount experiences that we have made real by putting them into words and to speculate about this function of language ("Sketch of the Past" 71);

7. to analyze our own sentences and sequences to become more aware of our own stylistic practices; then to analyze these stylistic practices in terms of our own positions of gender, race, class, age, and so on (*Room* 81);

8. to practice strict imitation and revisionary imitation, comparing both to determine which, if either, is helpful in improving our understanding of language function or our own writing processes (*Room* 766, 88; *Diary* 3: 119);

9. to analyze our audiences via Woolf's gendered scheme—that is, men in general, men in particular, women in general, women in particular—determining whether or not this scheme has any validity for improving our critical abilities and our writing processes (*Room* 88, 111; *Diary* 5: 127; "22 Hyde Park Gate" 152; Gordon xiv);

10. to critique Woolf's language imperative to accept what works, to discard what does not, and to create what

may; then to employ this imperative as topoi for reading and writing ("Men and Women" 195);

11. to argue why we do or do not believe that gendered invention strategies exist, using Woolf's British Museum scene as an example (*Room* 30);

12. to analyze the importance of money and leisure time for writers (e.g., men, women, and students) from different cultures (*Room* 4);

13. to consider whether or not we feel trapped within patriarchal languages, logics, and rhetorics; to reflect on the different ways of being trapped; and to wonder, like the narrator in *A Room of One's Own*, whether it is worse to be locked in or out of these structures (24).

Likewise, Daly's Anglo-American feminist theory of rhetoric reminds feminist composition teachers that we can challenge ourselves and our students with the following reading and writing possibilities:

1. to read, for example, excerpts from Aristotle's *Rhetoric* and debate the efficacy of studying patriarchal rhetorical theory for our own writing process (*Gyn/Ecology* 8);

2. to critique a text in terms of Daly's foreground and Background truths; and to critique the categories of foreground and Background truths (3, 26);

3. to read and write about multicultural fairy tales and myths, giving special attention to gender and analyzing their (un)common threads and metaphors (13–14, 75, 88);

4. to imitate Daly's language play via etymology or stipulative definitions, perhaps using her *paradise* analysis as a model—all in an attempt to make language more visible in terms of how it constructs categories and makes certain claims (im)possible in different cultures (7);

5. to read, for example, Cicero's discussion of the five canons of rhetoric—invention, arrangement, delivery, memory, style—and compare these canons to Daly's feminist reversals or Non-Canons—Spinning, Dis-ordering, Be-Spelling, Re-membering, Be-Speaking (*Wickedary* 96, 118, 65, 92–93, 65); then, to employ both schemes in different reading and writing situations in order to determine what kinds of issues and questions each raises and ignores;

6. to read a text and determine whether or not the methods of patriarchal logic that Daly identifies—such as, particularization, reversal, tokenism, Sado-Ritual Syndrome—exist (*Beyond* 5; *Gyn/Ecology* 8, and 130–35; *Wickedary* 243–47); then, to analyze the function of these methods in terms of gender and its intersection with other differences;

7. to identify metaphors in our culture, as in rap music, soap operas, an *Atlantic* essay, and the evening news; to critique how this metaphoric power of language generates gendered cultural values (*Pure Lust* 25, 327–33, 407); then, to discuss how this gendered value is complicated by race, sexual orientation, geography, and so on;

8. to contemplate how Daly's concepts of new hearing (*Gyn/Ecology* 424), new contexts (*Beyond* 189), new speech (159), and new words (*Gyn/Ecology* 340) could have implications in academic discourses, family discourses, job interview discourses, and so on; and to contemplate if and how these concepts could encourage considerations of differences;

9. to critique Daly's concept of Realizing Presence, considering our roles, our language's roles, and our social matrix's roles in this process; and to determine this concept's role in our writing processes (*Pure Lust* 149);

10. to debate the power of naming—for instance, Adam's naming in the Bible, women's taking their husband's

names, corporations' naming their products, and Daly's
Feminist Naming (*Gyn/Ecology* 24);

11. to argue the communicative (im)possibilities of a
feminist writing process like Daly's, which is so indi-
vidualized yet which is held up as a model for all women
(23);

12. to consider Daly's eight deadly sins—deception, processions, professions, possessions, aggression, obsession, assimilation, elimination, fragmentation—as topoi and as
rhetorical language moves (*Wickedary* 70–71);

13. to contemplate methodicide and its role in each
student's writing process (82).

Finally, Rich's Anglo-American feminist theory of rhetoric reminds feminist composition teachers that we can challenge ourselves and our students with the following reading and writing
possibilities:

1. to identify, analyze, and compare the politics of location from which we have spoken, are speaking, and are
spoken ("Notes" 212; "Split at the Root" 123); and to
critique these positions in terms of gender, class, race,
sexual orientation, and so on, and in terms of their various intersections;

2. to consider when, why, how, where, and for whom we
fall into dreams of a common language ("Origins" 1.12),
or silence ("Cartographies"),[23] or playing it safe; then
to determine if and how these moves affect our writing
processes;

3. to explore how Rich's metaphor, "the eye of the outsider," fosters re-vision of our own politics of location as
well as of patriarchal myths, laws, sports, education, enter-
tainment, sexuality, and so forth ("What Does" 3; "When
We Dead Awaken" 35); then, to examine how this gendered metaphor compares with composition theorists'

definitions of revision; and to consider if and how Rich's re-vision informs our own writing processes;

4. to analyze how Rich's three kinds of silence—stasis ("An Unsaid Word"), secret planning ("Cartographies"), and lying ("Women and Honor" 187)—function in terms of gender, race, class, and their intersections; and to determine how these intersections influence our reading and writing processes;

5. to critique textual strategies used by women and by men in particular positions, trying to determine to what extent style depends upon context, particular writing strategies, and/or authorial consciousness ("When We Dead Awaken"); and to critique our styles in terms of our conclusions;

6. to compose our own theories of rhetoric, using our own bodies as the site of these theories' emergence; then to critique the possibilities and limits of these theories for other readers, writers, and speakers in and beyond our class ("Notes" 210–14);

7. to listen to our unconscious—acknowledging that we can never fully hear or control it, recognizing that we are treading into potentially painful territory and that we are not trained therapists, yet questioning where, when, why, and how the unconscious informs our reading/writing processes ("Poetry and Experience" 89);

8. to listen to the many voices that inform an issue ("Notes" 231)—for example, critiquing the pluralism that attempts to accept all these voices, questioning the conservatism that attempts to validate only one "right voice," and considering what other positions are (im)possible;

9. to analyze why women and women's writing are dangerous to patriarchy's values and very existence; and to contemplate the possibility and feasibility of being "dangerous" ("From an Old House" 16.1–2);

10. to investigate whether or not Rich's invention strategies—questioning, remembering, storytelling, describing, reading between lines, analyzing the symbolic, deconstructing women's texts, educated guessing, intuitive rememberings based on the facts at hand, and disobeying—are useful topoi for analyzing reading assignments, including student texts, and for generating our own texts (*On Lies* 14; "Resisting" 148; "Disobedience" 78);

11. to explore differences between Anglo-American feminisms and African American feminisms and Hispanic feminisms, and so on ("Resisting" 151; "North American Tunnel Vision" 165); to determine how these differences inform our own politics of location, whether we consider ourselves feminist or not; and to analyze marked signifiers—such as, *natural* woman or *born* mother—that patriarchal critics associate with these feminisms so as to dismiss them with charges of essentialism and separatism;

12. to analyze academic discourse, recognizing how it silences particular voices and is sustained by others ("Cartographies"); and to consider our own marked voices, written and spoken, in terms of this analysis;

13. to critique whether or not Rich's metaphors of centers, borders, and blurred borders are useful constructs for analyzing society, the university, families, and so on; to consider whether the border meanings are actually *unspeakable* in the center ("It Is the Lesbian" 199); to determine what kinds of power, if any, the borders and blurred borders possess for generating new insights ("Contradictions" 29.11–12); and finally, to speculate about the border's influence on reading and writing.

Many other common and particular threads might be identified in Woolf's, Daly's, and Rich's feminist theories of rhetoric and then pulled through to pedagogy in many different ways. And I invite readers to do so, to determine for themselves just how these theories and their pedagogical possibilities may or may not inform their pedagogies. For as I previously mentioned, these theories and pedagogical possibilities are not grids that can be laid onto all composition classrooms to insure a feminist pedagogy. Feminist ideologies cannot be so easily institutionalized nor patriarchal ideologies so easily displaced. Instead, these theories and pedagogical possibilities should be put into play with our already existing pedagogies, whether our pedagogies are feminist or not. In this way, these theories and pedagogical possibilities challenge all of us—based on whatever particular ideology we might embrace—to consider gender and other differences within the social matrix. What makes such considerations of theory and pedagogy so exciting to us and so confusing to our students is that the results of our considerations differ wildly. I believe that it is time to take responsibility for our excitement and not leave making sense of our differences only to students.

Inconclusive Musings, or Is Walter Ong Asking the Right Question?

In 1972, Walter Ong asked whether or not traditional rhetoric could survive coeducational classrooms (615). Perhaps a better question to ask is, *Should* traditional rhetoric survive coeducational classrooms? If we read traditional rhetoric as a fixed, patriarchal structure, then the answer is probably *no*. But if we read it as an always emerging textual practice that is deeply embedded in our social matrix and indelibly inscribed on our bodies, then the answer is probably *yes*. And the reason for this yes is one of the very same reasons that Aristotle gives in book one of his *Rhetoric*: "we must be able to employ persuasion . . . on both sides of a question . . . [so] that, if another man argues unfairly, we on our part may be able to confute him" (1355a.30–35). Yet this quotation rings slightly off-key when the antecedent for *we* becomes *women* or *feminists*. Such a reading challenges the genderblindness of rhetorical theory, practice, and education. As such, it hits patriarchal nerves. Ong responds by arguing that traditional rhetoric could not survive coeducational classrooms; other theorists argue that it survives just fine and functions equally well for women as for men.

Feminist scholars have tried to interrupt this binary. In that spirit, perhaps Ong may be read differently, as discerning that the presence of women and feminists in the classroom has the potential to make genderblindness visible. Once visible, it may be put into words. Once put it into words, it may be made "real" within commonsense logic. Once made real, it and its intersections with other blindnesses presumed by patriarchal education may be called into question and resisted—again and again. Among the means of resistance are Woolf's, Daly's, and Rich's feminist theories of rhetoric. For they recognize, validate, and address Bathsheba's dilemma and, as such, possess potential for educating Bathsheba and everyone else in feminist literacies.

The possibilities of feminist literacies are Woolf's, Daly's, and Rich's contributions to rhetoric and composition studies. Despite recurring back-to-basics movements, we all know that teaching composition encompasses more than simply presenting rules for students to memorize and then magically translate onto paper. Teaching composition entails creating possibilities for students to see, to question, to shape, to rethink, to craft—all in hopes of continually making their ideas and feelings sensible to themselves and others. Teaching composition entails encouraging students to engage actively in their own reading, writing, speaking, listening, and thinking processes, that is, to become literate. When feminist literacies are one of its goals, teaching composition means all of the above, plus a commitment to foregrounding how gender and other differences complicate these processes. Woolf's, Daly's, and Rich's feminist theories of rhetoric help me articulate this commitment. They echo in my head when I design syllabi around two or three questions that will enable my students and me to entertain feminist questions; when I plan reading and writing assignments that ask students to generate their own questions and their own forms for pursuing these questions; when I design collaborative activities that allow students to design questions that drive class discussions; and when I evaluate students' writings based on criteria that we have negotiated at all stages of the writing process—from assignment, to peer review, to evaluation.

The feminist literacies fostered inside composition classrooms should also inform students' lives outside the classroom. In this sense, my concerns for students echo Woolf's, Daly's, and Rich's concerns for women: I want students to leave my classes with a respect for language, especially the ways in which gender and other differences construct, and are constructed by, language; with a more attuned ear for language; with a sharper eye for language; with a more sensitive feel for language; with a respect for others and their languages; with a recognition that the brain is only one factor in generating knowledge and truths; and with a realization that education is more insight than intellect, more achieved than received. And, yes, I would like them to love Virginia Woolf, Mary Daly, and Adrienne Rich as much as I do. But I try not to be too pushy. For the one truth that has remained constant for me pedagogically is: forcing students to talk about feminisms as given truths or forcing them adopt a feminist perspective is counter-productive. Only by creating spaces in which they could question my claims about gender and other differences—and question my claims in terms of their own issues—have we ever generated *committed* readings, writings, and discussions about feminist issues. Yet even when such readings, writings, and discussions emerge, I never forget a corollary truth: whatever my intentions, my status as "teacher" no doubt precludes complete honesty by certain students.

For me, complicating my own truths and questions with the pedagogical possibilities of Woolf's, Daly's, and Rich's Anglo-American feminist theories of rhetoric is just one step toward articulating a feminist composition pedagogy. Such a move may prepare me to walk into a writing classroom, but what happens next depends upon the particular mix of students I face. If I want them to move beyond savvily asking me, "But what do *you* want me to do?" I need to respect them enough to ask what they expect of the class, what they expect of themselves, and what they expect of me; then I need to put their expectations into play with my own assumptions and actions. When gender and other differences are respected, such non-Socratic dialogues[24] can model a feminist pedagogy in which students and teachers may educate themselves and each other by asking: what is (im)possible to be questioned, who gets to frame the questions, and who gets to respond? In the process of questioning Bathsheba's dilemma, students and teachers may discover that their purpose is not so much to find "the answer" as to see where their questions may lead. My hope is that students and teachers may also discover that their questions may lead not to the defensiveness of denial, not to the paralysis of pluralism, but to the politics of always evolving locations. From such committed positions within ever emerging fields of difference(s), we can argue actions and attitudes into, and out of, existence. One such action, one such attitude is recognizing, validating, and addressing Bathsheba's dilemma.

Notes
Works Cited
Index

Notes

1. Bathsheba's Dilemma

1. Women's speech has traditionally been stereotyped as "polite, emotional, enthusiastic, gossipy, talkative, uncertain, dull, and chatty" while men's speech has been described as "capable, direct, rational, illustrating a sense of humor, unfeeling, strong (in tone and word choice), and blunt" (Kramarae 58). Scholars in communication studies (e.g., Karlyn Kohrs Campbell, Theodora Martin) and socio-linguistic studies (e.g., Robin Lakoff, Cate Poynton, Julia Penelope, Dale Spender) have sought to disprove these stereotypes. Lakoff researched differences in how women use langauge and how women are portrayed through language. She discovered that women use more specific names for colors, more adjectives and tag questions, and more courteous, meaningless particles ("oh dear" as opposed to "shit") than men do; that more words referring to women have derogatory connotations than do words referring to men; and that more contextualized linguistic study is needed ("Language" 60–67). Lakoff's importance lies in the dialogues she has initiated. Valian questions Lakoff's method ("Is women's speech inferior to men's?"), her linguistic definitions ("Do men and women really speak a different language?"), and her politics ("What is the relationship between linguistics and social change?") (68). Fortunata calls for more emphasis on social context than Lakoff provides (82). Kuykendall argues that only by examining the social context of a remark can we accurately reflect on gender biases and assumptions and that such reflection can influence social change (144). Multicultural scholars expose the "whiteness" of the above claims. Silvera and Gupta argue that women of color have been made invisible or forced into the margins by white feminists who attempt to initiate feminist reform by colonizing, rather than by understanding local politics and procedures. Albrecht and Brewer expose conflicting strategies for building and maintaining alliances across cultures and offer strategies for negotiating these differences in the workplace, political organizations, neighborhoods, and homes.

Women's writing has suffered from the same "commonsense" stereotypes as women's speech. Anglo-American literary theorists have constructed three positions from which to refute such stereotyping. First, Joyce Carol Oates calls for an individual, sexless writing in which writers transcend political aims while being simultaneously grounded in them. Second, Ellen Moers argues that

175

differences exist between the way men and women write, that is, differences in the images that historical situations afford women and men; but Moers's interchangeable use of *male* and *female* with *masculine* and *feminine* hints at a reductive, essentialist concept of biological difference, and her focus on *female* and *male* posits monolithic concepts that erase difference(s) between and among individuals, a move that parallels what Gates calls the trap of authenticity (" 'Authenticity' " 26). And, third, Mary Ellmann defines masculine and feminine writing, with the former asserting an authority missing in the latter, a position that privileges cultural influence more than biology and allows differences in women's writing to be perceived as empowering, not divisive (M. Eagleton 200–207). For other conceptual schemas of Anglo-American women writing, see Showalter, *Sister's Choice*; and Jacobus.

Women's writing as theorized in French feminist theories implies a closer tie between women's speech and women's writing than appears within the Anglo-American tradition. Informed by poststructuralist and psychoanalytic theories of language, writers such as Monique Wittig, Hélène Cixous, and Luce Irigaray construct feminine styles of writing that have been described as "open, nonlinear, unfinished, fluid, exploded, fragmented, polysemic, attempting to 'speak the body,' i.e., the unconscious, involving silence, incorporating the simultaneity of life as opposed to or clearly different from logical, nonambiguous, so-called 'transparent' or functional langauge" (Makward 96); and as having the qualities of "mutuality, porousness, intimacy, recontacting a both/and, using both sides of the brain, nonhierarchic, anti- or multi-climactic, wholistic, lacking distance . . . perhaps didactic" (DuPlessis 282). Ironically, the argument for *l'écriture féminine* unfolds via traditional deductive logic: since Western structures innately represent "the masculine" and repress "the feminine," constructing a feminine style becomes essential if women are to write themselves into being. The accompanying call to "write the body" is a call to decenter phallocentrism and logocentrism from its privileged "head" position and to textually construct the rhythms of a woman's body.

African American feminist theories have theorized women's writing differently. Morrison claims that real differences in women's writing comes not between men and women but between African American and Anglo-American women ("Interview" 117–131). hooks maintains that white women may need to escape silence by coming to voice but that black women already have voices, which only need to find cultural spaces in which to be valued ("Talking Back" 6–7). Morrison also claims that "struggling with and through a language that can powerfully evoke and enforce hidden signs of racial superiority, cultural hegemony, and dismissive 'othering' of people and langauge" forces her to consider "the pervasive use of black images and people in expressive prose"; "the shorthand, the taken-for-granted assumptions that lie in their usage"; and "the sources of these images and the effect they have on the literary imagination and its product" (*Playing* x). Lorde discusses connections between language, feeling, and freedom: "The white fathers told us: I think, therefore I am. The Black mother within each of us—the poet—whispers in our dreams: I feel, therefore I can be free. Poetry coins the language to express and charter this revolutionary demand, the implementation of that freedom" ("Poetry" 38).

2. My use of the term *symbolic* derives from Kristeva's division of human experience into the semiotic and symbolic realms (*Revolution*). Her terms, in turn, echo Lacan's division of human existence into three orders: the real (the anatomical order that cannot be known, which exists before the ego and the formation of the drives); the *imaginary* (the order where a child totally identifies with the world and cannot distinguish a space between self and others, particularly the Mother; Kristeva renames this order the semiotic); and the *symbolic* (the order of language and loss of identity in which the lack of the latter triggers continual repressions of this lack and, hence, gives rise to the unconscious and the power of the phallus). My subsequent discussions of the symbolic also assume a familiarity with other terms in French discourse theories: for example, Derrida's *logocentrism*, which privileges the Logos as a metaphysical presence; Lacan's *phallocentrism*, which privileges the phallus as the source/position of power; and Cixous's combination of the two terms into *phallogocentrism* (Moi 105).

3. Cameron argues that debates about Bathsheba's dilemma have actually positioned themselves into two widely defined moves: criticism and critique (*Feminist Critique* 2–3). The first move assumes that to change the world, we must change the world's words: language use must be revised if women are to construct a space in which to express themselves. Changing the generic *he*, the animal nicknames associated with women, the tentative use of tag questions, the words and definitions in dictionaries, and so on, are commonly proposed strategies within this school of thought. The main problem with this *catch-22* is its frequent refusal to critique the function and structure of language. Often disassociating language and thought, theories within this position imply a contradictory proposition: meanings are socially constructed through language; therefore, language must be changed if societal change is to occur. The enormous gap hidden by the previous semicolon is the problem of location of agency. Where do individual subjects stand to break their socialization, to discern problems with their language use, and to change their own usage? Inside language? Outside language? Somewhere else? Notice that the function of

language changes at different points of this inquiry. When locating problems, these theories posit language as an all-powerful socializing function. But when addressing problems, these theories reduce language to a positivistic tool-like object that individual subjects may employ to effect conscious language change—a necessary but limited conclusion.

Cameron's second move, critique, assumes that to change the world and Woman's/women's positions within it, feminists must rethink Woman's/women's relation to language and to the dominant discursive practices. Feminists must "examine the conditions upon which [Bathsheba's dilemma] exists, calling into question the assumptions it is based on" (*Feminist Critique* 2). Such a philosophical critique would call into question the truth conditions of cultural assumptions about gender, class, sex roles, and so on, thus enabling feminists to describe, demystify, and revise their multiple cultural locations. This position also assumes a more consistent function of language than the first. At the interwoven points of locating and addressing problems, language embodies a powerful socializing function within which exist spaces for the construction of agency. Such a critique heralds a more conscious use of language while simultaneously acknowledging its partial function, its limitations.

4. Different disciplinary approaches to Bathsheba's dilemma are as follows. Sociolinguist Lakoff proclaims that women and men speak separate languages, with women being discriminated against in the ways they are taught to use language and the way language uses them ("Language"). Literary theorist Showalter claims that women are simply silenced, denied access to the dominant language that could potentially empower them ("Feminist Criticism"). Psychoanalytic and literary theorist Cixous writes that *féminine jouissance* is so repressed in phallogocentric language that women (and those men who are unafraid of the feminine) must construct their own *écriture féminine*, writing in white ink to invoke the absent feminine and thus materialize their bodies and their voices ("Laugh of the Medusa"). Linguist and psychoanalytic theorist Kristeva argues that women are born into the Symbolic with desires and language positions that differ from men's ("Women's Time"). African American feminist theorists Childers and hooks assert that race is a silenced discourse for white feminists ("Conversation"); furthermore, hooks claims that the internalized racism and sexism of academic rhetoric terrorizes black women ("Black and Female"). Political scientist Hawkesworth classifies four separate but progressive stages of feminist consciousness: the rhetorics of oppression, reason, difference, and vision. And speech communication theorist K. K. Campbell claims that nineteenth-century women orators developed a gender-related feminine style, based on the crafts of motherhood and housewifery,

with which any woman in a powerless situation may empower herself (*Man Cannot Speak*).

5. For feminist challenges to literary traditions, see Gilbert and Gubar; and Showalter, *Literature*. For feminist challenges to historical traditions, see Lerner; Anderson and Zinsser; and Bridenthal, Koonz, and Stuart. For feminist challenges to philosophical traditions, see Nye; and Waithe. Bizzell posits a slightly different research agenda for feminist challenges to the rhetorical traditions: (1) read traditional rhetorical theories as a resisting reader; (2) recover women who have written about rhetoric; and (3) include women who have not necessarily focused on rhetoric but whose work might reconceptualize rhetorical studies (51).

6. Both stances have precedents in feminist literary studies. In the late sixties and early seventies, literary texts were reread to expose patriarchal prejudices (Millett) and to foreground "images of women" (Cornillion). In the midseventies, women's texts were read and constructed into a separate tradition of women's literature (Showalter, "Feminist Criticism" 247–50); such a move assumes that focusing on men's texts denigrated the importance of women's texts, validating the latter only in terms of the former. Today, men's and women's literary texts are once again being read together.

7. To avoid repeating the awkward phrase, "women and/or feminists," I will simply use "feminist" because it implies an ideological stance that both includes women and challenges the dominant logic and rhetoric.

8. Cixous and Clément debate whether or not master discourse (one of Lacan's four-part classification of discourse) may be revised, with Clément arguing that the master discourse is a necessary means for women to attain power, while Cixous argues for a new definition of power achieved via *lécriture féminine*. Bauer argues that the Bakhtinian concept of carnival provides the means for disrupting the master discourse (*Feminist Dialogics*). And Yaeger argues that a search for women's joy and delirium will rupture, and expose ruptures in, the master discourse.

9. Although this study foregrounds feminist theories of rhetoric, other studies might just as importantly focus on women's rhetoric(s), theories of women's rhetoric(s), or women's theories of rhetoric. They might examine feminine rhetoric(s), theories of feminine rhetoric(s), or feminine theories of rhetoric. They might study feminist rhetoric(s) or even theories of feminist rhetoric(s). As becomes readily apparent, a wealth of research possibilities emerges (Jarratt, "Special Issue"). What also becomes readily apparent is that these possibilities may occupy different spaces in relation to one another and in relation to received traditions of rhetorical theories. For example, a woman's theory of rhetoric may or may not be considered feminist; conversely, a feminist the-

ory of rhetoric may or may not be written by a woman. These multiple possibilities create the demand for certain defining moves.

10. Much debate has arisen recently about the need for/problem of separating sex and gender. See Gallop 35–37; Moi 12–15; and Showalter, "Introduction."

11. For a historical classification of *feminist*, see Banks, who divides feminism into four movements: the Early Years, 1840–1870 (Protestant feminism, equal rights feminism, and socialist feminism); the Golden Years, 1870–1920 (moral reform feminism, female superiority feminism, and suffragist feminism); the Intermission, 1920–1960; and the Modern Movement, 1960 to the present (liberal feminism and radical feminism).

12. When discussing cross-cultural research possibilities, questions of appropriation, colonization, and tokenism often emerge. For example, see Lee; and hooks, *Talking Back*. Both argue that identity politics should neither trap us nor be ignored. Lee argues that identity politics are not biologically determined but culturally determined, that is, that at this particular cultural moment a black director needed to make *Malcolm X* because a white director could not have appreciated the subtleties of African American culture. hooks argues that "[o]ften a scholar with the same intellectual qualifications as his or her white colleague, who also has the authority of lived experience, is in the best possible position to share information about that group" and that "problems arise not when white women choose to write about the experiences of nonwhite people, but when such material is presented as 'authoritative' " (44, 48). For an excellent exploration of appropriation and race, see Anzaldua.

13. For a consideration of Burke and poststructuralist language assumptions, see Nelson, "Writing."

14. Not all feminist critics would agree. See Stimpson, Introduction; and Walker 552–53, 568–69.

15. Barthes argues that only two predominant images of style, or language function, have actually been theorized: the apricot and the onion ("Style and Its Image" 99). Aligning himself with the latter image, Barthes posits a "working hypothesis" of language function as "*transformations*, derived either from collective formulas (of unrecoverable origin, literary or preliterary) or, by metaphoric interplay, from idiolectal forms . . . essentially a memory" (98). The text-as-apricot image represents a form/content dichotomy, wherein content is perceived as a closed system of meaning (the pit) while form is perceived as interchangeable outward appearances (the skin) that only decorates meaning. The text-as-onion image represents a process by which the signified instantaneously emerges as another signifier as one layer of the text gives way to the next, with the reader never uncovering, or even conceiving of or searching for, a fixed core of meaning. In both cases, Barthes argues

the following: "[W]hat should govern the stylistic task is the search for models, for patterns: sentential structures, syntagmatic cliches, divisions and clausulae of sentences; and what should animate this task is the conviction that style is essentially a citational procedure, a body of formulas, a memory . . . , an inheritance based on culture and not on expressivity. . . . [T]hese models are only the depositories of culture (even if they seem very old); they are repetitions, not foundations; citations, not expressions; stereotypes, not archetypes" (99).

16. Lakoff stipulates certain language functions that belong to women and men and that result in "linguistic imbalances" (*Language and Woman's Place* 43; qtd. in Ryder 531): women, for example, have more names for colors than men; men, on the other hand, use more expletives publicly. Cixous's medusa recovers the monster/hysteric position for women, positing it as a position of strength. For Ryder, this binary traps women into adopting social roles that are totally determined by language (e.g., Lakoff) or having to resort to madness (e.g., Cixous). For an in-depth discussion of this binary, see Ryder 530–31. For a history of this debate, see A. O. Hill.

17. Stimpson claims that language must function as a "plea" against violence, cruelty, afflictions, and despair, and as a "plea, too, for such pleas to mean enough to work, here, in the space of this world" (*Meanings* xx).

18. For another account of this binary division of the textual and the cultural, see Watts. Specifically, Watts argues that the "linguistic left" has "promoted a spurious view of politics and power" grounded in poststructuralist theories of language, that its political agenda is "narrowly elitist and overly intellectual," and that it "unintentionally reinforces many features of the modern state that it purports to abhor."

19. This move presumes a definition of ideology similar to the one posited by Cixous and Clément: "For me ideology is a kind of vast membrane enveloping everything. We have to know that this skin exists even if it encloses us like a net or like closed eyelids. We have to know that, to change the world, we must constantly try to scratch and tear it. We can never rip the whole thing off, but we must never let it stick or stop being suspicious of it" (145).

20. To investigate different methods of rhetorical historiography, see Kennedy; Fogarty; Corbett; Burke, *Rhetoric of Motives*; Richards; Todorov; Covino, *Wondering*; Bizzell and Herzberg; and Lunsford.

21. Natanson posits a multilayered, progressively abstract definition when he argues that rhetoric may refer to all of the following: (1) rhetorical intention in speech or writing, (2) the technique of persuasion, or methodology, (3) the general rationale of persuasion, or theory, and (4) the philosophy of rhetoric, or the cri-

tique of theory (379). Bizzell and Herzberg follow suit, situating rhetoric as "the practice of orator; the study of the strategies of effective oratory; the study of the persuasive effects of language; the study of the relation between language and knowledge; the classification and use of tropes; and, of course, the use of empty promises and half-truths as a form of propaganda" (1).

22. Aristotle's *Prior Analytics* posits three types of syllogisms: scientific, dialectic, and rhetorical (the enthymeme). The first assumes true premises and conclusions; the second assumes probable premises and true conclusions; the third assumes probable premises and conclusions. His *Rhetoric* discusses the enthymeme and cites two types—the demonstrative enthymeme, which proves a proposition, and the refutative enthymeme, which disproves one (bk. 2, ch. 22); he also cites the four types of facts upon which an enthymeme may be based—probabilities, examples, infallible signs, fallible signs (bk. 2, ch. 25).

23. See, for example, Deuteronomy 17:6 and Numbers 30:35. Both citations refer specifically to the death penalty. But the importance of witnesses (read "men") is stressed throughout Exodus, Leviticus, Numbers, and Deuteronomy. Interestingly, an Old Testament sexual harassment case that invalidates the testimony of two men while simultaneously validating one woman's virtue is relegated to the Apocrypha as the Book of Daniel and Susannah.

24. Interrogations of presence have attempted to erase traces of authorial agency in the making of meaning and, instead, have foregrounded the functions of readers, institutional structures, and language. See Barthes, "Death of the Author"; Foucault; and Derrida, "Structure, Sign, and Play."

25. Partly because of the title of his article "The Death of the Author," Barthes is often misread as eliminating any type of agency. Because he asserts that the death of the author allows the birth of the reader, a type of readerly agency emerges. While the writer is a reader of the world, she or he cannot control the meanings in the texts that are constructed for other readers.

26. A special edition of *Feminist Studies* (Spring 1988) focuses on the intersections of poststructuralism and feminism. Poststructuralist critics Rabine, Scott, and Poovey (re)consider the concept of agency as a way of empowering real-life speaking/writing women, but their concepts of agency are not monolithic presences or static identities but rather are multidimensional processes; that is, these scholars explore the interwoven agencies of reader, text, author, cultural institutions, language, and so on. Also see Weedon; and Walker.

27. For another inquiry into the intersections of rhetoric and composition and critical theory in terms of agency, see Miller.

28. For other critiques of Bitzer's rhetorical situation, see Larson; Wilkerson; Pomeroy; Patton; Kaufer; and Vatz. For a different per-

spective of rhetorical situation, see Black. Black's methodology, which may be described as the inverse of Bitzer's, consists of "rhetorical strategies, rhetorical situations, and audience effects," all of which work to comprise a complex web of events that Black calls "rhetorical transaction" (134). Black's concept of rhetorical transaction, which subsumes situation, implies that an act can be separate from and greater than the situation from which it arose.

29. For more information on feminist methods of historiography, see Abel, *Coming to Terms*; Scott, "Gender"; Smith-Rosenberg; Harstock, *Money*; and Newton and Rosenfelt.

30. Aristotle's Ideal States are discussed in his *Politics*, book 2, which cites theoretical examples from Plato's *Republic*, Plato's *Laws*, Phaleas of Chalcedon, and Hippodamus of Miletus, as well as practical examples of Sparta, Crete, and Carthage.

31. The institutionalization of rhetorical pedagogy is discussed in Secor and Charney; and Murphy.

32. For an example, see Moi, 19–173.

33. Nye details the attack against perceived essentialism in Anglo-American radical feminisms:

> Radical feminists, having theorized a world of warring wills, cannot so easily escape their own theory. . . .
> . . . Early radical feminists catalogued in detail the socialization of women, but socialization did not excuse women's capitulation. Socialization implies an intact female self which may be influenced but which can also refuse to accept the rewards of collaboration and courageously accept the pain of non-conformity. Gender identity and the choice of sexual object, however, may not be accessible to conscious change. . . .
> Nor is there any positive prognosis in radical feminist theory for a woman's refusal to be a fellow traveller. . . . In each case, feminist theory and practice continues to operate within the space of Satrean metaphysics . . . [that] is inadequate to feminist practice. (102)

See also, Judith Butler, 1–34, who echoes this problem. Conversely, hooks discusses how such dismissals of essentialism also include dismissals of identity politics. She calls for the recovery of an identity politics that is not static and not solely a concern of Anglo-American feminists: "We return to 'identity' and 'culture' for relocation, linked to political practice—identity that is not informed by a narrow cultural nationalism masking continued fascination with the power of the white hegemonic other. Instead identity is evoked as a stage in a process wherein one constructs radical black subjectivity. . . . [I]t is crucial to radically revise notions of identity politics, to explore marginal locations as spaces where we can best become whatever we want to be while remaining committed to liberatory black liberation struggle" ("Radical Black Subjectivity" 20). Likewise, Fuss asks us to reconsider essentialism, not as the fixed binary opposite to difference but as a philosophical construct in flux. To do so, she claims, "The question we should be asking is not 'is this text essentialist (and therefore "bad")?' but rather, 'if this text is essentialist, *what motivates its deployment?* How does the sign "essence" circulate in various contemporary critical debates? Where, how, and why is it invoked? What are its political and textual effects?' " (xi). Similarly, Daly posits an essentialism in flux, which she calls "Real Presence" or Realizing the Presence of our past and future Selves; see *Pure Lust* 148.

34. The perceived male/female separatism is most frequently associated with Rich's and Daly's texts. While their separatist moments cannot be denied, such a male-centered gaze too easily dismisses the importance of these feminist theories and erases the fact that a woman's wanting to focus on women and fight patriarchy is not synonymous with androcide.

A more insidious separatism is charged against Anglo-American feminists by feminists of color. Silvera and Gupta claim: "So often we hear women's publications, presses, organizations excuse all white publications and groups with the cry that they cannot 'find' a woman of colour. We were never lost" (6). Poet Dionne Brand claims: "[white feminists] like us to join with them and struggle with them—but just as a symbol" (Silvera and Gupta 12). And Prabha Khosla claims: "[The concept of revolution is] where the white women's movement gets its role models—the women with guns, the women fighting are Vietnamese, Nicaraguan, Chinese women, not lily-white women. Yet nobody has said point blank, 'Look who our heroes are' " (Silvera and Gupta 27). Michelle Wallace argues that white feminists sometimes use African American culture as "the starting point for white self-criticism," or according to bell hooks, "as though [African American culture] exists solely to suggest new aesthetic and political directions white folks might move in" (qtd. in hooks, "Radical Black Subjectivity" 21).

35. de Lauretis rejects the idea that a missing premise of innate female essence must necessarily be supplied in radical feminist theories: "Why [supply the premise] at all? What is the purpose, or the gain, of supplying a missing premise . . . in order to construct a . . . feminism which thus becomes available to charges . . . based on the very premise that had to be supplied?" (264).

36. In this sense, ideology becomes more than a set of doctrines. It becomes "the ways in which what we say and believe connects with the power-structure and power-relations of the society we live in . . . the modes of feeling, valuing, perceiving, and believing

which have some kind of relation to the maintenance and reproduction of social power" (T. Eagleton 14–15). This definition may be expanded for feminism by asserting that "[o]nly a concept of ideology as a *contradictory* construct, marked by gaps, slides, and inconsistencies, would enable feminism to explain how even the severest ideological pressures will generate their own lacunae" (Moi 26). Within this theory of ideology, the cultural and the textual are interwoven. For ideological beliefs are not only manifested in (un)stated cultural behaviors but are also "translated into literary forms and conventions that at once encode and perpetuate those values" (Boone). Interestingly, Burke proposed a similar relationship between ideology and textuality in his 1935 address, "Revolutionary Symbolism in America"; drawing heavily from Burke's address, Lentricchia claims that "the substance, the very ontology of ideology . . . in a broad but fundamental sense is revealed to us *textually* and must be grasped (read) and attacked (reread and rewritten) in that dimension" (24). Only then will cultural change become possible.

2. Minting the Fourth Guinea

1. Last minted in 1813 and worth approximately 21 shillings, guineas are still used to quote prices of luxury items in Britain.
2. For accusations of class naïveté in *Three Guineas*, see Showalter, *Literature* 294–95; and Leavis. Conversely, for celebrations of feminist subversions in *Three Guineas*, see Moi 14; Caughie, *Woolf and Postmodernism* 113–43; and Benstock 123–62.
3. Woolf's knowledge of rhetoric may have been largely Platonic. We know Woolf had read Plato by 1900, for in that year she embarrassed her half brother George Duckworth and scandalized the Dowager Countess of Carnavon and her sister Mrs. Popham by discussing a risque passage from Plato (Bell 1.77). Other notes in Bell's biography of his aunt indicate that Woolf was reading Plato in 1908 and again during the years 1923–25 (1.139, 2.105). Citations in her notebook indicate that she read the *Symposium* in July 1908 and the *Phaedrus* in May 1909 (Silver 168, 169).
4. For a survey of Woolf's essays about women and writing, see Barrett 1–35.
5. The conference was held at Lincoln University, a traditionally black college, in Jefferson City, Missouri, in June 1993, under the direction of Jane Lilienfeld and the Virginia Woolf Society.
6. Woolf describes her successful "androgynous" writer as follows: "she wrote as a woman, so that her pages were full of that curious sexual quality which comes only when sex is unconscious of itself" (*Room* 93). For differing interpretations of this concept, see

Marcus, *Languages of Patriarchy* 136–62; Minow-Pinkney 158–59, 184–86, 189–90; Transue 2–9, 77; and Jones.

7. For other readings of Woolf and rhetoric, see Moi 1–18; Furman 45–54; and Ratcliffe 401–5.

8. For a survey of contemporary linguistic attempts to reconceptualize stylistics from a feminist perspective, see Ryder.

9. This third strategy echoes K. K. Campbell's call for a feminist critique of discourse that will challenge our "fundamental assumptions" about rhetoric by focusing on women's "highly inventive, developing strategies that go far beyond argument as traditionally understood" ("Sound of Women's Voices" 214, 213).

10. For a discussion of how women have found pleasure, and emancipation, through language, see Yaeger.

11. Woolf specifically cites an example: a moment shortly after her mother died when she lay on the grass at Kensington Garden reading poetry ("Sketch of the Past" 93).

12. For an extended discussion of ellipses in *Three Guineas*, see Benstock 123–62.

13. For discussions of naming, see Cameron, *Feminist Critique* 99–198.

14. For linguistic debates about the use of "Miss," Mrs." and "Ms.," see Levin; Purdy; and Soble.

15. Woolf discusses the intertextuality of her own work in her diaries: "Anyhow thats the end of six years floundering, striving, much agony, some ecstasy: lumping the Years and 3Gs together as one book—as indeed they are" (*Diary* 5: 148).

16. This anticipation of danger is common to children from dysfunctional families; in Virginia Woolf's case, she and her sister Vanessa were sexually abused by their stepbrother: "Yes, the old ladies of Kensington and Belgravia never knew that George Duckworth was not only father and mother, brother and sister to those poor Stephen girls; he was their lover also" ("22 Hyde Park Gate" 155).

17. For a psychoanalytic discussion of Woolf's concept of author, see Ferrer 1–7. Also, in an unpublished essay, Embser argues that Woolf's concept of anger in *A Room of One's Own* expands the concept of anger in Aristotle's *Rhetoric*. When juxtaposed, these two definitions construct a space for women's and feminists' emotions, particularly anger, in argumentative theory.

18. The argument of *A Room of One's Own* parodies Plato's parody by unfolding as follows: the introduction defines the terms *women* and *fiction* (3–4); the narration of facts establishes the identity of the narrator, the purpose of the essay, and her experiences at Oxbridge and Fernham (5–24); the proof section investigates what men have written about women, what women have written about women, and what women like Mary Carmichael can hope to achieve with £500 and a room of their own (25–94); the refutation section opens with a digression (95–105) and then anticipates the concerns of the narrative audience (Fernham women stu-

dents who are present) and the authorial audience (educated men who are not) (106–10); finally, the peroration is a call to action for the young women to prepare the way for Judith Shakespeare (110–14).

19. For differing interpretations on Woolf's arrangement strategies, see Guiguet; Farrell; and E. C. Jones. Guiguet argues that "it would be vain to seek in this book for any strict method. It is rather a series of vignettes with commentary, illustrating her two chosen themes" (170); Farrell argues that Woolf employs a "male" method of formal rhetoric and a "female" method of indirection (919); Jones complicates Farrell's argument by dismissing the Jungian premises that border on biological determinism and by asserting that Woolf "creates . . . a form which is at once fragmented and unified . . . through two modes of discourse: . . . the 'story' . . . [and] the formal rhetorical argument" (229).

20. Irigaray also posits a type of imitation, mimeticism, that feminists may employ to disrupt the dominant ideology by mimicking male discourse; also, see Moi for a discussion of Irigaray's mimeticism, 139–43.

21. Although listing every important discussion of Woolf's style is impossible, I have found three extremely useful poststructuralist readings: "Introduction: Who's Afraid of Virginia Woolf? Feminist Readings of Woolf" (Moi); "Ellipses: Figuring Feminisms in Three Guineas" (Benstock); and, especially, "Narrative Structures and Strategies" and "Nonfictional Prose" (Caughie, *Woolf and Postmodernism*). Caughie's chapters acknowledge the popular novel/essay split in Woolf criticism, but her reading of Woolf's texts undermines this divide. For an extended discussion of the politics of Woolf's style in her novels, see Transue. Her "Works Cited" is valuable for scholarship before 1986.

22. Woolf makes this claim about audience in 1927 when preparing an Oxford lecture later published as "The Narrow Bridge of Art."

23. In *Gyn/Ecology*, Daly reveals how women have traditionally been socialized to serve as the voice of patriarchy; she cites examples such as mothers and grandmothers binding young girls' feet in China, holding them down for genital mutilation in Africa, and taking them to gynecologists for hysteria in nineteenth-century America (134–77, 223–92).

24. hooks comments on this Victorian game of manners that still thrives within academic feminisms: "I am startled by the dichotomy between the rhetoric of sisterhood and the vicious way nice, politically correct girls can deal with one another, do one another in, in ways far more brutal than I ever witnessed in shoot and cut black communities" ("Third World" 90).

25. For the definitive discussion of Woolf's (di)vision of art and politics, see Marcus, " 'No More Horses' "; see footnote twelve (286–87) for a summary of the 1938 reviews of *Three Guineas*, which

appeared in *Time and Tide*, *The Spectator*, *The New Statesman*, *Nation*, and *New Republic*. For other discussions of Woolf's (di)vision between art and politics, see Marcus, *Languages of Patriarchy* xi–xv; and *A Feminist Slant* 132–50; Ferrer 6–7; Barrett 20–24; and Minow-Pinkney 187–96.

26. Woolf makes a distinction between literature (horses) and propaganda (donkeys) in *Three Guineas*, labeling this text a donkey. Her lament that mixing the two might result in "no more horses" (170) inspired Marcus's article of the same name.

3. De/Mystifying HerSelf and HerWor(l)ds

1. For the source of Daly's thrice-born Athena concept, see Nicholson.
2. For Daly's autobiographical accounts of her evolving radical feminism, see the "Autobiographical Preface to the 1975 Edition," *Church* 5–14; the 1990 New Intergalactic Introduction, *Gyn/Ecology* xi–xliv; and, of course, her autobiography, *Outercourse*.
3. Daly claims that patriarchal scholarship is "writing that erases itself" and "even at its best, continues and participates in the Righteous Rites of female slaughter/erasure" (*Gyn/Ecology* 120). Also see 126, 133, 143–52, 170–77, 203–22, 288–92, 306–12.
4. Daly defines patriarchy as follows:

> n 1: a society manufactured and controlled by males: FATHERLAND; society in which every legitimated institution is entirely in the hands of males and a few selected henchwomen; society characterized by oppression, repression, depression, narcissism, cruelty, racism, classism, ageism, objectification, sadomasochism, necrophilia; joyless society, ruled by Godfather, Son, and Company; society fixed on proliferation, propagation, procreation, and bent on the destruction of all Life 2: the prevailing religion of the entire planet, whose essential message is necrophilia. (*Wickedary* 89)

5. Aristotle discusses his definitions of essence in the *Metaphysics* (1.7.315–21). For critiques of this position, see Fuss xi, 71–72.
6. See Locke, 1.27–29, who defines real (or Aristotelian) essentialism as assuming an irreducible, unchanging essence and nominal essentialism as assuming that essence is a linguistic construction. For an extended discussion of feminism and essentialism, see Fuss.
7. For discussions of why feminisms should not attempt to redefine essentialism, see Judith Butler vii; and de Lauretis 267.
8. Daly distinguishes between Be-ing and be-ing as follows: Be-ing is the "Ultimate/Intimate Reality, the constantly Unfolding Verb of Verbs which is intransitive, having no object that limits its dyna-

mism (*Wickedary* 64); be-ing is "actual participation in the Ultimate/Intimate Reality—Be-ing, the Verb" (65).

9. For an extended discussion of how rhetoric emerges at the intersection of myth, language, and ideology, see Burke, *Rhetoric of Motives* 101–10. This relationship is most evident, and applicable to Daly's project, in Burke's seventh definition of *ideology*: an "inverted genealogy of culture, that makes for 'illusion' and 'mystification' by treating ideas as primary where they should have been treated as *derivative*" (104).

10. Feminists have sometimes accused Daly of colonizing another culture's myths by viewing them from a Euro-American perspective. See Lorde, "Open Letter" 66–71.

11. To honor Daly's (theory of) language play, I use her spelling and punctuation when referring to her concepts. For example, I use the verb "dis-cover" purposely here to reflect Daly's meaning: "uncovering the Elemental Reality hidden by the hucksters, frauds, and framers of phallocracy; finding the treasures of women's Memory, Knowledge, History that have been buried by the grave diggers of patriarchal re-search" (*Wickedary* 118).

12. Influences on Daly's concept of metaphor include: Jaynes 48; Langer 14; Morton; Rich, *Dream*; Tillich 1.163; and the work of Julia Penelope (Stanley). See *Pure Lust* 25–30, 421).

13. Daly defines the term *metapatriarchal* as follows:

> [B]ecause the prefix *meta* has multiple meanings. It incorporates the idea of "postpatriarchal," for it means occurring later. It puts patriarchy in the past without denying that its walls/ruins and demons are still around. Since *meta* also means "situated behind," it suggests that the direction of the journey is into the Background. Another meaning of the prefix is "change in, transformation of." This, of course, suggests the transforming power of the journey. By this I do not mean that the women's movement "reforms" patriarchy, but that it transforms our Selves. Since *meta* means "beyond, transcending," it contains a built-in corrective toreductive notions of mere reformism. (*Gyn/Ecology* 7)

14. In *Pure Lust* Daly identifies deception as the Eighth Deadly Sin, that is, "the most crucial one, which the fathers, of course, omit" (x). The other seven are Professions (pride); Possession (avarice); Aggression (anger); Obsession (lust); Assimilation (gluttony); Elimination (envy); Fragmentation (sloth) (x). In the Medieval period a debate arose as to whether the deadly sins should number seven or eight; like Daly, Gregory the Great championed lying, or deceit, as the eighth sin (Bloomfield 60–67).

15. Daly defines "mind-bindings" as "layers of crippling patriarchal thought patterns comparable to the footbindings which mutilated

millions of Chinese women for over one thousand years: master-minded myths and ideologies meant to mummify the spirit and maim the brain" (*Wickedary* 211).

16. Daly defines "plastic passions" as "those blobs in inner space which preoccupy and paralyze their victims—predominantly women—draining our energies, perverting us from the pursuit of Pure Lust" (*Pure Lust* 200); she defines "potted passions" as "feelings that fragment and distort the psyche, masking Passion, making Pyrognostic Lust incomprehensible" (206).

17. See duBois 169–83, who also analyzes this phenomenon in her feminist critique of classical philosophy.

18. For a critique of Daly's method, see Nye, who argues that Daly's theory falls into the utopian trap of many Anglo-American radical feminisms because it assumes that something essentially female about women can be recovered and used to empower women (101). For other sides to this debate, see Spender 53–54, 165–71, 181–89, 228–29; and Penelope 35–38, 213, 218–23).

19. For an extended discussion of how Daly connects rhetoric and magic, see *Pure Lust* 79–123. Covino, *Magic* also explores the intersections of rhetoric and magic in Mary Daly's texts. For more on connections between rhetoric and magic, see Gorgias, who argues that two arts of witchcraft and magic are errors of the soul and deceptions of opinion; Burke, *Rhetoric of Motives* 40–42, 44; and *Rhetoric of Religion*; and Blankenship.

20. To unpack Daly's definition of *methodicide*, we need to examine the terms of her definition. *Nonquestions* are "genuinely Questing Questions; Canny Questions frequently raised by women and erased by men and their henchwomen in the elementary schools of snooldom," a *snool* being a "normal inhabitant of sadosociety, characterized by sadism and masochism combined" (*Wickedary* 87, 227). And *nondata* are "information that is disruptive and disturbing to pedants and therefore banned from the categories and classifications of academented re-search, theory, and method" (86). Also see *Beyond* 7–12 and *Gyn/Ecology* 23–24. The debate about feminism and its relation to methodology has haunted the contemporary feminist movement; see Harding, *Feminism and Method* 1–14.

21. Dr. Jones is Professor of Theology at Florida State University.

22. To demonstrate how her concept of Realizing reason differs from foreground constructions of realism, Daly compares her concept to Platonic realism, Aristotelian realism, and nominalism (*Pure Lust* 160–61). Drawing on a "medieval tradition of 'theological ethics,' " Daly also locates reason as one of the eight "quasi--integral" parts of prudence (265–74).

23. The following is Barbara's explanation for why she suddenly saw herself as a radical feminist:

I used to—when I'd go in the bookstore and I'd see books about radical feminism—I'd have this fear. And I'm a great reader, but oh I wasn't going to read that! And I always had this great fear that, oh, they would just be angry books. I don't know, I would have this awful fear. And then when Bonnie was reading stuff from *Gyn/Ecology* I thought, "God, why have I been so afraid of those books," . . . and if anything there's a connectedness. That *really* did help me, that really helped me because up until that point I felt like no other woman thought this way, that I was terribly radical and alone. (Mann xli)

24. Speaking in tongues, Daly argues, is evidence of psychological rebellion against strictures imposed by language (*Beyond* 166). For critical discussions of Daly's Feminist Naming, see Rich, "That Women Name Themselves" 10; and Reading.

25. The following are reviews that Daly predicts for her text: "I saw this coming in 1968," from a Conservative Catholic; "Despite her disclaimers, she still *belongs* to the Judeo-Christian tradition," from a Liberal Protestant Professor; and "She should join the Unitarian Universalists," from a Unitarian Universalist (*Church* 48).

26. For an opposing argument, see Fraser 93–100. In her critique of Kristeva's work on "avant-garde aesthetic production," Fraser argues that such language play, "irrespective of content," is indeed mere formalism (95).

27. For a discussion of the limits and possibilities of feminist naming, see Cameron, *Feminist Critique* 99–198.

28. For critiques of radical feminism and language theory as they apply to Daly, see Alcoff; Cameron, "Why Is Language" 12–20; Nye 95–103, 175, 178; Ruthven 36–50, 96; Weedon 6–7, 132–35.

29. Daly's manuever is reminiscent of Callicles' move in Plato's *Gorgias*. Callicles refuses to participate in (and thus repudiates) the dialectical method; as a result, Socrates is forced into a rhetorical monologue, the very type of discourse that he purportedly most mistrusts.

30. Like Burke, Daly is intrigued by how language functions at the level of the word and "the Word," what Burke in *Rhetoric of Religion* calls logology and Logology. What Daly foregrounds is the gendered function: "Such extensions/incarnations of the collectively supreme patriarchal Word (Lie) in secular as well as sacral society requires the discrediting of women's own words, although patriarchally instilled delusions will be accepted from the mouths of women after these have been tested and corroborated. This follows the tradition of Christian gospel: The words of the women who had 'seen' the risen Christ were at first discredited, but the

error of those who disbelieved the women was rectified when the reports were confirmed by male witnesses" (*Gyn/Ecology* 91).

4. Re-Visioning the Borderlands

1. Zimmerman notes in her review of *Blood, Bread, and Poetry* that Rich's second step of acknowledging particular locations "is particularly urgent because each of 'us' . . . places the I and the we at the center of a world-view, de-centering and marginalizing all other I's and we's" (5).
2. Rich has found many forums for her writings. In addition to her four anthologies of collected prose, Rich's essays have appeared in a diverse group of publications, such as *Freedomways, Signs, Women's Studies Quarterly, Boston Review, Massachusetts Review, College English, New York Review of Books, American Poetry Review, Chronicle of Higher Education*, and *Heresies: A Feminist Magazine of Art and Politics*.
3. Hereafter, prose will be cited by page numbers; poems, by line numbers.
4. Although Rich employs her father as a symbol of patriarchy in her prose and poems, she also argues that "I have to claim my father" if she is to move forward in her life and understand herself and her roots, particularly her Jewish roots ("Split at the Root" 100).
5. See Rich's first footnote in the foreword to *Blood* for more information about her antiseparatism; she is especially opposed to separatism if it is based on essential, biological differences (viii). Also see "Compulsory Heterosexuality" 72–74.
6. For arguments advocating separatism, see Valeska.
7. For different perspectives, see Hartman 11–29; and Rabine 11–28. The former posits a theory of agency; the latter calls it into question.
8. Harding discusses the absolutism/relativism dichotomy, exposing it as located within absolutist logic and arguing for a concept of different truths situated in a different logic ("Who Knows?" 111–12).
9. Scheman explores the importance of simultaneously theorizing the particular and the interconnectedness of particulars (184–86).
10. See Gough. In "Compulsory Heterosexuality," Rich argues that the eight characteristics which Gough claims enforce patriarchy also enforce heterosexuality within patriarchy: "men's ability to deny women sexuality or to force it upon them; to command or exploit their labor to control their produce; to control or rob them of their children; to confine them physically and prevent their movement; to use them as objects in male transactions; to cramp their creativeness; or to withhold from them large areas of society's knowledge and cultural attainments" (36).
11. Standpoint theory originated in Marx and Engels's, and eventually Lukacs's, concepts of a "proletarian standpoint." This theory as-

sumes that people are what they do, that is, produce, and that doing/producing from the standpoint of the proletariat (a class position) offers the most productive means for demystifying capitalistic societies and overturning their social inequities. See Marx and Engels. Rich analyzes the impossibilities of such marxist politics for feminists: "Much of what is narrowly termed 'politics' seems to rest on a longing for certainty even at the cost of honesty, for an analysis which, once given, need not be reexamined. Such is the deadendedness—for women—of Marxism in our time" ("Women and Honor" 193).

Feminist theorists have reconceptualized standpoint theory in terms of gender, refusing the marxist claim that "the woman question" will be taken care of once class equality is attained. As Harding describes it: "a feminist standpoint is not something anyone can have by claiming it, but an achievement. (A standpoint differs in this respect from a perspective.) To achieve a feminist standpoint one must engage in the intellectual and political struggle necessary to see nature and social life from the point of view of that disdained activity which produces women's social experiences instead of from the partial and perverse perspective available from the 'ruling gender' experience of men" ("Conclusion" 185). For another discussion of how standpoint theory evolved from marxist thought to feminist theory, see Harstock, "Feminist Standpoint" 159–64. Also see, Ardener; Collins; Harding, "Who Knows?" 103–7; Noddings; Showalter, "Feminist Criticism" 260–66; and Smith, "Women's Perspective" and *Everyday World*.

12. Rich positions women near edges or borders; see "On Edges," "Contradictions" 29, "Turning," and "For a Friend in Travail."
13. For an analysis of Rich's dream of a common language, see Hedley, 50–59.
14. bell hooks argues that African American women do not need to recover their voices; they already have them. What African American women need is a cultural space in which audiences will respect their voices; see "Talking Back" 6.
15. Rich examines her own family's silence about the "secret" of her father's Jewishness in "Split at the Root."
16. Rich claims that lying emerges through words, through bodies, and through silence ("Women and Honor" 186, 188). For more on the connection between lying and silence, see "When We Dead Awaken," "Women and Honor," "Anti-Feminist," and "Disloyal to Civilization."
17. Rich claims that women's ideas and work have "been made to seem sporadic, errant, orphaned of any tradition of its own"; she cites Virginia Woolf as an example, arguing that Woolf's socialism and feminism have been overshadowed by her Bloomsbury association (*On Lies* 111–12).
18. For a comparison of global and local locations, see Dupré.

19. For Rich's discussions of how Anglo-American feminisms have limited use for African American women, see "Disloyal to Civilization" and "Resisting."
20. Judith Butler argues that debates about radical feminisms too often center on unanswerable questions of "the *origin* and *cause*" of female essence rather than around critiques of female essence as the "*effect* of institutions, practices, and discourses" that write our cultures and ourselves; such debates emerge from a fear of indeterminancy (vii–viii).
21. Rich believes that disobedience forces us to critique our strategies of complicity and guilt. She wonders "if guilt, with its connotations of being emotionally overwhelmed and bullied, or paralyzed, is not more a form of defensive resentment or self-protection than an authentic response to the past and its warts" ("Disobedience" 82).
22. Rich argues that women should pursue two goals simultaneously: "You can question generalizations which are made from a white perspective as if they applied to all women. You can, at the same time, be searching for the patterns of history shared by women everywhere" ("Resisting" 154).
23. For further discussions of how language has the power to affect the personal and the cultural, see "Turning" 4.8–11; "Implosions" 4–5; and "Burning" 3.7–9.
24. For a discussion of how Rich's father and famous male poets affected her developing style as a poet, see "Split at the Root" 113; and "Blood" 170–175. Also see "Adrienne Rich" 342 in *Current Biography*.
25. Rich's claims about the intersections of poetry and politics are reminiscent of Burke's discussion of "the moral aspect of poetic meaning" (*Philosophy of Literary Form* 146–49) and of "rhetoric and poetics" (*Language as Symbolic Action* 295–302).
26. Rich credits Mary Daly with conceptualizing the image of new spaces on the boundaries of patriarchy in *Beyond God the Father*; see "When We Dead Awaken" 49.

5. Educating Bathsheba and Everyone Else

1. Woods argues that the body assumed by traditional rhetorical pedagogy is male (24).
2. For a reading of Hegel's master-slave dialectic that challenges humanistic readings, see Davis 33–45, 370. He argues that the "subtle ways in which either position [of domination or submission] can triumph make it impossible to identify these projects with gender or to target one project as the cause of our ills" (38).
3. See Derrida, *Spurs* 109–11, who sums up Nietzsche's position as follows: "man is master because he takes, but the woman is the master because she gives" (qtd. in Nye 223).

4. In response to these erasures, feminists such as Bauer and hooks attempt to break through this theoretical framework. Bauer claims that feminists need to assert a new mastery—"feminist and dialogic" rather than "monologic and authoritarian" ("The Other 'F' Word" 387); hooks claims that feminists need to construct oppositional classrooms in which students can come to voice even while feeling afraid and at risk ("Toward a Revolutionary" 53).
5. For a critique of Woolf's description of patriarchal education, see Meisenhelder 190–92.
6. Because many women's colleges were based on patriarchal models, including the premise that colleges must train women to earn livings, Woolf advised in *Three Guineas* that her solicited guinea be spent on petrol and that the following course of action be taken: "Take this guineas and with it burn the college to the ground. Set fire to the old hypocrisies. Let the light of the burning building scare the nightingales and incarnadine the willows. And let the daughters of educated men dance round the fire and heap armful upon armful of dead leaves upon the flames. And let their mothers lean from the upper windows and cry, 'Let it blaze! Let it blaze! For we have done with this "education"'" (36).
7. In *Gyn/Ecology*, Daly describes patriarchal scholarship as "'writing that erases itself'... [that] continues and participates in the Righteous Rites of female slaughter/erasure.... [W]hat we are confronted with is not exactly untruth but a partially suppressed truth, which becomes absorbed, belittled, and discarded in the reader's mind" (120).
8. Lather claims that traditional pedagogies are driven by the "Enlightenment equation of knowing, naming, and emancipation" in addition to the concept of presence; and she exposes the problems with these Enlightenment concepts (131). For a defense of these Enlightenment concepts, see Dillon 86.
9. The most noted leftist challenges to patriarchal pedagogy come from the critical pedagogies of Stanley Aronowitz, Henry Giroux, Paulo Freire, and Ira Shor. As defined by Aronowitz and Giroux, critical pedagogies demand and construct "transformative intellectuals" who can "emerge from and work with any number of groups, other than and including the working class, that advance emancipatory traditions and cultures within and without alternative public spheres" (*Education Still under Seige* 45); as such, critical pedagogies assume the "task of making the pedagogical more political and the political more pedagogical" (46). Giroux unpacks this claim even more:

> Radical education doesn't refer to a discipline or a body of knowledge. It suggests a particular kind of practice and a particular posture of questioning institutions and received assumptions. I would say in a general way that the basic prem-

ises of radical education grew out of the crisis in social theory. More specifically, we can distinguish three traits: radical
education is interdisciplinary in nature, it questions the fundamental categories of all disciplines, and it has a public mission
of making society more democratic. This last point is perhaps
the principal reason why radical education as a field is so exciting. We can take our ideas and apply them. (*Border Crossings*
10)

According to Freire, such education resides in particular pedagogies, not blanket methodologies: "any teacher who rigidly ad-
heres to the routines set forth in teaching manuals is exercising authority in a way that inhibits the freedom of students, the
freedom they need to exercise critical intelligence through which
they appropriate the subject matter" ("Letter" 214).

These marxist-based critiques of patriarchal pedagogy are also
self-reflective and self-critical. For example, Aronowitz and Giroux
argue that, at worst, critical pedagogy been reduced to an "emphasis on technique and procedure . . . , focusing almost exclusively on
issues of dialogue, process, and exchange" (*Postmodern Education*
117); however, they also argue that, at best, critical pedagogy is
"a form of engaged practice . . . [that] calls into question forms of
subordination that create inequities among different groups as they
live out their lives" (118). For additional definitions and discussions of critical pedagogy, see Aronowitz and Giroux, *Education
under Seige*; Giroux, *Border Crossings* and *Theory and Resistance*;
Freire, *Pedagogy of the Oppressed*; Paine; Shor and Freire; and
Shor, *Culture Wars*.

Feminists debate the effectiveness of critical pedagogies for feminist agendas. For example, Jarratt reads critical pedagogies as sophistic pedagogies and, thus, deems them useful to feminist
projects (*Sophists* 107–12), and Schneidewind joins Freire in rejecting the banking concept of education (179). On the other hand,
Luke and Gore argue that critical pedagogies are actually deeply
patriarchal, unmasking only structural differences of class within
traditional enlightenment ideals and giving only a brief nod to differences of gender and race (9). Luke and Gore, no doubt, base
this claim on the fact that, except for Giroux's *Border Crossings*,
which has a chapter entitled "Modernism, Postmodernism, and
Feminism," most critical pedagogy texts foreground social oppressions in general with only passing references to feminism or gender. This fact, however, does not invalidate critical pedagogies; it
simply leaves room for feminist theorists/teachers to fill the gaps
left open by these pedagogies. For arguments that demystify the
function of gender and pose alternative postcritical pedagogies, see
three particularly insightful articles: Orner; Ellsworth; and Lewis.

10. David Lusted's definition is employed by several feminist educators in Luke and Gore.
11. For an excellent bibliography of research studies about feminist pedagogy, see Luke. For a discussion of feminists' experiences in the classroom, see Eichhorn et al.
12. For a discussion of a more nurturing, less confrontational feminist pedagogy, see Frey.
13. For other definitions of feminist pedagogies, see Culley and Portuges; Guy-Sheftall 310; Henry; C. E. Hill; Hollis; Jarratt, *Sophists* 112–17; Ladson-Billings and Henry; Omolade; Osborn 258–59; Shrewsbury; Sills 30; and Weiler.
14. In "Teaching Language," Rich complicates this equation with class variables.
15. Many education studies have proved that women and men experience the same classroom differently. For example, Lavine cites Candace West and Don Zimmerman's conversational studies of same-sex and different-sex conversations to explain some of these differences (137–39), and Statham et al. study the role of gender in instruction, in students' in-class responses, in teacher evaluations, and so on.
16. Paine separates content and strategy approaches to pedagogy, and he critiques each one (561). Spivak, however, refutes this split and argues that "teaching is a question of strategy. That is perhaps the only place where we actually get any experience in strategy, although we talk a lot about it" (146).
17. My claim contradicts some other feminists claims: for example, Hollis bases her argument on the assumption that much composition theory is "*implicitly*" feminist (340).
18. West provides an excellent analysis of how these political positions obfuscate the real questions and problems in matters of race (11–20).
19. Ellsworth echoes this plea for empowerment, noting that critical educational "literature offers no sustained attempt to problematize [the professor/teacher's] stance and confront the likelihood that the professor brings to social movements (including critical pedagogy) interests of her or his own race, class, ethnicity, gender, and other positions. S/he does not play the role of disinterested mediator on the side of the oppressed group" (101).
20. For critiques of the term *empowerment*, see the following: Gore, who provides a history of the term's use and explores its dangers for feminist discourse; and Ellsworth, who argues that this term as well as the terms *student voice, dialogue*, and *critical* are actually "repressive myths that perpetuate relations to domination" (91).
21. Every graduate teaching assistant, instructor, and rhetoric and composition faculty member has felt this theory/pedagogy split, which perpetuates and results from the university class system in this

country. North identifies this split as the different values associated with theory and lore.

22. Cowell outlines just such a pedagogical strategy. To help students acknowledge their "distrust [of] words and themselves," she asks them to explore the "magic" of language in terms of " 'the semantic derogation of women' " (147).

23. For a discussion of women's silences and their pedagogical implications, see Annas.

24. In an unpublished essay, English argues convincingly for the need for non-Socratic dialogues.

Works Cited

Abel, Elizabeth, ed. *Coming to Terms: Feminism, Theory, Politics.* New York: Routledge, 1989.

————. "Matrilineage and the Racial 'Other': Woolf and Her Literary Daughters of the Second Wave." Third Annual Virginia Woolf Conference. Jefferson City, MO, 13 June 1993.

"Adrienne Rich." *Current Biography.* 1976: 342–45.

Albrect, Lisa and Rose Brewer, eds. *Bridges of Power: Women's Multicultural Alliances.* Philadelphia: New Society, 1990.

Alcoff, Linda. "Cultural Feminism versus Post-Structuralism: The Identity Crisis in Feminist Theory." *Feminist Theory in Practice and Process.* Ed. Micheline R. Malson et al. Chicago: U of Chicago P, 1989. 295–326.

Anderson, Bonnie and Judith Zinsser. *A History of Their Own.* 2 vols. New York: Harper, 1988.

Annas, Pamela J. "Silences: Feminist Language Research and the Teaching of Writing." Caywood and Overing 3–19.

Anzaldua, Gloria, ed. *Making Face, Making Soul = Haciendo Caras: Creative and Critical Perspectives by Women of Color.* San Francisco: Aunt Lute Foundation, 1990.

Ardener, Shirley, ed. *Perceiving Women.* New York: Halstead, 1978.

Aristotle. *Metaphysics, Books 1–9.* Trans. Hugh Tredennick. Cambridge: Harvard UP, 1947.

————. *Politics.* Trans. Ernest Barker. New York: Oxford UP, 1980.

————. *Prior Analytics.* Trans. Robin Smith. Indianapolis: Hackett, 1989.

————. *The Rhetoric and the Poetics of Aristotle.* Trans. Rhys Roberts. 1954. New York: Modern Library, 1984.

Aronowitz, Stanley and Henry Giroux. *Education under Siege.* South Hadley, MA: Bergin, 1985.

————. *Education Still under Seige.* 2d ed. Westport, CT: Bergin, 1993.

————. *Postmodern Education: Politics, Culture, and Social Criticism.* Minneapolis: U of Minnesota P, 1991.

Auden, W. H. "Foreword to *A Change of World.*" Rich, *Rich's Poetry* 125–27.

199

Augustine. *On Christian Doctrine*. Trans. D. W. Robertson. Library of Liberal Arts 80. New York: Bobbs, 1958.

Ballif, Michelle. "Re/Dressing Histories; or, On Re/Covering Figures Who Have Been Laid Bare by Our Gaze." *Rhetoric Society Quarterly* 22 (1992): 91–98.

Banks, Olive. *Faces of Feminism: A Study of Feminism as a Social Movement*. 2d ed. New York: Basil Blackwell, 1986.

Barrett, Michèle, ed. *Virginia Woolf: Women and Writing*. New York: Harcourt, 1979.

Barthes, Roland. "The Death of the Author." *Rustle of Language* 49–55.

———. "The Old Rhetoric: An Aide-Mémoire." *The Semiotic Challenge*. Trans. Richard Howard. New York: Hill and Wang, 1988. 11–94.

———. *The Rustle of Language*. Trans. Richard Howard. Berkeley: U of California P, 1986.

———. "Style and Its Image." *Rustle of Language* 90–99.

———. *S/Z*. Trans. Richard Miller. New York: Hill and Wang, 1974.

Bauer, Dale. *Feminist Dialogics*. Albany: SUNY P, 1988.

———. "The Other 'F' Word: The Feminist in the Classroom." *College English* 52 (1990): 385–96.

Beale, Walter. "Rhetoric in the Vortex of Cultural Studies." Keynote Address. Rhetoric Society of America Conference. Minneapolis, 21 May 1992.

Beja, Morris, ed. *Critical Essays on Virginia Woolf*. Boston: Hall, 1985.

Belenky, Mary Field, Blythe McVicker Clinchy, Nancy Rule Goldberger, and Jill Mattuck Tarule. *Women's Ways of Knowing*. New York: Basic Books, 1986.

Bell, Quentin. *Virginia Woolf: A Biography*. 2 vols. New York: Harcourt, 1972.

Belsey, Catherine. "Constructing the Subject: Deconstructing the Text." Newton and Rosenfelt 45–64.

Benstock, Shari. *Textualizing the Feminine: On the Limits of Genre*. Norman: U of Oklahoma P, 1991.

Biesecker, Barbara. "Coming to Terms with Recent Attempts to Write Women into the History of Rhetoric." *Philosophy and Rhetoric* 25 (1992): 140–61.

Bitzer, Lloyd. "The Rhetorical Situation." *Philosophy and Rhetoric* 1 (1968): 1–14.

Bizzell, Patricia. "Opportunities for Feminist Research in the History of Rhetoric." *Rhetoric Review* 2 (1992): 50–57.

Bizzell, Patricia and Bruce Herzberg, eds. *The Rhetorical Tradition: Readings from Classical Times to the Present*. Boston: Bedford Books-St. Martin's, 1990.

Black, Edwin. *Rhetorical Criticism: A Study in Method*. New York: MacMillan, 1965.

Blair, Hugh. *Lectures on Rhetoric and Belles Lettres*. Ed. Harold Harding. 2 vols. Carbondale: Southern Illinois UP, 1965.

Blankenship, Jane. " 'Magic' and 'Mystery' in the Works of Kenneth Burke." Simons and Melia 128–55.

Bloomfield, Morton. *The Seven Deadly Sins: An Introduction to the History of a Religious Concept, with Special References to Medieval English Literature*. East Lansing: Michigan State UP, 1952.

Boone, Joseph. "How Feminist Criticism Changes the Study of Literature." *Chronicle of Higher Education* 8 July 1987: 76.

Bridenthal, Renate, Claudia Koonz, and Susan Stuart, eds. *Becoming Visible: Women in European History*. 2d ed. Boston: Houghton, 1987.

Brodkey, Linda. "The Discourse of Difference and Consensus." *Academic Writing as Social Practice*. Philadelphia: Temple UP, 1987.

Burke, Kenneth. *Language as Symbolic Action*. Berkeley: U of California P, 1966.

———. *The Philosophy of Literary Form*. 3d ed. Berkeley: U of California P, 1973.

———. *A Rhetoric of Motives*. 1950. Berkeley: U of California P, 1969.

———. *A Rhetoric of Religion: Studies in Logology*. Berkeley: U of California P, 1970.

Butler, Johnnella E. "The Difficult Dialogue of Curriculum Transformation: Ethnic Studies and Women Studies." Butler and Walter 1–19.

Butler, Johnnella E. and John C. Walter. *Transforming the Curriculum: Ethnic Studies and Women's Studies*. Albany: SUNY P, 1991.

Butler, Judith. *Gender Trouble: Feminism and the Subversion of Identity*. New York: Routledge, 1990.

Cameron, Deborah, ed. *Feminism and Linguistic Theory*. New York: Macmillan, 1985.

———. *The Feminist Critique of Language*. New York: Routledge, 1990.

———. "Why Is Language a Feminist Issue?" *Feminist Critique* 1–30.

Campbell, George. *The Philosophy of Rhetoric*. Ed. Lloyd Bitzer. Carbondale: Southern Illinois UP, 1988.

Campbell, Karlyn Kohrs. *Man Cannot Speak for Her*. 2 vols. New York: Praeger, 1989.

————. "The Sound of Women Voices." *Quarterly Journal of Speech* 75 (1989): 212–20.

Cassiodorus Senator. *An Introduction to Divine and Human Readings*. Trans. Leslie W. Jones. Rpt. New York: Norton, 1969.

Caughie, Pamela. "Passing and Pedagogy." *College English* 54 (1992): 775–93.

————. *Virginia Woolf and Postmodernism: Literature in Quest and Question of Itself*. Urbana: U of Illinois P, 1991.

Caywood, Cynthia, and Gillian R. Overing, eds. *Teaching Writing: Pedagogy, Gender, and Equity*. Albany: SUNY P, 1987.

Cereta, Laura. *Laura Cereta, Quattrocentro Humanist*. Ed. Albert Rabil, Jr. Binghamton, New York: Center for Medieval and Early Renaissance Studies, 1981.

Childers, Mary, and bell hooks. "A Conversation about Race and Class." Hirsch and Fox Keller, 60–81.

Christian, Barbara. "Layered Rhythms: The Case of Toni Morrison and Virginia Woolf." Third Annual Virginia Woolf Conference. Jefferson City, MO, 12 June 1993.

Cicero. *De Oratore, Books 1 and 2*. Trans. E. W. Sutton and H. Rackham. 1942. Cambridge: Harvard UP, 1948.

————. *Topica*. Trans. H. M. Hubbell. Cambridge: Harvard UP, 1949.

Cixous, Hélène. "The Laugh of the Medusa." Trans. Keith Cohen and Paula Cohen. *Signs* 1 (1976): 875–93.

Cixous, Hélène, and Catherine Clément. "A Woman Mistress." *The Newly Born Woman*. Trans. Betsy Wing. 1975. Minneapolis: U of Minnesota P, 1986. 136–46.

Cliff, Michelle. "Virginia Woolf and the Imperial Gaze: A Glance Aslant." Third Annual Virginia Woolf Conference. Jefferson City, MO, 11 June 1993.

Collins, Patricia Hill. "Learning from the Outsider Within: The Sociological Significance of Black Feminist Thought." Hartman and Messer-Davidow 40–65.

Comfort, Juanita. "Scenes of Self-Authorization: A Black Graduate Student Writes Herself into the Profession." Workshop Presentation. Conference on College Composition and Communication. Nashville, 16 Mar. 1994.

Corbett, Edward P. J. *Classical Rhetoric for the Modern Student*. 3d ed. New York: Oxford UP, 1990.

Cornillon, Susan Koppelman, ed. *Images of Women in Fiction*. Bowling Green, OH: Bowling Green Popular UP, 1972.

Covino, William. *The Art of Wondering: A Revisionist Return to the History of Rhetoric*. Portsmouth, NH: Heinemann, 1988.

———. *Magic, Rhetoric, and Literacy: An Eccentric History of the Composing Process.* Albany: SUNY P, 1994.

Cowell, Pattie. "Valuing Language: Feminist Pedagogy in the Writing Classroom." Caywood and Overing 147–49.

Culley, Margo, and Catherine Portuges, eds. *Gendered Subjects: The Dynamics of Feminist Teaching.* Boston: Routledge, 1985.

Daly, Mary. *Beyond God the Father: Toward a Philosophy of Women's Liberation.* Boston: Beacon, 1973.

———. *The Church and the Second Sex.* 1968. Boston: Beacon, 1985.

———. *Gyn/Ecology: The Metaethics of Radical Feminism.* 1978. Boston: Beacon, 1990.

———. *Outercourse: The Be-Dazzling Voyage.* San Francisco: Harper, 1992.

———. *Pure Lust: Elemental Feminist Philosophy.* Boston: Beacon, 1984.

Daly, Mary, and Jane Caputi. *Websters' First New Intergalactic Wickedary of the English Language.* Boston: Beacon, 1987.

Davis, Walter. *Inwardness and Existence: Subjectivity in/and Hegel, Heidegger, Marx, and Freud.* Madison: U of Wisconsin P, 1989.

de Lauretis, Teresa. "Upping the Anti in Feminist Theory." Hirsch and Fox Keller 255–70.

de Pisan, Christine. *Treasure of the City of Ladies: Or the Book of Three Virtues.* Trans. Sarah Lawson. New York: Viking Penguin, 1985.

Derrida, Jacques. *Spurs: Nietzsche's Styles.* Trans. Barbara Harlow. Chicago: U of Chicago P, 1978.

———. "Structure, Sign, and Play in the Discourse of the Human Sciences." *Writing and Difference.* Trans. Alan Bass. Chicago: U of Chicago P, 1978. 278–94.

Dillon, George. "Argumentation and Critique: College Composition and Enlightenment Ideals." Gere 84–98.

duBois, Page. *Sowing the Body: Psychoanalysis and Ancient Representation of Women.* Chicago: U of Chicago P, 1988.

DuPlessis, Rachel Blau. "For the Etruscans." Showalter, *Criticism* 271–91.

Dupré, John. "Global versus Local Perspectives on Sexual Difference." Rhode 47–62.

Eagleton, Mary, ed. *Feminist Literary Theory.* New York: Basil Blackwell, 1986.

Eagleton, Terry. *Literary Theory: An Introduction.* Minneapolis: U of Minnesota P, 1983.

Eichhorn, Jill, et al. "A Symposium on Feminist Experience in the Composition Classroom." *CCC* 43 (1992): 297–322.

Ellman, Mary. *Thinking about Women*. New York: Harcourt, 1968.

Ellsworth, Elizabeth. "Why Doesn't this Feel Empowering? Working through the Repressive Myths of Critical Pedagogy." Luke and Gore 90–119.

Embser, Elvira. "The Attendent Sprite on Power: Reading Woolf to Reread Aristotle's Concept of Anger." Unpublished essay.

English, Todd. "When Rhetoricians Read Plato: *The Phaedrus* and the Dynamics of Seduction." Penn State Rhetoric Conference. State College, PA, 8 July 1992.

Farrell, Thomas. "The Female and Male Modes of Rhetoric." *College English* 40 (1979): 909–21.

Fell, Margaret. *Women's Speaking Justified*. Ed. David J. Latt. Los Angeles: William Andrews Clark Memorial Library, U of California, 1979.

Ferrer, Daniel. *Virginia Woolf and the Madness of Language*. Trans. Geoffrey Bennington and Rachel Bowlby. New York: Routledge, 1990.

Flynn, Elizabeth. "Composing as a Woman." *CCC* 39 (1988): 423–35.

Fogarty, Daniel. *Roots for a New Rhetoric*. New York: Russell, 1968.

Fortunata, Jacqueline. "Lakoff on Language and Women." Vetterling-Braggin 81–92.

Foucault, Michel. "What Is an Author?" Harai 141–60.

Frank, Francine, and Paula Treichler. *Language, Gender, and Professional Writing*. New York: Commission on the Status of Women in the Profession, MLA, 1989.

Fraser, Nancy. "The Uses and Abuses of French Discourse Theory for Feminist Politics." *Boundary2* 17 (1990): 82–101.

Freire, Paulo. "Letter to North-American Teachers." Shor, *Freire for the Classroom* 211–14.

———. *Pedagogy of the Oppressed*. Trans. Myra Bergman Ramos. 1970. New York: Continuum, 1989.

Frey, Olivia. "Equity and Peace in the New Writing Class." Caywood and Overing 93–105.

Furman, Nelly. "Textual Feminism." *Women and Language in Literature and Society*. Ed. Sally McConnell-Ginet, Ruth Borker, and Nelly Furman. New York: Praeger, 1980. 45–54.

Fuss, Diana. *Essentially Speaking: Feminism, Nature and Difference*. New York: Routledge, 1989.

Gallop, Jane. *Around 1981: Academic Feminist Literary Theory.* New York: Routledge, 1992.

Gates, Henry Louis. " 'Authenticity,' or the Lesson of Little Tree." *New York Review of Books* 24 Nov. 1991: 1, 26–30.

———. *The Signifying Monkey: A Theory of Afro-American Literary Criticism.* New York: Oxford UP, 1988.

Gere, Anne Ruggles, ed. *Into the Field: Sites of Composition Study.* NY: MLA, 1993.

Giddens, Anthony. *The Constitution of Society: Outline of the Theory of Structuration.* Berkeley: U of California P, 1984.

Gilbert, Sandra. "What Do Feminist Critics Want? A Postcard from the Volcano." Showalter, *Criticism* 29–45.

Gilbert, Sandra, and Susan Gubar. *The Madwoman in the Attic.* New Haven: Yale U P, 1979.

Gilligan, Carol. *In a Different Voice: Psychological Theory and Women's Development.* Cambridge: Harvard UP, 1982.

Giroux, Henry. *Border Crossings: Cultural Workers and the Politics of Education.* New York: Routledge, 1992.

———. *Schooling and the Struggle for Public Life: Critical Pedagogy in the Modern Age.* Minneapolis: U of Minnesota P, 1988.

———. *Theory and Resistance in Education: A Pedagogy for the Opposition.* South Hadley, MA: Bergin, 1983.

Glenn, Cheryl. "Sex, Lies, and Manuscripts: Refiguring Aspasia in the History of Rhetoric." *CCC* 45 (1994): 180–99.

Gordon, Mary. Foreword. Woolf, *Room* vii–xiv.

Gore, Jennifer. "What We Can Do For You! What *Can* 'We' Do for 'You'?: Struggling over Empowerment in Critical and Feminist Pedagogy." Luke and Gore 54–73.

Gorgias. *Encomium of Helen.* Ed. D. M. McDowell. Bristol, Eng.: Bristol Classical, 1982.

Gough, Kathleen. "The Origin of the Family." *Toward an Anthropology of Women.* Ed. Rayna Reiter. New York: Monthly Review, 1975. 69–70.

Greene, Maxine. Foreword. Luke and Gore ix–xi.

Grimaldi, William. *Aristotle, Rhetoric 1: A Commentary.* Bronx: Fordham UP, 1980.

———. *Aristotle, Rhetoric 2: A Commentary.* Bronx: Fordham UP, 1988.

Grimke, Sarah. *Letters on the Equality of the Sexes and Other Essays.* Ed. Elizabeth Ann Bartlett. New Haven: Yale UP, 1988.

Guiguet, Jean. *Virginia Woolf and Her Works*. Trans. Jean Stewart. London: Hogarth, 1965.

Guy-Sheftall, Beverly. "A Black Feminist Perspective on the Academy." Butler and Walter 305–11.

Harai, Josue, ed. *Textual Strategies: Perspectives in Post-Structuralist Criticism*. Ithaca, NY: Cornell UP, 1979.

Harding, Sandra. "Conclusion: Epistemological Questions." *Feminism and Method* 181–90.

———, ed. *Feminism and Method*. Bloomington: Indiana UP, 1987.

———. "Who Knows? Identities and Feminist Epistemology." Hartman and Messer-Davidow 100–120.

Hardy, Thomas. *Far from the Madding Crowd*. 1874. New York: Macmillan, 1974.

Harkin, Patricia, and John Schilb, eds. *Contending with Words: Composition and Rhetoric in a Postmodern Age*. New York: MLA, 1991.

Harstock, Nancy. "The Feminist Standpoint: Developing the Ground for a Specifically Feminist Historical Materialism." Harding, *Feminism and Method* 157–80.

———. *Money, Sex, and Power: Toward a Feminist Historical Materialism*. Boston: Northeastern UP, 1985.

Hartman, Joan E. "Telling Stories: The Construction of Women's Agency." Hartman and Messer-Davidow 11–34.

Hartman, Joan E., and Ellen Messer-Davidow, eds. *(En)Gendering Knowledge: Feminists in Academe*. Knoxville: U of Tennessee P, 1991.

Hawkesworth, Mary E. "Feminist Rhetoric: Discourses on the Male Monopoly of Thought." *Political Theory* 16 (1990): 444–67.

Hedley, Jane. "Surviving to Speak New Languages: Mary Daly and Adrienne Rich." *Hypatia* 7 (1992): 40–62.

Henry, Annette. "African-Canadian Women Teachers' Activism: Recreating Communities of Caring and Resistance." *Journal of Negro Education* 61 (1992): 392–405.

Hiatt, Mary P. "The Feminine Style." *CCC* 29 (1978): 222–26.

Hill, Alkette Olin. *Mother Tongue, Father Time: A Decade of Linguistic Revolt*. Bloomington: Indiana UP, 1986.

Hill, Carolyn Eriksen. *Writing from the Margins: Power and Pedagogy for Teachers of Composition*. New York: Oxford UP, 1990.

Hirsch, Marianne, and Evelyn Fox Keller, eds. *Conflicts in Feminism*. New York: Routledge, 1990.

Hollis, Karyn. "Feminism in Writing Workshops: A New Pedagogy." *CCC* 43 (1992): 340–46.

hooks, bell. "Black and Female: Reflections on Graduate School." *Talking Back* 55–61.

———. "Race and Feminism: The Issue of Accountability." *Ain't I a Woman: Black Women and Feminism.* Boston: South End, 1981. 119–58.

———. "Radical Black Subjectivity." *Yearning* 15–22.

———. "Talking Back." *Talking Back* 5–9.

———. *Talking Back: Thinking Feminist, Thinking Black.* Boston: South End, 1989.

———. "Third World Diva Girls: Politics of Feminist Solidarity." *Yearning* 89–102.

———. "Toward a Revolutionary Feminist Pedagogy." *Talking Back* 49–54.

———. " 'When I Was a Young Soldier for the Revolution': Coming to Voice." *Talking Back* 10–18.

———. *Yearning: Race, Gender, and Cultural Politics.* Boston: South End, 1990.

Horner, Winifred, ed. *The Present State of Scholarship in Historical and Contemporary Rhetoric.* Rev. ed. Columbia: U of Missouri P, 1990.

Howe, Florence. "Identity and Expression: A Writing Course for Women." *College English* 32 (1971): 863–71.

Irigaray, Luce. *Speculum of the Other Woman.* Trans. Gillian C. Gill. Ithaca, NY: Cornell UP, 1985.

Jacobus, Mary, ed. *Women's Writing and Writing about Women.* London: Croom Helm, 1979.

Jarratt, Susan. "Feminism and Composition: The Case for Conflict." Harkin and Schilb 105–23.

———. *Rereading the Sophists: Classical Rhetoric Refigured.* Carbondale: Southern Illinois UP, 1991.

———, ed. "Special Issue: Feminist Rereadings in the History of Rhetoric." *Rhetoric Society Quarterly* 22 (1992).

Jaynes, Julian. *The Origin of Consciousness in the Breakdown of the Bicameral Mind.* Boston: Houghton, 1976.

Johnson, Barbara. *A World of Difference.* Baltimore: Johns Hopkins UP, 1987.

Jones, Ellen Carol. "Androgynous Vision and Artistic Process in Virginia Woolf's *A Room of One's Own.*" Beja 227–39.

Jones, William. Discussion. Conference on The Spiritual Dimension of Social Change. University of Missouri-Columbia. 30 Oct. 1992.

Jong, Erica. "Alcestis on the Poetry Circuit." *The Norton Anthology of*

Literature by Women. Eds. Sandra Gilbert and Susan Gubar. New York: Norton, 1985. 2357–58.

Kaufer, David. "Point of View in Rhetorical Situations." *Quarterly Journal of Speech* 65 (1979): 171–86.

Kempe, Margery. *The Book of Margery Kempe.* Ed. W. Butler-Bowdon. New York: Devin-Adair, 1944.

Kennedy, George. *Classical Rhetoric and Its Religious and Secular Traditions.* Chapel Hill: U of North Carolina P, 1980.

Knoblauch, Charles, and Lil Brannon. *Rhetorical Traditions and the Teaching of Writing.* Upper Montclair, NJ: Boynton, 1984.

Kramarae, Cheris. "Proprietors of Language." *Women and Language in Literature and Society.* Ed. Sally McConnell-Ginet, Ruth Borker, and Nelly Furman. New York: Praeger, 1980. 58–68.

Kristeva, Julia. "From Symbol to Sign." *The Kristeva Reader.* Ed. Toril Moi. Oxford: Blackwell, 1986. 62–73.

———. *Revolution in Poetic Language.* NY: Columbia U P, 1984.

———. "Women's Time." Trans. Alice Jardine and Harry Blake. *Signs* 7 (1981): 13–35.

Kuykendall, Eleanor. "Feminist Linguistics in Philosophy." Vetterling-Braggin 132–46.

Ladson-Billings, Gloria, and Annette Henry. "Blurring the Borders: Voices of African Liberatory Pedagogy in the United States and Canada." *Journal of Education* 172 (1990): 72–89.

Lakoff, Robin. "Language and Woman's Place." Vetterling-Braggin 60–67.

———. *Language and Woman's Place.* New York: Harper, 1975.

Langer, Suzanne. *Philosophy in a New Key.* New York: New American Library, 1942.

Larson, Richard. "Lloyd Bitzer's 'Rhetorical Situation' and the Classification of Discourse." *Philosophy and Rhetoric* 3 (1970): 165–68.

Lassner, Phyllis. "Feminist Responses to Rogerian Rhetoric." *Rhetoric Review* 8 (1990): 220–31.

Lather, Patti. "Post-Critical Pedagogies: A Feminist Reading." Luke and Gore 120–37.

Lavine, Ann. "Subject Matter and Gender." Caywood and Overing 135–43.

Leaska, Mitchell A. Introduction. Woolf, *The Pargiters* vii–xxii.

Leavis, Queenie. "Caterpillars of the World Unite." Rev. of *Three Guineas,* by Virginia Woolf. *Scrutiny* Sep. 1938: 210–11.

Lee, Spike. Guest Appearance. *The Tonight Show*. NBC. Los Angeles. 7 Jan. 1993.

Lentricchia, Frank. *Criticism and Social Change*. Chicago: U of Chicago P, 1983.

Lerner, Gerda. *The Creation of Patriarchy*. Oxford: Oxford UP, 1986.

Levin, Michael. "Vs. Ms." Vetterling-Braggin 217–22.

Levine, Judith. "White Like Me: When Privilege Is Written on Your Skin." *Ms.* Mar.-Apr. 1994: 22–24.

Lewis, Magda. "Interrupting Patriarchy: Politics, Resistance, and Transformation in the Feminist Classroom." Luke and Gore 167–91.

Lipscomb, Drema. "Sojourner Truth: A Practical Public Discourse." Lunsford.

Locke, John. *An Essay Concerning Human Understanding*. Oxford: Clarendon, 1975.

Lorde, Audre. "Age, Race, Class, and Sex" *Sister* 114–23.

———. "An Open Letter to Mary Daly." *Sister* 66–71.

———. "Poetry Is Not a Luxury." *Sister* 36–39.

———. *Sister Outsider*. Trumansburg, NY: Crossing, 1984.

Luke, Carmen. "Feminist Politics and Radical Pedagogy." Luke and Gore 25–53.

Luke, Carmen, and Jennifer Gore, eds. *Feminisms and Critical Pedagogy*. New York: Routledge, 1992.

Lunsford, Andrea, ed. *Reclaiming Rhetorica*. U of Pittsburgh P, in press.

Lunsford, Andrea, and Lisa Ede. "Rhetoric in a New Key: Women and Collaboration." *Rhetoric Review* 8 (1990): 234–41.

Lusted, David. "Why Pedagogy?" *Screen* 27 (1986): 2–14.

Makward, Christiane. "To Be or Not to Be . . . a Feminist Speaker." *The Future of Difference*. Ed. Hester Eisenstein and Alice Jardine. Boston: Hall, 1984. 95–105.

Mann, Bonnie. "*Gyn/Ecology* in the Lives of Women in the Real World." Daly, *Gyn/Ecology* xxxiv–xliii.

Marcus, Jane. " 'No More Horses': Virginia Woolf on Art and Propaganda." *Women's Studies* 4 (1977): 265–90.

———. "Pathologies: The Virginia Woolf Soap Operas." Second Annual Virginia Woolf Conference. New Haven, CT, 14 June 1992.

———. "Thinking Back through Our Mothers." *New Feminist Essays on Virginia Woolf*. Ed. Jane Marcus. Lincoln: U of Nebraska P, 1981. 1–30.

————. *Virginia Woolf: A Feminist Slant*. Lincoln: U of Nebraska P, 1983.

————. *Virginia Woolf and the Languages of Patriarchy*. Bloomington: Indiana UP, 1987.

Martin, Theodora. *The Sound of Our Own Voices: Women's Study Clubs, 1860–1910*. Boston: Beacon, 1987.

Marx, Karl, and Frederich Engels. *The German Ideology*. Ed. C. J. Arthur. NY: International, 1970.

Meisenhelder, Susan. "Redefining 'Powerful' Writing: Toward a Feminist Theory of Composition." *Journal of Thought* 20 (1985): 184–95.

Miller, Susan. *Rescuing the Subject: A Critical Introduction to Rhetoric and the Writer*. Carbondale: Southern Illinois UP, 1989.

Millett, Kate. *Sexual Politics*. 1969. London: Virago, 1977.

Minow-Pinkney, Makiko. *Virginia Woolf and the Problem of the Subject*. New Brunswick, NJ: Rutgers UP, 1987.

Moers, Ellen. *Literary Women: The Great Writers*. New York: Doubleday, 1976.

Moi, Toril. *Sexual/Textual Politics*. New York: Routledge, 1985.

Morrison, Toni. "Interview with Claudia Tate." *Black Women Writers at Work*. Ed. Claudia Tate. New York: Continuum, 1983. 117–31.

————. *Playing in the Dark: Whiteness and the Literary Imagination*. Cambridge: Harvard UP, 1992.

Morton, Nelle. *The Journey Is Home*. Boston: Beacon, 1985.

Mountford, Roxanne. "Feminist Theory and Classical Rhetoric: Connection, Rejection or Transformation?" Conference on College Composition and Communication. San Diego, 2 Apr. 1993.

————. "The Feminization of *Ars Praedicandi*." Diss. Ohio State U, 1991.

Murphy, James, ed. *A Short History of Writing Instruction*. Davis, CA: Hermagoras, 1990.

Natanson, Maurice. "The Limits of Rhetoric." *Contemporary Theories of Rhetoric: Selected Readings*. Ed. Richard Johannesen. New York: Harper, 1971. 371–80.

Neel, Jaspar. *Plato, Derrida, and Writing*. Carbondale: Southern Illinois UP, 1988.

Nelson, Cary. *Recovery and Repression*. Madison: U of Wisconsin P, 1989.

————. "Writing as the Accomplice of Language: Kenneth Burke and Poststructuralism." Simons and Melia 156–73.

Neverow, Vara. "A Room of One's Own as a Model of Composition Theory." Third Annual Virginia Woolf Conference. Jefferson City, MO, 11 June 1993.

Newton, Judith, and Deborah Rosenfelt. "Introduction: Toward a Materialist-Feminist Criticism." *Feminist Criticism and Social Change: Sex, Class, and Race in Literature and Culture*. Ed. Newton and Rosenfelt. New York: Meuthen, 1985. xv–xxxix.

Nicholson, Catherine. "How Rage Mothered My Third Birth." *Sinister Wisdom* 1 (1976): 40–45.

Noddings, Nel. "Ethics from the Standpoint of Women." Rhode 160–173.

North, Stephen. *The Making of Meaning in Composition: Portrait of an Emerging Field*. Portsmouth, NH: Heinemann, 1987.

Nye, Andrea. *Feminist Theory and the Philosophies of Man*. New York: Routledge, 1988.

Oates, Joyce Carol. "Is There a Female Voice? Joyce Carol Oates Replies." M. Eagleton 208.

Omolade, Barbara. "A Black Feminist Pedagogy." *Women's Studies Quarterly* 21 (1993): 31–39.

Ong, Walter. "Review of Brian Vickers' *Classical Rhetoric in English Poetry*." *College English* 33 (1972): 612–15.

Orner, Mimi. "Interrupting the Calls for Student Voice in 'Liberatory' Education: A Feminist Poststructuralist Perspective." Luke and Gore 74–89.

Osborn, Susan. " 'Revision/Re-Vision': A Feminist Writing Class." *Rhetoric Review* 9 (1991): 258–72.

Paine, Charles. "Relativism, Radical Pedagogy, and the Ideology of Paralysis." *College English* 51 (1989): 557–70.

Patton, John. "Causation and Creativity in Rhetorical Situations." *Quarterly Journal of Speech* 65 (1979): 36–55.

Penelope, Julia. *Speaking Freely: Unlearning the Lies of the Fathers' Tongues*. New York: Pergammon, 1990.

Plato. *Plato 1: Euthyphro, Apology, Crito, Phaedo, Phaedrus*. Trans. H. N. Fowler. Cambridge: Harvard UP, 1977.

Pomeroy, Ralph. "Fitness of Response in Bitzer's Concept of Rhetorical Discourse." *Georgia Speech Communication Journal* 4 (1972): 42–71.

Poovey, Mary. "Feminism and Deconstruction." *Feminist Studies* 14 (1988): 61–66.

Poynton, Cate. *Language and Gender: Making the Difference*. 1985. Oxford: Oxford UP, 1989.

Purdy, L. M. "Against 'Vs. Ms.' " Vetterling-Braggin 223–28.

Quintilian. *The* Institutio Oratoria *of Quintilian.* Trans. H. E. Butler. 4 vols. Cambridge: Harvard UP, 1920–22.

Rabine, Leslie Wahl. "A Feminist Politics of Non-Identity." *Feminist Studies* 14 (1988): 11–32.

Ramus, Peter. *Arguments in Rhetoric against Quintilian (1549).* Trans. Carole Newlands and James J. Murphy. DeKalb: U of Northern Illinois P, 1983.

Ratcliffe, Krista. "A Rhetoric of Textual Feminism: (Re)reading the Emotional in Virginia Woolf's *Three Guineas. Rhetoric Review* 11 (1993): 400–16.

Reading, Peter. "Canny and Cockaludicrous." Rev. of *Websters' First New Intergalactic Wickedary of the English Language,* by Mary Daly with Jane Caputi. *Times Literary Supplement* 3–9 June 1988: 622.

Rhode, Deborah, ed. *Theoretical Perspectives on Sexual Difference.* New Haven: Yale UP, 1990.

Rich, Adrienne. *Adrienne Rich's Poetry.* Ed. Barbara Charlesworth Gelpi and Albert Gelpi. New York: Norton, 1975.

———. "The Anti-Feminist Woman." *On Lies* 69–84.

———. "As If Your Life Depended on It." *What Is Found* 32–33.

———. "An Atlas of the Difficult World." *Atlas* 3–28.

———. *An Atlas of the Difficult World: Poems 1988–1991.* New York: Norton, 1991.

———. "Blood, Bread, and Poetry." *Blood* 167–87.

———. *Blood, Bread, and Poetry: Selected Prose 1979–1985.* New York: Norton, 1986.

———. "The Burning of Paper Instead of Children." *Rich's Poetry* 47–50.

———. "Cartographies of Silence." *Dream* 16–20.

———. *A Change of World.* New Haven: Yale UP, 1951.

———. "Compulsory Heterosexuality and Lesbian Existence." *Blood* 23–75.

———. "Contradictions." *Your Native Land* 81–111.

———. "Dearest Arturo." *What Is Found* 22–27.

———. "The Demon Lover." *Rich's Poetry* 37–40.

———. *The Diamond Cutters and Other Poems.* New York: Harper, 1955.

———. "Disloyal to Civilization: Feminism, Racism, Gynephobia." *On Lies* 275–310.

———. "Disobedience and Women's Studies." *Blood* 76–84.

——. "The Distance between Language and Violence." *What Is Found* 181–89.

——. "Diving into the Wreck." *Rich's Poetry* 65–68.

——. *Diving into the Wreck, Poems 1971–1972.* New York: Norton, 1973.

——. *The Dream of a Common Language: Poems 1974–1977.* New York: Norton, 1978.

——. "Eastern War Time." *Atlas* 35–44.

——. "Education of a Novelist." *Your Native Land* 37–40.

——. "For a Friend in Travail." *Atlas* 51.

——. "From an Old House in America." *Rich's Poetry* 76–85.

——. "I Am in Danger—Sir—." *Rich's Poetry* 31.

——. "If Not with Others, How?" *Blood* 202–9.

——. "Images for Godard." *Rich's Poetry* 51–53.

——. "Implosions." *Rich's Poetry* 41.

——. "In the Evening." *Rich's Poetry* 36.

——. "Invisibility in Academe." *Blood* 198–201.

——. "It Is the Lesbian in Us. . . . " *On Lies* 199–202.

——. *Leaflets.* New York: Norton, 1969.

——. "The Lioness." *Dream* 21–22.

——. "Natural Resources." *Dream* 60–67.

——. *Necessitites of Life.* New York: Norton, 1966.

——. "Nights and Days." *Dream* 45–46.

——. "North American Time." *Your Native Land* 33–36.

——. "North American Tunnel Vision." *Blood* 160–66.

——. "Notes Toward a Politics of Location." *Blood* 210–31.

——. *Of Woman Born: Motherhood as Experience and Institution.* 1976. New York: Norton, 1986.

——. "On Edges." *Rich's Poetry* 42.

——. *On Lies, Secrets, and Silence: Selected Prose 1966–1978.* New York: Norton, 1979.

——. "Origins and History of Consciousness." *Dream* 7–9.

——. "Paula Becker to Clara Westhoff." *Dream* 42–44.

——. "Planetarium." *Rich's Poetry* 45–46.

——. "Poetry and Experience: Statement at a Poetry Reading (1964)." *Rich's Poetry* 89.

——. "Power." *Dream* 3.

214   Works Cited

———. "Power and Danger: Works of a Common Woman." *On Lies* 247–58.

———. "Resisting Amnesia: History and Personal Life." *Blood* 136–55.

———. *Snapshots of a Daughter-in-Law.* New York: Norton, 1963.

———. "Snapshots of a Daughter-in-Law." *Rich's Poetry* 12–16.

———. "The Soul of a Women's College." *Blood* 188–97.

———. "Sources 22." *Your Native Land* 25.

———. "Sources 24." *Your Native Land* 27.

———. "Split at the Root: An Essay on Jewish Identity." *Blood* 100–23.

———. "The Stranger." *Rich's Poetry* 65.

———. "Taking Women Students Seriously." *On Lies* 237–45.

———. "Teaching Language in Open Admission." *On Lies* 51–68.

———. "That Women Name Themselves." Rev. of *Gyn/Ecology*, by Mary Daly. *New York Times Book Review* 4 Feb. 1979: 10+.

———. "Three Conversations." *Rich's Poetry* 105–22.

———. "Through Corralitos under Rolls of Cloud." *Atlas* 46–50.

———. *Time's Power: Poems 1985–1988.* New York: Norton, 1989.

———. "To Invent What We Desire." *What Is Found* 214–16.

———. "Toward a More Feminist Criticism." *Blood* 85–99.

———. "Toward a Woman-Centered University." *On Lies* 125–55.

———. "Toward the Solstice." *Dream* 68–71.

———. "Transcendental Etude." *Dream* 72–77.

———. "Turning." *Time's Power* 51–55.

———. "Twenty-One Love Poems." *Dream* 25–36.

———. "An Unsaid Word." *Rich's Poetry* 3.

———. "A Valediction: Forbidding Mourning." *Rich's Poetry* 53–54.

———. "What Does a Woman Need to Know?" *Blood* 1–10.

———. *What Is Found There: Notebooks on Poetry and Politics.* New York: Norton, 1993.

———. "When We Dead Awaken: Writing as Re-vision." *On Lies* 29–49.

———. *The Will to Change.* New York: Norton, 1971.

———. "A Woman Dead in Her Forties." *Dream* 53–58.

———. Women and Honor: Some Notes on Lying." *On Lies* 185–94.

———. *Your Native Land, Your Life: Poems.* New York: Norton, 1986.

Richards, I. A. *The Philosophy of Rhetoric.* New York: Oxford UP, 1936.

Richardson, Eudora Ramsey. *The Woman Speaker: A Hand-Book and Study Course on Public Speaking.* Richmond, VA: Whittet, 1936.

Ricoeur, Paul. *The Rule of Metaphor.* Trans. Robert Czerny. Toronto: U of Toronto P, 1979.

Rose, Phyllis. *Women of Letters: The Life of Virginia Woolf.* New York: Oxbridge UP, 1978.

Royster, Jackie Jones. "Intersecting Race, Gender, and Ethnicity in a Feminist Perspective." Conference on College Composition and Communication. San Diego, 31 Mar. 1993.

Ruthven, K. K. *Feminist Literary Studies: An Introduction.* 1984. New York: Cambridge UP, 1990.

Ryder, Mary. "Feminism and Style: Still Looking for a Quick Fix." *Style* 23 (1989): 530–44.

Sackville-West, Vita. "New Novels." *Listener* 2 (6 Nov. 1929): 620. Rpt. in Beja 18–19.

Scheman, Naomi. "Who Wants to Know?: The Epistemological Value of Values." Hartman and Messer-Davidow 179–204.

Schneidewind, Nancy. "Feminist Values: Guidelines for Teaching Methodology in Women's Studies." Shor, *Freire for the Classroom* 170–79.

Schulkind, Jeanne. Introduction. Woolf, *Moments of Being* 11–24.

Scott, Joan. "Deconstructing Equality-Versus-Difference: Or, the Uses of Post-Structuralism for Feminism." *Feminist Studies* 14 (1988): 33–49. Rpt. in Hirsch and Fox Keller 134–48.

———. "Gender: A Useful Category of Historical Analysis." Abel 81–100.

Secor, Marie, and David Charney, eds. *Constructing a Rhetorical Education.* Carbondale: Southern Illinois UP, 1992.

Shepherd, Deneen. "Empowering Basic Writers to Negotiate Their Differences within Academic Boundaries." Workshop Presentation. Conference on College Composition and Communication. Nashville, 16 Mar. 1994.

Shor, Ira. *Critical Teaching and Everyday Life.* Boston: South End, 1980.

———. *Culture Wars: School and Society in the Conservative Restoration.* 1986. Chicago: U of Chicago P, 1992.

———, ed. *Freire for the Classroom: A Sourcebook for Liberatory Teaching.* Portsmouth, NH: Heinemann, 1987.

Shor, Ira, and Paulo Freire. *A Pedagogy for Liberation: Dialogues on Transforming Education.* South Hadley, MA: Bergin, 1987.

Showalter, Elaine. "Feminist Criticism in the Wilderness." *Criticism* 243–70.

———. "Introduction: The Rise of Gender." *Speaking of Gender.* Ed. Showalter. New York: Routledge, 1989. 1–13.

———. *A Literature of Their Own.* Princeton, NJ: Princeton UP, 1977.

———, ed. *The New Feminist Criticism.* New York: Pantheon, 1985.

———. *Sister's Choice: Tradition and Changes in American Women's Writing.* New York: Oxford UP, 1991.

Shrewsbury, Carolyn. "What Is Feminist Pedagogy." *Women's Studies Quarterly* 21 (1993): 3–17.

Sills, Caryl. "College Composition with a Focus on Gender." *Transformations: The New Jersey Project Journal* 2 (1992): 30–35.

Silver, Brenda. *Virginia Woolf's Reading Notebook.* Princeton, NJ: Princeton UP, 1983.

Silvera, Makeda, and Nila Gupta. "The Issue Is 'Ism: Women of Color Speak Out." *Fireweed: A Feminist Quarterly.* Ed. Silvera and Gupta. 1983. Toronto: Black Women and Women of Colour, 1989. 5.

Simons, Herbert, and Trevor Melia, eds. *The Legacy of Kenneth Burke.* Madison: U of Wisconsin P, 1989.

Smith, Dorothy. *The Everyday World as Problematic: A Feminist Sociology.* Boston: Northeastern UP, 1987.

———. "Women's Perspective as a Radical Critique of Sociology." Harding, *Feminism and Method* 84–96.

Smith-Rosenberg, Carrol. "Writing History: Language, Class, and Gender." *Feminist Studies/Critical Studies.* Ed. Teresa de Lauretis. Bloomington: Indiana UP, 1986. 31–53.

Soble, Alan. "Beyond the Miserable Vision of 'Vs. Ms.' " Vetterling-Braggin 229–48.

Spender, Dale. *Man Made Language.* 2d ed. London: Routledge, 1985.

Spivak, Gayatri. Interview with Ellen Rooney. *Differences* 1 (1989): 124–56.

Stanton, Elizabeth Cady. "Speech at the Seneca Falls Convention, 1848." K. K. Campbell, *Man Cannot Speak.* Vol. 2, 41–70.

Statham, Anne, Laurel Richardson, and Judith A. Cook. *Gender and University Teaching: A Negotiated Difference.* Albany: SUNY P, 1991.

Stewart, Maria W. Miller. "Lecture Delivered at the Franklin Hall." K. K. Campbell, *Man Cannot Speak.* Vol. 2, 1–10.

Stimpson, Catherine. Introduction. *Feminist Issues in Literary Scholarship.* Ed. Shari Benstock. Bloomington: Indiana UP, 1987. 1–6.

———. *Where the Meanings Are: Feminism and Cultural Spaces.* New York: Routledge, 1988.

Swearingen, C. Jan. "Rereading Aspasia: Reconstructions of Gender, Public and Private." Rhetoric Society of American Conference. Norfolk, VA, 20 May 1995.

Tedesco, Jane. "Women's Ways of Knowing/Women's Ways of Composing." *Rhetoric Review* 9 (1991): 246–256.

Terrell, Mary Church. "What It Means to Be Colored in the Capitol of the United States, 1906." K. K. Campbell, *Man Cannot Speak.* Vol 2, 421–32.

Tillich, Paul. *Systematic Theology.* 3 vols. Chicago: U of Chicago P, 1951–63.

Todorov, Tsvetlan. *Theories of the Symbol.* Trans. Catherine Porter. 1977. Ithaca, NY: Cornell UP, 1982.

Tompkins, Jane. "Me and My Shadow." *New Literary History: A Journal of Theory and Interpretation* 19 (1987): 169–78.

Transue, Pamela. *Virginia Woolf and the Politics of Style.* Albany: SUNY P, 1986.

Truth, Sojourner. "Speech at the Women's Rights Convention, Akron, Ohio, 1851." K. K. Campbell, *Man Cannot Speak.* Vol. 2, 99–102.

Valeska, Lucia. "The Future of Female Separatism." *Building Feminist Theory.* Ed. Charlotte Bunch et al. New York: Longman, 1981.

Valian, Virginia. "Linguistics and Feminism." Vetterling-Braggin 68–80.

Vatz, Richard. "The Myth of the Rhetorical Situation." *Philosophy and Rhetoric* 6 (1973): 154–61.

Vetterling-Braggin, Mary, ed. *Sexist Language: A Modern Philosophical Analysis.* Lanham, MD: Littlefield, 1988.

Waithe, Mary Ellen, ed. *A History of Women Philosophers.* 2 vols. New York: Kluwer, 1989.

Walker, Cheryl. "Feminist Literary Criticism and the Author." *Critical Inquiry* 16 (1990): 551–71.

Watts, Steven. "Academe's Leftists Are Something of a Fraud." *Chronicle of Higher Education* 29 Apr. 1992: 40A.

Weedon, Chris. *Feminist Practice and Poststructuralist Theory.* New York: Basil Blackwell, 1987.

Wehr, Demaris. "Fracturing the Language of Patriarchy." Rev. of *Pure Lust,* by Mary Daly. *New York Times Book Review* 22 July 1984: 14.

Weiler, Kathleen, ed. *Women Teaching for Change: Gender, Class and Power.* South Hadley: Bergin, 1988.

Wells, Ida B. "Southern Horrors: Lynch Laws in All Its Phases." K. K. Campbell, *Man Cannot Speak.* Vol. 2, 385–420.

West, Cornel. *Race Matters.* Boston: Beacon, 1993.

Whately, Richard. *Elements of Rhetoric.* Ed. Douglas Ehninger. Carbondale: Southern Illinois UP, 1963.

Wilkerson, K. E. "On Evaluating Theories of Rhetoric." *Philosophy and Rhetoric* 3 (1970): 83–96.

Wittig, Monique. *Les Guérillères.* Trans. David LeVay. New York: Viking-Penguin, 1971.

Woods, Marjorie Curry. "Among Men—Not Boys: Histories of Rhetoric and the Exclusion of Pedagogy." *Rhetoric Society Quarterly* 22 (1992): 18–26.

Woolf, Virginia. *Collected Essays.* Ed. Andrew McNeillie. 4 vols. London: Chatto, 1967.

———. "Craftsmanship." *The Death of the Moth and Other Essays.* New York: Harcourt, 1942. 198–207.

———. *The Diary of Virginia Woolf.* 5 vols. Ed. Anne Olivier Bell and Andrew McNeillie. New York: Harcourt, 1977–84.

———. "Dorothy Richardson." Barrett 188–92.

———. *The Essays of Virginia Woolf.* 5 vols. Ed. Andrew McNeillie. New York: Harcourt, 1988.

———. "Jane Austen." Barrett 109–20.

———. "Men and Women." *Essays of Virginia Woolf.* Vol. 3, 192–95.

———. *Moments of Being.* New York: Harcourt, 1976.

———. *Orlando: A Biography.* 1928. London: Hogarth, 1990.

———. *The Pargiters: The Novel-Essay Portion of The Years.* Ed. Mitchell A. Leaska. New York: Harcourt, 1977.

———. "Professions for Women." Barrett 57–63.

———. *A Room of One's Own.* 1929. New York: Harcourt, 1957.

———. "A Sketch of the Past." *Moments of Being* 64–137.

———. "Speech of January 21, 1933." *The Pargiters.* xxvii–xliv.

———. *Three Guineas.* 1938. New York: Harcourt, 1966.

———. "22 Hyde Park Gate." *Moments of Being* 142–155.

———. "Women and Fiction." Barrett 43–52.

———. "Women Novelists." Barrett 68–71.

———. *A Writer's Diary.* Ed. Leonard Woolf. 1951. New York: Harcourt, 1981.

Worsham, Lynn. "Reading Wild, Seriously: Confessions of an Epistemophiliac." *Rhetoric Society Quarterly* 22 (1992): 39–62.

Yaeger, Patricia. *Honey-Mad Women: Emancipatory Strategies in Women's Writing.* NY: Columbia UP, 1988.

Zimmerman, Bonnie. "Disobedient Daughter." Rev. of *Blood, Bread, and Poetry,* by Adrienne Rich. *Woman's Review of Books* 4 (1987): 5–6.

Index

Krista Ratcliffe is an assistant professor of English at Marquette University. She received her Ph.D. in rhetoric and composition from Ohio State University and currently teaches undergraduate courses in rhetorical theory, freshman and advanced writing, professional writing, and women's literature, as well as graduate courses in rhetoric and composition history, theory, and pedagogy. She has published articles about Adrienne Rich's feminist composition pedagogy and Virginia Woolf's textual feminism, feminist stylistics, and rhetorical theory. Her current interest is a book-length project that explores the possibilities of women's multicultural autobiographies for rhetoric and composition studies.